THE PLEASANT VALLEY FLYING SAUCER MASSACRE

BY ALLAN C. KIMBALL

D1104423

COVER PHOTO BY A. ELI COHEN

SUN COUNTRY PUBLICATIONS
WIMBERLEY, TEXAS

THE PLEASANT VALLEY FLYING SAUCER MASSACRE
by Allan C. Kimball

ISBN 978-0-578-61999-6

Cover photo by A. Eli Cohen

Sun Country Publications, Inc.
P.O. Box 1482
Wimberley, TX 78676

THE PLEASANT VALLEY FLYING SAUCER MASSACRE

CHAPTER 1:
DECLOAKED BY THE SUIT

She was not invisible and this bothered her.

This bothered her a little less than it might have otherwise because she had the darkness and the woods around her. She was *kunoichi* and·was used to becoming invisible at will. She had never worn this suit before so it would require practice which was something she should have done more of before. She had scouted. Only twice before but the last one paid off. She found a chicken ranch not a half-mile from here, It was full of poultry so she brought her packet and had to wear this blasted suit. Rural Texas towns were wonderful because livestock of all types and sizes were everywhere, she thought. More than enough wild turkeys and buzzards, too. She knew they wouldn't need all the longhorns, hogs, horses, llamas, deer, and goats she also found. So many goats. It seemed to her that's what this Hill Country was: all limestone, cedar and goats.

Her nose itched. She couldn't scratch it through her helmet so she willed the itch to go away. It did. She was *kunoichi*; she could will away the worst pain so an irritating itch was insignificant. Should be. The itch returned. She knew it was only because she was trying not to think about it, and when you did that you only thought about it more. She concentrated on her mission. She walked carefully in the thick underbrush among the cedars and the occasional oak. She made little noise. That bothered her. She should be making no noise whatsoever but the suit and its bulky boots were made for protection not stealth. Damn her nose itched. She willed it away again.

The sky was deeply overcast, hiding most of a crescent moon. She was glad of that, but had noticed some time ago that because the suit was light colored it was far more reflective than she wanted it to be. She made a mental note to check on the availability of a black suit. Maybe she could dye this one somehow. She wriggled her nose at the itch. She gave up trying to get rid of it. Why wasn't she issued a black suit? The air inside the suit was stale. She wanted fresh air, but she had endured far worse than this. The damn suit was distracting her in a way she had never been before and she knew that was dangerous. She was *kunoichi*; she had to be in control.

She heard what she thought was a hiss and worried that the suit had a leak but the hiss escalated into a soft growl. She crouched, setting down her packet to free both hands, looking for an animal. She saw none. She stood and looked around carefully, stepping to the edge of the woods to look up and down the hill. She saw nothing, but the growl grew.

Then the light hit her.

CHAPTER 2:
THE SLEEPYHEAD AND THE SPACEMAN

"Fred is dead."

The words on the phone didn't register in Ray Strider's mind. He wanted more sleep. He blinked his eyes several times then looked at the digital clock radio on the bedside table that told him the precise time in soothing green: 05:43 AM. He sighed and threw back the lightweight quilt on the bed. One hour and seventeen minutes before the radio would have turned itself on blaring whatever Bob FM in San Marcos was playing. He cleared his throat and his mind, gathering all his journalistic and investigative skills to ask the caller a typically insightful question.

"Hunh?"

"Fred is dead."

Ray recognized the bass voice of his friend LeRoi Nguyen who happened to be a Bigfoot County deputy sheriff. Ray swung his feet out of the bed and sighed—he thought he'd left these sorts of calls behind him when he left Houston and the *Post*. Both Freds he knew were relatively fit thirtysomethings and people like that rarely died in small towns, especially tiny ones like Pleasant Valley.

"Which Fred?" Ray asked. "Freddy Morgan or Fred Salgado?"

"Fred not Freddy."

"What happened?"

"Fred bought it on his bike sometime last night. He was taking that short cut from 12 over to County 666—"

"Huth Lane, the dirt road goes by Chicken Charley's place?"

"That would be the one," LeRoi said.

"But Fred was such a good bike rider. He didn't speed, always wore a helmet, never passed between cars or on the right. Heck, he didn't even drink."

"He was so good it makes you wonder why he bothered to ride a Harley. Nonetheless, he lost control of the bike but managed to dodge several cedars before he slammed head-on into a big oak probably five times as old as he was. He must have lain there for hours until Charley's mom noticed the path his bike cut into the brush when she was taking Charley down to school this morning. Fred was dead on the scene."

"C.O.D.?"

"We will not know officially for at least a few days. Our tiny county is not too high on the priority list over at the Austin M.E.'s joint."

Ray ran his right hand through his short, thinning hair several times; tried to blink away his insatiable craving for more sleep. But his stomach was already cramping, demanding that big bowel movement that never seemed to arrive. "Probably swerved to hit a deer."

"About one-point-five-million vehicles collide with deer every year in the United States. They are the number one road hazard throughout the Hill Country, so that is the most likely explanation," LeRoi said. "We have got his skid marks, you can see where he swerved to avoid something, so that is what we are guessing. You see one of our small white-tails on the road while you are driving your car or pick-up and you should drive right through it. If you are smart. It will mess up your car, but you will come through it OK. On a bike? Not so much."

"Critter tracks on the shoulder?"

LeRoi laughed up a snort. "Sure. We have all sorts of tracks out there. Take your pick—deer, dillos, possums, coons, rabbits, dogs, cats, skunks, turkeys, vultures, lizards, snakes. You are not in Houston anymore, city boy."

"I get it," Ray said.

"Well, we did have one set of tracks we are not sure of. Tracks of a person. They may not mean anything, though."

"Something out of the ordinary?"

"Tracks of one person coming out of the woods and going back again. The north side of the road is grass so we did not get anything on that side, the south side is mostly underbrush and trees so nothing there, and the caliche on the road is too rocky for anything definitive and the traffic rolls over them anyway, but that small strip of loose dirt on the south shoulder gave us a couple of good prints. Size eight-and-a-half."

"A woman?"

"Most common shoe size for adult women is seven-and-a-half, eight, so, yes, it was probably a woman. Could have been a small man. Could not tell from the impression the sole left which one. We have good pictures. What it reminded me of was that famous photograph of that footprint Buzz Aldrin left on the moon. Flat sole with symmetrical ridges from toe to heel."

Ray shook his head abruptly. "You saying Fred swerved to avoid hitting a spaceman?"

LeRoi snortled again. "No. No. I am just telling you what it reminded my over-active imagination of. What the footprints probably are is some woman wearing a pair of flip-flops. It is probably Charley's mom. We are checking all of that."

"Lookit, thanks for calling me. I appreciate it," Ray said. "You still on duty or will I see you at The Fork?"

"Me miss those cinnamon rolls? About eight maybe."

"See ya."

"Buh-bye."

Ray blinked and rubbed his eyes. He turned the bedside radio on. "WAR! HUNH, YEAH. WHAT IS IT GOOD FOR?" Edwin Starr's song reverberated around Ray's bedroom. Before Edwin could answer his own question, Ray turned the radio off. He coughed, reached for a tissue, and blew his nose on the way into the bathroom. He punched on the bathroom radio to listen to an Austin news/talk station that would give him the day's weather in between blatherings from the hosts and callers, sat on the commode and read a little from *Sports Illustrated*. He gave up after fifteen minutes produced only a few rabbit pellets.

Instead of the typical political give-and-take on the radio, this morning was filled with people speculating on a UFO reported southwest of the city, out over the Hill Country. Most of the callers and two of the hosts felt the sighting was due to various herbs Austinites were known to favor smoking. The third host, a retired cop, opined that unknown flying objects certainly existed because so many had been reported for hundreds of years. Why, they were even mentioned in the Bible. Trouble was, he said, no one had yet figured out what they were—extraterrestrials, manifestations from another dimension, reflections from car windshields—who knew?

Ray let a single laugh up from his throat. He washed his face and slathered on shaving cream. As he negotiated the razor around his face, he tried to map out his day.

The news about Fred would mean driving up to the county seat in Wallaceville to get the official report from the sheriff's office, then he'd have to get the funeral details, then he'd have to contact Fred's family. Who was it? A daughter and an ex-wife in Leakey. Janice was the daughter's name, but he couldn't remember if he knew the ex's. He hoped he could get that from the S.O., too. Then write up the story and obit information. Find a photo of Fred. He was certain he had one in the files from the Ice Cream Social the last Fourth of July when Fred rode his Harley festooned in American and Texas flags in the parade. He'd drive out to Chicken Charley's and talk to her mom, Sarah. He'd go by the accident scene and take a picture or two. Maybe grab a snap of one of the footprints LeRoi told him about, if they hadn't been trampled over by cops and curious passersby and the wrecker driver the S.O. would have called in by now to haul the bike out. Then write it all up in some pithy fashion. He escaped the city and bought this weekly paper for this?

"Work! What is it good for? Absolutely nothing!" That's what Starr should have sung.

CHAPTER 3:
BIG ROLL CONFABULATION AT THE FORK

Ray slathered butter on an oat bran muffin to make it taste a little less like cardboard. He yawned. He was at his usual table on the deck outside the Fork in the Road restaurant, the only one of the three restaurants in town that opened for breakfast.

"Where's everybody else?" asked Angie, the live-in sweetie of Fork owner Tom Dilligara, as she removed the "Reserved" sign from his table and set down a carafe of coffee.

"Oh, they'll be here pretty soon."

"When did you take to muffins? My rolls aren't good enough anymore?"

"I consider those colossal maple pecan cinnamon rolls to be your personal contribution to the betterment of society," Ray said. "I'd much rather have a Big Roll. But I'm after the fiber right now. I need a bowel movement more."

She patted him on the head as she walked away. "Too much information, Ray."

He sat on the deck and inhaled the warm April air tinged with wildflowers. On days like this he couldn't imagine being any place else. This day would be perfection if it weren't for his constipation, lack of sleep, work lurking, and Fred dying.

"Wha'd'you know good?" Trey Burleson said as he sat down next to Ray.

Ray shook his head. "Fred's dead."

"Oh, my gravy." Trey poured a cup of coffee from the carafe on the table. "On his motorcycle?"

"He lost control of his bike and smashed head-on into a rather large oak. Best guess right now is between midnight and dawn. Once the S.O. gets a T.O.D. from the M.E. we'll know better."

Trey whistled amazement, cutting a slice from a Big Roll—a cinnamon roll so large it could almost have substituted for a hub cap. Instead of being covered in vanilla icing like most such rolls, this one was drenched in maple frosting dotted with pieces of pecans. After eating the slice, he asked, "And how'd you find out?"

"LeRoi called me," Ray said after drinking some orange juice. "Don't that just knock your dick in the dirt? Most cops I've ever known don't care much for civilians and newspaper folk even less, much less call 'em smooth up with scoops early in the morning."

Ray smiled. "You're jealous."

"I ain't jealous."

"Yeah, you are, but you have no need to be. You and I have been friends much longer and we have an unbreakable bond between us, you know."

"I know, I know," Trey said, nodding his head. "I reckon I'll never get used t' friendly cops."

"I'm not sure I'd call LeRoi friendly," Ray said.

"Is t'you."

"See, you are jealous."

Trey shook his head firmly, slowly, rolling his eyes at the same time as he adjusted the glasses that kept sliding down his nose.

"I keep telling you," Ray said, gesturing with half of his muffin.

"Yeah, yeah, this Cowboy Action Shooting thing."

"You need to come out and watch us some day, then you'll understand."

"Why would I want t'watch a bunch of grown men—"

"And women and children..."

"And women and children play Cowboys and Indians with real guns? How schmaltzy can you get? I don't know about you, but I grew up a bit back."

"Lookit," Ray said. "It's fun and what's wrong with wanting to relive your childhood a little? But it's more than that. All the usual social differences don't exist on the range. We're all just cowboys. You become friends with people you might not even associate with out in the real world."

"Never try to teach a pig to sing," LeRoi Nguyen said, sitting down at the table carrying a Big Roll on a plate from the buffet. He poured a cup of coffee from the carafe. "You will just waste your time and annoy the pig."

As LeRoi settled into his chair, he tugged at his crisp green and tan uniform shirt to make certain the sewn-in creases lined up properly. The highly-polished, fist-sized gold star over his heart reflected the early morning sun. The morning was still cool, a sign it would remain pleasant in this little valley for the rest of the day.

"Did you make it out to the scene?" LeRoi asked Ray.

"Yeah, but you were already gone."

"Had to write up the report. That is two-thirds of my job, writing up reports after shit happens."

"Yeah, then I write up stories based on all those reports."

"A lot of trees die for all the words we put on paper."

"Small sacrifice. Otherwise, we'd both be out of jobs."

The men were quiet for a little while, enjoying their breakfasts. Well, LeRoi and Trey enjoyed theirs. Ray could only enjoy the company; he hated this muffin.

They formed a triangle, the three of them, sitting around the round table. Ray slouched in his chair, his feet propped up on an empty chair. LeRoi sat straight as a gun barrel. Trey leaned in heavily on his elbows, protecting his plate from potential predators like honeybees and butterflies.

LeRoi had been joining Ray and Trey here for only the past couple of days and in the quiet, as Ray looked around, he realized each of them sported mustaches and weighed in at 200 pounds, but they looked nothing alike. Decades separated their ages—Ray was oldest at sixty-eight, LeRoi youngest at thirty-six, and Trey was fifty-one until Saturday. Ray was a deep tan with black eyes and had closely-cropped hair that once was black before it turned white. He stood six-feet-two. Trey was five-eight but appeared shorter because of his stocky, muscular build and tendency to waddle just a little as he walked. He was pale and pulled his long blond hair into a single braid that his wife Solange fixed for him every morning. LeRoi was three inches taller than Ray, had almond-shaped eyes, and was the same color as the icing on his roll.

Trey cut another piece from his roll. "I seen Fred just Wednesday at Rotary. What happened?"

"We do not know yet. The Evidence Chick is still out there poking around. Probably swerved to avoid hitting a deer," LeRoi said.

"Or a spaceman," Ray said, toasting his orange juice glass toward the deputy.

Trey looked confused. LeRoi laughed.

"So tell me," Ray said, "did the flying saucer report remind you of the moon landing or did you make that part up just to get a rise out of me?"

"I had just run on that call before I made the scene at the accident and I guess space was in my subconscious when I saw the footprint. I did not make it up."

"I feel like some camel in the Klondike," Trey said.

"We found a footprint that reminded me of that picture of the astronaut footprint on the moon," LeRoi said to Trey. His eyes closed momentarily as he savored his first bite of the cinnamon roll. "Likely just a flip-flop."

Trey leaned back and pushed his glasses back up his nose. "Flying saucers? People get so eat up with the dumb ass the next thing you know they'll say they've been abducted by aliens. Wonder why all those alien abduction stories involve anal probing?"

"Obvious," LeRoi said. "The bright lights and examination table and anal probe are repressed memories of a baby on a changing table getting its temperature taken with a rectal thermometer."

Ray, Trey and LeRoi sat on the deck listening to the sound of water burbling over the boulders in the adjacent river. LeRoi savored a cigar.

"Still no rain headed our way?" Trey asked Ray.

Ray shook his head no. "Ten-day forecast says nothing at all. Much more of this and the Dark Fork'll be dry this summer and there goes the tourist season."

"Why'd they call it tourist season if you can't shoot 'em?" Trey asked.

The deck the men sat on overlooked the Dark Fork of the Bigfoot River. The splitting of the river and its later merging just a mile away created The Island, the downtown shopping area. The Fork in The Road was built on the north end of The Island at the junction of Ranch Road 12 and County Road 666.

The Dark Fork's bed was interrupted in many places by boulders that were actually tips of the same batholith that formed The

Island, and these various-sized boulders created a series of Class II rapids (Class III after a heavy rain) that every weekend during warm weather attracted hundreds of urban refugees who needed to wash away the stress of their metropolitan lives by bumping their butts over the rapids while splayed out in inner tubes, preferably with a beer-infested cooler wedged into a tube tethered onto their own. Ray believed the only good thing about tubing was that you could drink beer and piss in the same place at the same time. Plus the view of female tubers dressed in the latest, and skimpiest, of bikini and thong bathing suits, and those times when one of those nubile lasses would tump over and momentarily lose her top.

No one came to the Fork for its Big Rolls—as scrumptious as they were—nor for the Jalapeño Chicken Fried Steak nor Southwest Caesar Salad. They came for the view. The entire west side of the restaurant was made up of large picture windows, all looking over the Dark Fork and the pleasant valley scene created by the stream and the woods and the hills.

"Is it always this quiet on Mondays?" LeRoi asked.

"Monday through Thursday is, unless it's a holiday," Ray explained. "Fridays through Sundays the place is swarmed with impatient fathers and squealing children and oblivious mothers. Sometime yesterday all the tourists SUVed back to whichever Austin-Dallas-Houston-San Antonio Standard Metropolitan Statistical Area they escaped from and today our little village isn't even fully awake yet. I know I'm not."

Trey pointed across the river. "What's'r illustrous civic leader doin' out'n the rock with Bubba? They ain't shmoozin'."

Ray scowled, looking over his shoulder toward the river. "Crap," he mumbled, sipping some juice. Across the river, on the 15-foot pink granite boulder that dominated the far bank of the Dark Fork stood Mayor Jubal T. Gruntle and his business lackey Bubba Thibodeaux.

Ray shook his head, knowing that at some point he'd have to confront the mayor and ask him what was going on and the mayor would be his usual obstreperous self and Ray would write some relatively innocuous story in this Thursday's *Pleasant Valley Picayune* that would upset the mayor needlessly. Ray strained his eyes, trying to read their lips. Among the tricks he'd learned in Naval Intelligence many decades ago that helped him in the journalism trade was how to read lips and how to read papers upsidedown across desks.

"Crap," Ray said again.

"Maybe Jubal T's goin't'put in a miniature golf course behind Frontier Gulch," Trey said. Ray replied with a positive hoisting of his eyebrows. "Make more sense than all those fake gunfights every Saturday and Sunday out on the streets with fake store fronts."

LeRoi drank down about half of his cup of coffee in one swallow. "Recalls a time in Pleasant Valley's history that never existed."

They all nodded and finished their food.

Whenever Jubal T. had one of his preposterous ideas, Ray knew it meant more work for him. He made small talk with his friends while keeping a careful eye on the pair on the big rock across the Dark Fork. After the Dark Fork merged with the main stream, the Bigfoot flowed into the Blanco River just five miles downriver. The Bigfoot River and the county were named for the famous Texas Ranger William "Bigfoot" Wallace.

"Greg finally got a job," Trey said. "He'll be selling stuff down at Moondog Music. Turns out they're adding a cashier position and goin' all plastic. That's about all them college students use anyway, debit or credit. No checks 'cause too many of them bounce an' they can never figure out how to make one out proper, an' no cash 'cause they've had a lot of break-ins over the past year. So just plastic. Scan the CD or LP, zip the card through the reader, here's your receipt and thanks for your business, come again soon. Means he has to commute to San Marcos everyday and Robby gives him a ride, but his last class is later than Greg works so Greg has to walk up t' the college and wait around at the LBJ Center for him."

"Maybe him being around all those students will give him the idea that maybe he, too, might want to roam the hills of Texas State trying to track down some sort of degree," Ray said.

"In pursuit of what? I did not think the lad knew what he wanted to be when he grew up," LeRoi said, swallowing another half cup of black coffee.

"Greg wants to be a rock star," Trey said.

"Umm-hum," Ray said, "but does he want to become a rock

star? Sits on your back porch all hours of the day and night playing that guitar."

"Mandolin, too, now," LeRoi corrected.

"'Sides, you can't be lazy and play an instrument that much. He's good at it, y'know," Trey said. "Solange believes he's an Indigo Child."

"What's that supposed to mean?" Ray asked.

"It's a kid got a strong indigo aura. Seems a lot more being born these days. They don't conform, don't like authority, strive for world peace, stuff like that. Marks an increase in the collective consciousness. Some even supposed t' be psychic. She believes it means Greg is destined for great things."

Ray cocked an eyebrow. "That'll be the day."

"He's only sixteen, cut him some slack. Did you know what you wanted t' do with the rest of your life when you was sixteen? I didn't and I'm still not sure if I do."

"I knew when I was seven," Ray said.

"Twelve," LeRoi added.

"Least he's got a job at the right place," Ray said. "Meet a lot of musicians down there. Maybe he'll get a regular gig from one of them. If any of them actually play that rockabilly Greg seems to prefer."

Trey pointed to the front door with his coffee cup. "Getting busy."

The trio had been the only customers, but now they watched a couple come in and sit down—newlyweds staying at one of the three dozen B and Bs in the village, Ray guessed. Ray didn't think they fit together as a couple. The man was more than a head shorter than the woman, was overweight but handsome and jovial. Ray clucked his tongue when he spotted the blue light flashing in the man's left ear. The woman was tall, thin and severe with bleached-out, shortly-cropped white hair. She was also beautiful.

Ray turned to LeRoi. "So where did this UFO report come from?"

"Billy."

"Oh, crap," Ray sighed, mentally adding to his Monday to-do list.

LeRoi nodded. "Saw the UFO at two-thirty-five a.m. Called 9-1-1 and then called every radio station and TV station in a sixty-mile radius. Every 9-1-1 needs a report filed on it and since yours truly is the only Bigfoot County deputy sheriff in our little village I am the one who gets the call at two-forty a.m. from dispatch so I am the one who gets to drive out to his old fifth-wheeler. Billy sitting on a rickety rocking chair outside smoking a hand-rolled cigarette and nursing a Lone Star. Tells me he does not want to be beamed up and have his butt probed by gray-skinned aliens. Tells me the county needs to do something about it."

"Got t' be the county's responsibility 'cause you can't trust the feds 'cause they're in cahoots with the aliens ever since that crash in Roswell and now they're reverse engineering a starship at Area 51," Trey laughed, wiping his last piece of cinnamon roll through a dollop of glaze on his plate.

"What are cahoots anyway and how do you get in them?" LeRoi asked.

Ray kept trying to suck out a tiny piece of muffin from the empty socket between two back molars. "I think it's some Scandinavian term."

"Well, that old coot is getting to be a pain. Coot. That a Scandinavian term, too?"

"I think," Ray said.

"Radio news would not have paid any attention to one call, but several people called in sightings. Some trucker out on 306, a goat farmer near Canyon Lake, that weird group of vortex seekers out of Austin that stays up Saturday and Sunday nights looking to the skies. More folks than Billy saw something."

"I imagine it was just some aircraft, probably military since the San Antonio bases are so near." Ray said. "Besides, Billy's 80 and even though we love him we all know he's beginning to lose it. Heck, for the past year every time he sees me he calls me Bob. At one point I couldn't stand it anymore and I told him, 'Billy, I am not now nor have I ever been a Bob,' and he says back, 'Well, you look like a Bob.'"

The trio laughed. "That is Billy all right," LeRoi said. "I was thankful I got the accident call when I did to get me away from that old buzzard. Not that I liked what I was being called away to."

"Maybe he'll get some help from Anita down t' the Alt Medicine Clinic over t' Oak Hill. He's getting some EMDR done and they reckon that'll help," Trey said, pushing his glasses back up his nose.

"You know, if you'd get cable temples on your glasses like I have, you wouldn't have that problem," Ray said. "What's EMDR ?"

"Maybe the next pair. Eye Movement Desensitization and Reprocessing. They get him t' move his eyes back and forth while he's concentrating on a certain difficulty then she waves a light in his eyes and he follows the light and that's suppose to erase the problem," Trey explained.

"Think that'll work for Old Timer's Disease or whatever in heck he's comin' down with?" Ray asked.

Trey shrugged his shoulders.

"When scientists hooked up a pile of Jell-O to an EKG machine it got the exact same movements as the brain waves of a healthy adult man or woman," LeRoi said. "So our brains are pretty much like Jell-O anyway."

"EKG?" Ray said. "Isn't that for heart waves? Wouldn't it be an EEG that tracks brain waves?"

"Speaking of work, I have got to go. Paperwork to fill out. But I would love to know what that fat ass is doing up on the rock waving that piece of paper around," LeRoi said, pushing himself up from his chair. Trey and Ray followed.

"I got inserts t' print up by tomorrow morning or some newspaper editor's going t' be honked off at me," Trey said.

"Well then, I might as well do some work, too. Inquiring minds want to know," Ray said as they walked out. He pulled his cap on. "And I'm just the guy to find out."

The trio walked through the restaurant and out the door. As they stepped out to the sidewalk, fluffy white cottonwood seeds assaulted them.

"Damn," Trey said, waving them away from his face. "It's like snow flurries."

"More like chicken feathers," Ray said, spitting out one that had lodged in the corner of his mouth.

CHAPTER 4:
THE MAYOR SPEAKS

Holding two large pieces of paper, Mayor Jubal T. Gruntle stood next to Bubba Thibodeaux on a boulder. From their perch they could look out over the collaboration of cedar, cottonwood, oak, mesquite, and sycamore that stretched back from the grassy edge of the stream.

The only pimples on this bucolic scene were the shack that was Bigfoot Toobs and, almost hidden in some trees, Billy Faust's trailer that hadn't been off its blocks in twenty years. The only buildings along County Road 666 that followed the west bank of the Dark Fork were that damned shack, the broken-down trailer, and Frontier Gulch.

The Gulch was a true attraction and owning it was like having a license to print money. But Billy Faust owned the property his trailer and the shack were on. Billy's grandnephew Orin Spurlin rented large and small inner tubes, some with canvas bottoms tied on to accommodate coolers. Except for Billy's land, Jubal T. owned a full section west of the Dark Fork. If he owned the fifth-wheeler, it would be gone before the ink was dry on the deed. If he owned the shack, he could bulldoze the eyesore and rent tubes from one of the Gulch businesses. It could all be a part of the whole. It would fit in his plan. But Billy refused to sell. He just hadn't reached the right price yet, the mayor believed.

Jubal T. had rebuilt Frontier Gulch after years of it lying dormant and falling apart. Actually, Bubba rebuilt the Gulch in their first co-operative venture in what was a seventy/thirty partnership. Jubal T. put up the money so he got the seventy; Bubba was the contractor on the construction so he got the thirty. The mayor's contributions were the most important—money and ideas. Jubal T. was an idea man who had never been short on ideas. Now that he had an infusion of big bucks, he could make his next big idea a reality. His grand plan.

They stood on the boulder the mayor was already calling Gruntle Rock to anyone who would listen. Jubal T. had waddled up a ladder held by two men Bubba introduced as his "foreign exchange students." Jubal T.'s gaze kept shifting from the plat to the woods, trying to visualize the future, thinking that one day his touch would cover all the area west of Pleasant Valley, maybe all of Pleasant Valley itself. He needed just that one piece to make the puzzle complete. Couldn't wait for Bubba's CedarEater to chomp out a path through the sparse forest, his grader to level out the rocky soil. Have to keep an old oak or two, the odd cottonwood perhaps—Hill Country homebuyers expected that. He grabbed his cell phone and speed dialed a number with a quick punch of his meaty thumb. He needed his morning stock report.

"Gruntle Avenue. Sycamore Lane. Thibodeaux Street. Live Oak Drive. Margie Boulevard. Hackberry Drive. Dark Fork Loop. Cypress Lane," Jubal T. said, listening to the phone while pointing his finger in one direction then another.

"Yvette Road," Bubba said.

"I dunno. That doesn't sound like much of a street to me," Jubal T. said, punching off his stock report and punching up his messages.

"You've got a Margie Boulevard, I better to have an Yvette Road or I won't hear the end of it."

The mayor patted his graying red hair back in place after a wind gust exposed his combover. "Sure, sure. You're doing the street signs anyway. You can stick her in anyplace you want. Just doesn't sound like a real street to me."

"What's up?" Ray asked from the base of the rock.

Bubba looked down, but the mayor ignored the editor of the *Pleasant Valley Picayune* and continued to jabber away on his phone. Bubba just waved and mouthed a "good morning," raising his fist to an ear then a finger at Jubal T. to indicate the mayor was occupied with a call. The mayor rolled his eyes at that, figuring any idiot could see he was on the phone.

Finally, Jubal T. shoved his phone in a shirt pocket and glared down at Ray. "You say something?"

"I was wondering what brings the mayor of our fair village and his business partner to the top of a boulder in an empty field early one fine Monday morning."

"Why, you think that's news or something?" Jubal T. said, handing the plat papers back to Bubba who rolled them up and shoved them solidly under his arm. "Think I don't just enjoy the view?"

"You're the mayor, you're the news," Ray said. The mayor saw right through the little compliment.

Jubal T. squatted down, cautiously sliding his ample form down the boulder to the ladder. Ray held the ladder as the mayor and Bubba climbed down. Bubba's two illegal helpers sat sleepily in the shade of a sycamore, waiting to be summoned.

"I don't make news until I tell you," Jubal T. said, grabbing his phone again and pretending to thumb in a number.

"Now, we both know that's a load of crap," Ray said. "It's just an innocent little question. What're y'all up to?"

"Nothing. You understand the word 'no-thing'? Go Google it if you need to and leave us be. We've got work to do."

"Just doing my job," Ray said with a smile.

"Well, go do it someplace else."

Ray touched the brim of his Terlingua souvenir cap with the longhorn skull on it, turned and walked away. "I'll check in with Loreen later."

Loreen was the city secretary and Jubal T. despised it when she was distracted from working on important things the mayor had for her to do. "Damn liberal media always poking their nose where it don't belong," he said to Bubba as they walked towards Bubba's white F-250 extended-cab. "I'll tell him when I want him to know something and not before."

"He could make trouble for us if you're not careful," Bubba said.

"Hey, I've been mayor of this burg for thirteen years now and I know how to handle the press. Doing it before he bought that paper and I'll be doing it after he goes broke or leaves. Besides, I'm going to fix his nosy butt tonight at the council meeting when I introduce him to my secret weapon. Oh, yeah, that'll kill him."

Chapter 5:
Deep in the Heart of Professor Doctor Farvel Jerome Perittomatopolis's Laboratory

Professor Doctor Farvel Jerome Perittomatopolis, MD, PhD, AMORC, DDSM surveyed the brilliant white room and pronounced it good.

He'd punched four numbers in the key pad outside the door—one of only three people who had access—and when the door opened toward him the light cast by six banks of incandescent bulbs and reflecting off the stark walls was almost blinding. He'd let his eyes adjust as the door shushed and clicked automatically behind him. He took it all in, spread his arms wide, and said aloud to no one but himself, "Good." It was a rare evaluation for a man who rarely thought anything was good enough to be rated "good." He'd never used the term "very good" in his life, and used "excellent" only once and then only when he was describing to a roomful of his students Doctor Jonas Edward Salk's brilliant use of formaldehyde in inventing a theretofore-thought-impossible means of disease prevention.

Now, here, he would have all the tools necessary to gain fame equaled only by Doctor Salk. Not that he really wanted the fame slathered on by celebrities in this day and age. No. He desired only fame among his peers. He desired no contact with the hoi polloi, that great unwashed. That's why he became a plastic surgeon once he finished medical school. He went into practice with an ENT he'd George Clooneyized and who conducted all the interviews, collected all the money, and then Doctor Farvel Jerome Perittomatopolis (he hadn't yet become a professor at that time) would show up at the appointed hour and perform the requested surgery. That way he never had to come into social contact with people. (He didn't even like the word "people." Sounded too much like "pee" to suit him.) Bob a nose here, build up a chin there, yank back some slack facial tissue and tack it taut behind the ears, tuck up hundreds of saline bags into more breasts than he thought needed them. If it hadn't been for that unfortunate liposuction fatality then that inopportune breast implant explosion on the Continental airbus from Boston to Hamburg that followed, he'd still be a plastic surgeon.

He supposed that if he had testified on his own behalf at the board hearing, he might still be allowed in operating rooms, but those boards were all notoriously political and had their minds made up before the hearing was ever held anyway. What could he possibly say to persuade them to see his side? Those Boston Brahmins and he from Presque Isle, Maine. So he found work for three years teaching at Juan José Arévalo Autonomous University Medical School in Huehuetenango, Guatemala. Then he was recruited to do this research, the kind of research he was born to do.

Being in this small, out-of-the-way location was perfect for him since it limited social contact. He was staying in a bed-and-breakfast cottage and had standing orders for the owner to deliver to his cottage every day at exactly 6:30 AM a bagel and various spreads, hot water, three green tea bags—he took two of the tea bags to work with him so he could enjoy tea at 10 AM and 4 PM.

The precise internal alarm in his head woke him every day at 6:15 AM so that by the time he was finished with his morning ablutions in the bathroom, his breakfast was ready. While he was at work, someone changed the sheets and towels and cleaned up the cottage. It was a satisfactory arrangement.

He put on his lab coat. He'd had it made of an acrylic fiber so it wouldn't wrinkle or show stains. He bought only clothing made of the same material for the same reasons. It made his life simpler and easier. He paused.

Ah, just look at it. Designed to his specifications, the room was fifty feet long by thirty feet wide with the Clean Room taking up twenty feet on the far side, giving him what he considered an unequaled, atheistically pleasing, five-three-two ratio. Unfortunately, the walls and ceiling here were shoddy, made of dried out plywood instead of drywall or metal, which is what he would have preferred, but everything was painted a proper white.

Speed claves and anaerobic chambers and capillary electrophoresis reagents awaited on stainless steel tables in the Clean Room, a room that could be accessed by only one other person aside from him and then only with more coded numbers on a key pad and a thumb print placed on a lens reader. The main room had two rows of stainless steel tables; even the chairs and stools were made of stainless steel with aluminum mesh backs. Arrayed on the tables were cryogenic vials, microdispensers, thermal cycler plates, thermocouple probes, photoionization detector lamps, UV-transparent cuvettes, several auto claves, an entire phosphorimaging system and an immunoassay system. Ahhh. And the cryomatic, membrane, and vapor phase osometers. Perfect. A nepholometer—well, he really needed only one. Colony counters, four incubators, a spectrophotometer, a platlet profiler, a chemiluminescence and fluorescence reader, rotating tube shakers, two centrifuges (albeit small ones), two rotating tube shakers, two freezers, and three refrigerators. What more could he ask for?

That's what he was thinking at the moment, making notes on a small pad of what else he could ask for, when he heard the door behind him click and shush open. He'd just written down "baculoworkstation," when his first assistant—what was her name? Dinah? Diane? Dora? Whatever—stepped in to the lab.

This was the necessary evil of his research. He couldn't do everything by himself; he needed help. So he had been given two assistants. His top one, this one, he'd been told was also a medical doctor but she didn't talk or act like one. She asked too many questions and they hadn't even begun. She insisted on the serpentarium against the far wall, believing that somehow quick-acting venom could be of some use in the research, but, really, comparing venom and pathogens was worse than comparing apples and oranges, it was like apples and rhinoceroses.

She did keep meticulous notes, though, and he thought well of her for that. Plus, she was an excellent expeditor. She was the one who put together all this equipment and he had to give her top grades for that. It remained to be seen just how well she knew how to operate how much of it.

He just felt uncomfortable around her, as he did most women. After all, women were like ferns—they were pretty but they had no souls.

The other assistant he didn't particularly care for. That was—what was his name? He was terrible with names. He never saw—Jordan?—much but he wasn't assigned specifically to the lab anyway. Jergen?—was supposed to liaison with the community, get all the proper permits and make all the proper bribes so he could get work done in peace. As long as no ignorant, red-necked city inspector made to feel omnipotent with a nametag and a clipboard didn't come knocking at the front door and as long as he didn't have to go to pancake breakfasts and spaghetti suppers, he figured—Jorge?—was doing his job properly. He didn't particularly like the idea that his assistants were engaging in sexual relations with each other, but what could he expect since they did live together. It was just that emotional entanglements were never good.

He knew that first hand. He'd had sexual relations twice in his thirty-eight years and they had both gone badly.

The first time was after a dance in college with Bessa Mae Mucho?—something like that—the woman who sat next to him in human anatomy and with whom he'd been paired for their semester-ending autopsy. She helped him so much with his work in the class that he felt an obligation to go to the dance with her and, in fact, wanted to satisfy his curiosity about such social gatherings. He was too busy studying in high school to participate in such frivolous extra curricular activities. His parents, both surgeons in their late sixties by that time, lauded his study habits and he was happy to have their favor, which was infrequent.

Bessa? Bessy? and he had gone back to her apartment, fumbled into various states of undress, and then coupled quickly on the edge of her living room sofa. He recalled a line from some song by Patti Page? Peggy Lee? "Is that all there is?" He fumbled with tissues to clean up Bee May's private parts, then fumbled into the rest of his clothing and left without saying a word. He thought that was probably a mistake because the next Tuesday in class he asked her if she would like to go to see the new exhibit at the Museum of Science that explored human and comparative anatomy, health science, and physiology through the study of real human bodies. Why, it provided people with the unprecedented opportunity to discover the wonders of the body and dovetailed perfectly with their class. But she just shook her head no and never said another word.

Finally, after the next Thursday class, he asked her what was wrong and she told him, "You're a lousy lay," and huffed off down the hallway. This was a surprise to him because he had nothing to compare that particular skill to. Perhaps he was a failure in that department. It also surprised him that she would know the difference. After all, she was only 23.

Being the analytical person he was, that experience got him to wondering if the other boys in high school had been correct about him. They called him "fairy" and "sissy" enough. Perhaps he was, indeed, homosexual. If he were, that would explain his poor performance with Bessa Mae.

Which directly led to his second time. He looked over the postings on the large kiosk in the quadrangle and found one for a Student Gay and Lesbian Alliance meeting. He attended and became the focus of attention of a mildly handsome young man about his age. And a blond. He thought he preferred blonds. So he accepted an invitation back to the young man's apartment and after a few preliminaries engaged in sexual relations of a similar but different nature. He felt about the same as he had before, "Is that all there is?" This time the young man—Gary? Cary?— asked him for another date but he declined using as an excuse that Lent was beginning.

He really failed to understand what all the fuss was about such relations. Every now and then when he turned on the television the shows were full of relationship failures. He didn't own a set—such a waste of time. But he knew enough from his high school and college days to know that although the names of the shows might change, their content never did. And if celebrities couldn't get it figured out, how could an average person?

Not that he was average; he was in the top 1.2 percent of the national population. That's what his IQ test in grammar school declared. But when he had so much else to occupy his time, when would he ever get time to study the problem properly so he would get it correct if he wanted a third encounter? Well, the species needed to be propagated. He guessed. Sometimes he wondered, especially on days when he was ill and spent his time sipping tea and chicken soup, and reading *The Enquirer* as his mother always ordered.

"Doctor," Diana said, breaking his reverie.

"Yes?" He preferred to be called Professor Doctor, as they did in Europe for someone who was both a physician and a full university professor, but no one would oblige him here. At least they should also use his last name, especially since he was the director of this department. Certainly he deserved at least that much respect.

"Ah, Doctor Perittomatopolis," she said again.

"Oh, I'm sorry, I was trying to think of any other items we might need."

"I'm sure y'all'll have lots of time to figure it out, but, ah, I can't imagine what we might of forgot."

He clipped his pen to his note pad, sliding them into the left pocket of his white lab coat. "No one is perfect. Once the project actually gets underway, I am certain we will think of things we need and should have. I trust you will acquire those with the same promptness you did all of this. Quite remarkable, really."

"Thank you," she said. She stepped in front of him, trying to force him to look her in the eyes. He hated that. She always thought he wasn't paying attention unless he was looking directly at her. Why, he could divide his attention several ways at once and be aware of each and every one. Besides, she stood taller than he did and he really despised looking up to anyone. Whenever she did this, he knew, she perceived some problem that needed to be addressed. She was going to have to learn that he did not deal with problems. That was her job and—Jordan's? He dealt in solutions. "We feel we should alter the flight path so—"

He shoved his hands deep into his pockets and stepped back so he wouldn't be so close to her. "I don't care what you two think in fact. If a decision is to be made it should be made by the person who knows the most about the situation. That would, I'm certain, be the pilot."

"But you don't, ah, understand—"

"My dear woman, I don't have to understand. I just have to do my job, as you have to do your job and everyone in the agency must do his or her job, to the best of their abilities. We've each been chosen for certain skills. I am neither a pilot nor a navigator nor a meteorologist for that matter, nor are neither of you."

She nodded slowly He noticed her jaw tightening. "One more thing," she said. "Something that does concern us. The, ah, six dozen rats we ordered were delivered last night and I just set 'em aside and didn't inspect 'em until a little bit ago. A lot of 'em are dead and the rest appear sickly. I don't know if we just got sent a bad batch or maybe they caught something on the flight in. Whichever, they're all goners. We need to, ah, autopsy they little butts and make certain we don't have a pathogen loose here we don't want."

He rolled his eyes and waved his hands in the air. "I do not need to be dealing with this. We were scheduled to get underway tomorrow morning at precisely—" he pulled his phone from the coat pocket and scrolled through its calendar until he came to the right page. "Precisely eight-fifteen a.m. tomorrow. I do not want this schedule to be set back or interrupted. We have all of today, can we get a new batch?"

"Impossible, given the situation we have. We need to determine what kilt 'em first, before anything else. Otherwise, we could, ah, end up with another pile of dead rats. I doubt we could get any new ones before tomorrow anyway."

"Grain-consuming animal units."

"What?"

"More grain-consuming animal units. We have only one, I believe, the one you acquired this morning. We'll skip rattus norvegicus and go directly to where we have to ultimately. Gallus gallus domesticus," he said, patiently waiting for the light of recognition that never filled her eyes. "Poultry? Acquire more now."

"Um, I don't think—"

"Your job description doesn't include thinking," he said. He didn't like confrontations; he wanted action. "My job description includes the title of project director and designates me as the chief scientist."

Diana scowled. "More poultry."

Professor Doctor Farvel Jerome Perittomatopolis allowed himself a rare smile and nodded. "Gallus gallus domesticus."

CHAPTER 6:
A CHIGGER-CHICKEN-CATERPILLAR- FLYING SAUCER KIND OF DAY

The woman Ray nearly bumped into as he opened the front door to the *Picayune* office had just put her phone to her ear and didn't see him at all. When he said, "Excuse me," even though it wasn't his fault, she didn't hear him either but walked quickly to her Murano in the parking lot.

Chigger Montgomery, the paper's lone advertising rep stood behind the counter, filling out paperwork. "Quarter-page ad," she said to Ray. "Saint Christina Mirabilis's Easter Bazaar."

"What's so all-fired important she couldn't wait to get out the door before planting a cell phone on her ear?" Ray snapped.

As he walked by the counter to go to his office, Chigger walked up to him and kissed him on the cheek. "Good morning to you, too."

"What's the deal? I just don't get it. Do people do it just because they think it makes them look important? She's just a church secretary at Christina the Astonishing for crying out loud," he said, waving an arm. "Since when does being an American mean being entitled to life, liberty and pursuit of being someone special? You can now have a room full of trophies without ever winning a game. Your Jimmy Durante schnozz can be bobbed down to Jennifer Aniston's. You can get plastic bosoms that'll put old geezers' eyes out when you're 96 years old. Why, you're so special you have to be connected electronically to the entire rest of the world every minute of every day. You have your own blog and Facebook page and you tweet because you know millions will hang on your every word and you have the solution to world peace and a cure for allergies, but you can't even figure out what's for dinner."

"And what do you want for dinner?" she asked.

"Hunh?"

"Seriously? Somebody didn't get up on the right side a the bed this morning. Remember me? I'm the gal who wants to live in your house and cook half your meals and wash laundry every Saturday morning and squeeze your cute butt whenever I can, not just sell ads for your cute little newspaper. Remember the newspaper? Our livelihood? Is any of that coming back to you?"

Putting his arm around her in a half-hug, he pecked her on the cheek. "Sorry. I do get carried away sometimes, I guess. And, lookit, I appreciate the attention, really I do. But I don't think an earnest romance with me would work out. They usually don't."

"Why don't you let me take that chance?"

She pressed up against him, her breasts in tight, her chin on his chest. Keeping her head tilted down, she looked up at him through thick eyelashes. "I'm more than a roll in the hay. I'm a big girl now."

He felt her 24-year-old body and he realized she was correct; she was a big girl, in all the right places. He stepped back towards his desk. "Anatomy looks real good on you, kid, but I've got T-shirts older than you. Any messages?"

She scowled. "On a Monday morning? Naw."

"You heading out soon?"

"I'm the only one who generates revenue, so I guess I better."

"I'll be toiling over a hot computer all day, writing up Fred's accident, the UFO sighting—"

"What happened to Fred?"

"Got killed on his bike this morning."

Chigger sat down and lowered her head. "Seriously? I heard about the UFO thing, but I didn't know about Fred. I'm sorry. He was a nice guy."

"When all that's done I've got to pour over the council agenda. Nothing much on it so I should be able to write the story up in a bit then plug in a quote or two after the meeting."

Chigger rose, patted Ray on the cheek, retrieved her large canvas briefcase from her desk and left the office.

An hour later, at straight-up eleven o'clock, Ray was eating his morning dark chocolate Milky Way bar when Chicken Charley walked into the office.

Charlene Colvin was fourteen years old and looked about ten, her brown hair styled into an unfashionable mullet. She wore faded and torn jeans and a white T-shirt. Charley was never seen without one of her famous T-shirts, always white and always with a fat chicken with several eggs she had drawn on the front with a magic marker. Ray had profiled her a couple years back in the *Picayune*. She had been raising chickens in her back yard since she was nine and looked on her hobby as earnestly as a battlefield commander would a major offensive. She was so meticulous, she kept ledgers noting which hen laid how many eggs on which day.

"Shouldn't you be in school?" Ray asked her.

She looked somber and sat down in a reupholstered, reclining movie theater chair Ray had as a guest chair by the side of his desk. "In-service day, whatever that means," she said with a firm nod of her head making it so. She tapped the top of his desk with two fingers of her right hand. "Someone stole Gertrude."

"Gertrude?"

"Yes. Gertrude. From the west hen house. Adelle, Bernice, Carlotta, Denise, Eunice, Francesca, Gertrude, and Hortense. In the east pen I've got Ida, Jacqueline, Kathleen—"

"I get the idea," Ray said.

"Yes, well, Gertrude. She's one of five Dominiques I have, lays a lot of brown eggs, and she's the friendliest of the hens in either of the coops. She's quite docile. I let them roam in the yard during the day and always pen them up at night. When I went out to open the coops and spread hen scratch this morning, promptly at seven, I noticed right away that Gertrude was missing."

"Bobcat, coyote, fox?"

"Definitely not a coyote. Too big. If a coyote got in a coop, it would have to tear some of the chicken wire and the coop is intact. Bobcat or fox maybe, but I don't think so really because the hens would have made a big fuss. I always hear them when there's a predator lurking and I didn't hear anything unusual last night, so my conclusion is that someone stole Gertrude."

She sighed and slumped a little. "The other day I thought someone stole Kathleen because she was missing but she came back. I don't know how she got out. I checked and couldn't find any loose boards or gaps in the wire, but I was in a rush that night and maybe, just maybe, I forgot to put her in and she roamed off. But she came back. I found her in the yard yesterday. I guess she knows where the

32

best feed is."

She sighed and sat ramrod straight. "Anyway, since I had checked all the coops just the other day, I know Gertrude couldn't have gotten out and nothing could get in. Each of the coops has two latches on the doors, little bolts, one down at the bottom and one just taller than I am. Maybe a bobcat or raccoon could open the bottom one, but never the top. And if a predator could get it open, it certainly wouldn't latch it up afterwards. No. Someone stole Gertrude."

"Two things, Charley," Ray said, leaning toward the girl. "First, why would anyone want to steal just one of your chickens? Second, why are you telling me and not the cops?"

"I *called* 9-1-1 and they said it wasn't an emergency. They said they'd send someone out to file a report and the only one who showed up was the animal control lady and she was as confused as I was. She looked around and said same as you, a bobcat or a fox, and said she would set out some traps and I told her to go ahead but she was wasting her time. She patted me on the head like I was a little girl. If you put it in the paper, whoever did this might get ascared and not do it again."

"But why steal a chicken? You can get a bucketful for a couple bucks down in San Marcos. With biscuits and slaw."

"I don't *know*," Charley said. "What I do know is how to raise chickens and sell eggs and I think I do that pretty good—"

"You do it exceptionally well."

"Thank you. Will you put something in the paper?"

Ray stood and she followed. "I will. It might just be a missing-chicken report, but I'll get something in."

"Thank you," Charley said, handing him a photograph of Gertrude. She nodded her head firmly, and left.

At the door, Billy Faust almost bumped into Chicken Charley. He sidestepped and swept his hand down in a theatrical bow to let Charley pass through the door. He tipped his battered cowboy hat to her and mumbled, "Day, m'am." She nodded once, agreeing that it was, indeed, a day.

Billy trudged into the office.

Since Billy's driver's license had been revoked several years ago because of his failing eyesight and five minor accidents in a single year, Ray knew Billy had gotten to the Picayune by riding his girl's bicycle the three miles from his fifth wheel parked out on property he owned near Frontier Gulch. He was too fat and his legs were too short to ride a boy's bike.

"Do you know that the Catholics are raffling off a brand new Ford pickup? Most beautiful blue I ever did see on a car, makes me wish I could drive," Billy said, maneuvering his bulk into the movie chair.

"They're running an ad announcing it," Ray replied.

"Got a special on nanner splits at the Grab and Gobble, too. Sign says. I'll get me one on the way home they're so good. Had one yesterday before the sale went on, though, I mean to tell you, it was pure-D-wonderful. Should be even better on the two-for-one."
Ray found his reporter's notebook buried under some mail, opened it to a blank page, and after two failed attempts found a pen that worked.

"I'll have to check that out."

"But don't eat there. I think they been boiling them hot dogs since Groundhog Day. Get you some soft tacos at Santiago's then get dessert at the Grab. That's the way to go, by God."

"I agree. But what brings you to town, Billy. Not just the banana splits, I imagine," Ray said, knowing what Billy was there to tell him about and thankful the man had come in, saving Ray a trip out to Billy's holey trailer.

"Oh, no-siree-Bob. I just found out about the nanner split sale on my way in, so no, that's not it. D'you know you weren't here Monday? I came by but the office was closed up tight."

"Today is Monday, Billy. We're closed on Sunday."

"Mebbe so, mebbe so," Billy said. He paused for a bit, rolling his eyes upwards trying to see into his brain so he could find the answer, then slammed his fist down on the arm of the chair. "The flying saucers! I'm keeping track and it's been a couple weeks I've seen them, off and on… They used to take the weekends off, but no more. Started calling the county in on it but they don't seem to be interested at all. Why that colored depty he comes out and takes down all the information then nothing happens. When did they start letting coloreds carry guns, anyway? Course, you got to remember the Buffalo Soldiers over at Fort McKavett and those Seminole Negro Indian Scouts down

34

at Brackettville and all the black cowboys, I mean, they all had guns. Had to. Did a great job of taming the Texas frontier, too, you know. But civilized colored folks carrying weapons is a bit much, don't you think?"

"No, Billy I don't. Lots of white people I wouldn't want carrying firearms. And LeRoi is Vietnamese *and* black," Ray said, his notebook now resting on his right thigh, his left leg crossed over just above it. "But what about the flying saucers? They running guns to black terrorists?"

Billy shook his head with a sigh. "Now you're making fun of me. I'm just saying no one is doing anything about the flying saucers and the flying saucers are keeping me up nights. Can't get a good night's sleep. If you would write me up a story in the paper maybe the county would have to pay attention and do something. The radio did some."

"How are they keeping you awake? Too noisy?"

"They don't make nary a sound. A whoosh sometimes. That's how I know they aren't planes or whirleybirds. I rode on more than my fair share of whirleybirds in the Marines—Semper Fi—and they make a hell of a racket. These things don't make nary a sound. It's those damn lights. Those flashing lights in the sky and I can see them from my bedroom and they sometime shine them right in, but when they do that I know they're looking to beam me up, Scotty, and I hide out. I don't want no alien probes up in my private places, no-siree-Bob."

Ray finished his candy bar with his left hand, crumpling the wrapper and tossing it in the wastebasket under his desk. "Tell me how they're shining the lights in your bedroom. Do they land?"

"No, no. Well, now, I haven't seen any of 'em land. Not on my prop'ty leastways. Maybe they do in some secret place. But what I see, they just shine the lights around from the sky, like they're looking for me. Then I hide 'til they're gone."

"What color are the lights?"

"They're all kinds, you know. Mostly white lights but I've seen reds and greens and yellows, I think. All the colors of the rainbow. You notice how we don't see too many rainbows around Pleasant Valley? That's 'cause we're in the valley with these steep hills all around. The hills block the view. If we were up in Dripping or down at San Marcos where it's flatter, we'd see lots more rainbows. We get deprived because of our valleys. Not really fair. Every person deserves to see rainbows. I remember we were filming *Major Dundee* down in Durango down in Mexico and they waited for days for a big rain to come so they could get this dramatic shot and the rainbow after it. They got themselves a big, wonderful rainbow. This was as perfect a rainbow as any that ever lived and you know what? They cut that scene out. Left in the scene with that ugly, naked whore, though. Go figure Hollywood."

That 1965 film was Billy's main claim to fame. In it he'd played a horse thief who mumbled and laughed manically, enough to get him a screen credit for a speaking part. But his other film roles had all been as extras. If you looked closely enough, you could even spot him mugging in the background in a shop in the fake town of Needles during the Clint Eastwood and Kevin Costner film *A Perfect World* that they filmed down in Martindale and in Wimberley. But mostly, Billy played in every little theatre production in Pleasant Valley and nearby villages—Bulverde, Comfort, Fredericksburg, Kerrville, Kyle, San Marcos, Wimberley, even one on an army base in San Antonio. His impish attitude had earned him the nickname of "Little Devil" in the village and he was so well known that he was honored on the city limits signs that proclaimed, "Welcome to Pleasant Valley, Pop. 1707 and one Li'l Devil."

"Billy, I just don't know what I can do," Ray said. "Like I told you before, we need some corroborative evidence. I need another local witness or photos. Something."

Billy pushed himself up and limped out with Ray by his side. "What in the world would you do if a UFO came down and tried to abduct you?"

"Billy, if an alien took me back to his planet, he'd be fired."

"You just wait 'til they come for you, you won't be hollering about corroborative anything then. You'll just be hollering about your own behind."

"Good to see you, Billy," Ray said, patting his visitor on his back as he left the office.

"Damn fine to talk at you again, yes-siree-Bob. Always is."

Ray stood at the door, watching Billy ride off on his bicycle in the opposite direction of his home. Ray chewed a little on his lower lip, enjoying the spring breeze and cool temperatures. It would be blazingly hot enough in a couple of months so he felt he should enjoy the good weather while he could. He propped the door open to let the fresh air in, but stayed leaning against the doorjamb. A man well-liked in the village had wrecked his motorcycle and been killed, UFOs were zipping around the hills, the mayor was up to no good, and chickens were being stolen from little girls—this was more real news in two days than Pleasant Valley had seen all year and Ray's brain had already fired its daily allotment of synapses.

He felt a pang of pain in his chest, radiating up toward his right shoulder, thankful it didn't wander up to the left. Gas, he guessed. The pain dissipated and Ray polished his face with his left hand and took a deep breath. He wondered what Billy was seeing. He knew it had to be something, just like "The Caterpillar That Ate Sagemont."

At the *Post* early one morning in '76 he'd taken a call from a man who asked if he'd heard about the caterpillar that ate Sagemont and Ray thought it was a joke so he said, "No, tell me about it."

"Well, the caterpillar ate four houses in Sagemont," the man said. "Come out and look for yourself."

Ray had visions of 1950s' science fiction films, but only for a moment. He blew the tip off and laughed about it to Margaret, one of the assistant city editors, who immediately chastised him.

"Something's obviously going on in Sagemont. Go find out what it is," she ordered. It was a slow news day and he was the only reporter in. He bristled at getting orders from Margaret who was much younger than he was, but she was the boss and he was the new kid in the newsroom. So he grabbed his notebook and camera and headed south to one of the new subdivisions being built just outside what was then the Houston city limits. As he drove down one of the streets, he got chills up his spine and goose bumps on his arms for he saw a huge hole that went directly through a house, just as if a giant caterpillar had crawled and ate its way through it. He saw another house, then another, directly in line, all with the same scooped out look. He drove up and saw the fourth house had an object stuck inside it. The giant caterpillar? Yes. Actually, it was a normal-sized D8 Caterpillar, a large, tracked, earth-moving machine.

He flashed his press card to one of the Harris County deputies outside the house with the Caterpillar wedged in it. "What the hell happened?"

The deputy shook his head, whistled, and pointed a thumb over his shoulder to the other three houses. "Apparently, early this morning a couple of kids were playing on the Cat and somehow got it started and in gear and when it took off they jumped off. It just slowly moved in a straight line. Those other houses were unsold, so no one was inside. This one, the family's lived here a month. Comes in this house and a beam falls and hits the gear shift, putting it in neutral." In one smooth motion, the deputy shifted his hand forward, dropping his thumb and pointing ahead with his index finger. "Go inside and see where it stopped."

Ray went in. The husband was the only family member home; the wife and child were now at her parent's home in Galveston. Ray introduced himself, wrote down the man's impression of what had happened to his home, and with tears in his eyes the man led him to the blade of the Caterpillar. The blade rested on a bed. A bed where the couple's four-year-old daughter had slept.

"God stopped that machine," the man said. "I've never been a religious man, but we're going to church now. Every damn Sunday. Only God could've stopped that beast."

Were the Flying Saucers That Buzzed Billy similar to The Caterpillar That Ate Sagemont? And did they beam up Chicken Charley's chicken?

CHAPTER 7:
A PIRATICAL EXPEDITION

Sebastian "Bass" Teach and Henry "Red" Haught drove from their tiny rent-house on Hopkins Street to the Moondog entertainment supermarket in their candy-blackcherry Chevy Corsair convertible, meticulously restored to mint 1968 condition by Haught's father and given to him as a high school graduation present two years before. The skulls and crossed cutlasses on the driver's and passenger's doors were a recent addition. So was the Jolly Roger flying from the radio antenna.

Teach fancied that he looked just like a real pirate—he had an athletic build with rock hard abdominal muscles that were genetic rather than earned and stood five-foot-ten with flowing black hair and deep-blue-sea eyes.

Haught was a tall, thin, carrot-topped bundle of energy. With hair of such a blazing color and a last name like Haught, he was naturally nicknamed "Red" by everyone who knew him—just like his father and his grandfather. He was glad he didn't have any brothers and sisters because they would have also probably been called Red and that would have really confused things growing up. It was confusing enough as it was since his grandfather, invalided with osteoporosis, also lived with the Haughts so when the phone rang and someone asked for Red, whoever answered the phone had to question the callers about just which Red they wanted.

Tonight, the particular ensemble Red had chosen was a red and pewter Tampa Bay Buccaneer game jersey over baggy tan trousers with voluminous cargo pockets. His last name was personalized across the shoulders of the jersey that also displayed the number zero. Bass wore a black and silver Oakland Raiders T-shirt with the team logo of a one-eyed pirate in a football helmet silk-screened 18 inches high on the chest. The T-shirt also had the number zero silk-screened on the back. A black silk do-rag covered his hair. He wore baggy black trousers with voluminous cargo pockets. They were off on a piratical expedition.

Inside the used music/book/CD/LP/DVD store, they went immediately to the DVD section, picking out a Jeff Dunham comedy to rent then went up and down the aisles that had DVDs for purchase, picking up several. It was a shame, they both thought, that the store carried almost no pirate DVDs, at least none they didn't already have. They had all the *Pirates of the Caribbean* series and Errol Flynn's *Captain Blood*, of course. If you loved pirates, you had to have those. And they already did.

"Hey, mate, look at this," Red said, trying unsuccessfully to keep his voice down.

Bass looked over at the *Blackbeard the Pirate* DVD that Red held in his hand. "Aye, that's the good one—the one with Robert Newton!"

Red bowed his head a little. "God's gift to pirate movies, may his soul rest in peace."

"Aye. Great, great. There'll be something decent to watch again and again."

"We won't be bored by having to watch all these lame pornos," Red said, waving three copies in the *Girls Gone Wild* series.

"Oh-Oh," came a voice from behind the pair. Bass and Red turned to see Barry Eades and Sammy Bryson, two other Texas State sophomores. Sammy, a short goth with a bad black hair dye job, a pleated red mini-skirt, blood red platform sneakers, and a black tube top that jiggled when she giggled, pointed to the boys' shirts and said again, slower, "Zero and zero. Oh-Oh. Here's comes trouble." And giggled. She didn't know how not to.

Barry, her boyfriend, equaled her number of piercings, even though several were in different places, but she had a six-to-one advantage in the tattoo department. Red and Bass liked the pair because they looked like pirates, even if they weren't really into things piratical.

"Whazzup?" Barry asked.

"The usual," Bass said. "Ditched homework for some tunes and zooms."

"Dig it," Barry said. "You down for the weekend?"

"Up in the air," Bass said. "You?"

"Could have a high awe factor," Sammy said, almost in a whisper. It was her way of trying not to giggle and she failed. "I've never seen a gunfight before."

"Maybe we'll see you there," Red said.

"AMF," Barry said and the couple walked off.

"'Here comes trouble'?" Red said to Bass, who had picked up two old Westerns starring Gary Cooper.

"That's exactly what we want people to think, matey. Then they won't mess with us."

The two walked over to chairs between the gay-and-lesbian section and the current affairs section, in a back corner of the store. They looked around, then went to work quickly removing the shrink wrap from the DVDs and popping the cases open. Using a small device they had stolen from the Moondog on one of their previous expeditions, they removed the magnetic strips that would set off the alarm if taken past the cashier counter. Once clean, the DVDs went into ample cargo pockets.

Their passion for pirates began one Friday night when they were at Blanco High School and they had double-dated to the River Center movie theater along the River Walk down in San Antonio and saw one of the Pirates of Caribbean movies. Bass became curious about pirates. He checked a book out of the library and was drawn to an illustration of Blackbeard, the notorious pirate who often lit fuses on his straggly beard when boarding other vessels in order to strike fear into the hearts of his adversaries. In reading about Blackbeard, he discovered the pirate's real name was Edward Teach, the same as his grandfather. Now the notorious Edward Teach had buccaneered centuries before Bass's grandfather was born, but Bass made the logical assumption that he was certainly related to this bona fide pirate and that began his obsession with all things piratical. Red had followed Bass around like a puppy dog since the day they first met at recess in fifth grade. If Bass was into cowboys, so was he. If Bass was into space ships, so was he. When Bass got into pirates, so did he.

Now they walked up to the front of the store, pausing in the front sitting area near the magazines so they could stuff the crumpled plastic and the magnetic strips into the trash can by the table with the coffee pot on it. Bass dropped the rental DVD on the counter, produced his rental card, ran his father's credit card through the reader, was handed the rental back after he signed the electronic screen and, after Red bought a giant economy size pack of Good and Plenty, they left the store.

As they settled into the Corsair, they smiled and said in unison, "Pirates!"

CHAPTER 8:
THE SECRET WEAPON

The Tuesday evening Pleasant Valley City Council meeting was rolling along as Ray expected it to—boringly. He'd rather be at the dentist's. He noticed that the mayor was passing time in his usual way by doodling boobs on his copy of the agenda. The only citizen comment was from a woman complaining about her neighbor's dogs barking. Jubal T. advised her that was a county problem and to call the sheriff's department when the dogs disturbed her tranquility. Then the council accepted the resignation of someone from the Building Code Board and received a report from the chair of the Water and Wastewater Board about which areas of the village would be able to connect to the new sewer system and when. They listened to a proposed amendment to the 1,758-page sign ordinance and tabled it for more discussion, then discussed the budget process at an interminable length and Ray's chin bounced off his chest twice. At one point he had to suppress a terrible belch of gas.

The council walking out got Ray's attention. He read over the official agenda carefully, thinking perhaps he had missed something. No. The last item was "Executive Session to Discuss Personnel Matters." Seemed routine, but there was no mention elsewhere on the agenda about hiring or firing anyone. So why the session? He scowled and went to the men's room.

"You know, Pleasant Valley has been incorporated for thirteen years now and the county has an animal control department, even though it is just one person and she is terribly overworked, but you would think our mayor would know this and stop recommending citizens call the sheriff's office," LeRoi said to Ray when Ray emerged from the men's room wiping his hands on his jeans because no one had restocked the paper towel machine.

"Didn't know you signed on to be a dog catcher when you went to the academy, did you?"

LeRoi chewed on the unlit cigar that was usually wedged into the left corner of his mouth unless he was eating or talking to the high sheriff. "Rather shoot all them loose mutts anyway, but I can not do that, oh no, can not do that. That lady, she should get to know her neighbor maybe and resolve this the way folks always have for generations. But no. She is going to call 9-1-1 you wait and see, then they will call me and I will go out and talk to her, go talk to the neighbor, get everybody riled up and pissed off. Get other neighbors wondering what the cops are doing on their street. Jesus, can we all just get along?"

"Amen, brother."

"So what's happening? Meeting should be over by now."

"They're probably having an illegal session behind closed doors."

"Should I go bust in and bust them?"

"City attorney probably wouldn't like that — to say nothing of the mayor."

"No doubt. You and Chigger going over to Trey's birthday barbecue Saturday?"

"Only if he's marinating them in that bourbon sauce you make. Man, that stuff is good."

"Going to cook them on the grill, so I do not think he can use as much of the sauce as he usually does when he broils them, but they will have a fine taste for sure. I do not know if he can cook steak with the sauce."

"Chigger said she's going. I'll be there the God lord willing and the river don't rise. I assume you are, what with the free food and all."

"I will be there, assuming I do not have to solve some terrible crime. River rises and I will be real busy and you got a front-page story. How long has it been since we had a good soak?"

"Last August if memory serves, and it always does. Give you the exact date tomorrow morning if you're that curious. I believe it was around the twenty-third. I'm on the verge of forgetting what rain looks like."

"When you and that gal going to get serious anyway?"

"About the time you get your pesky into Doria."

"Hey, let us not go there."

Ray raised his eyebrows as he cocked his head to one side, hearing a noise. "You ain't."

The door behind the long council table swung open and the members retook their seats. With them came a stranger. Ray recognized him from the Fork in the Road that morning. He quickly scanned the audience and noticed the female half of the couple sitting in the front row. With other people around for comparison, he noticed that she was even taller than he thought, likely as tall as LeRoi.

Councilman Lamar Pendergrass moved that the village create the position of city manager in order to help the mayor run the village more efficiently and Councilwoman Doris Pirtle seconded it quickly. Jubal T. asked for those in favor and all said, "Aye."

"Motion passes," Jubal T. said, gaveling the motion into law.

Councilwoman Pirtle moved that George Jefferson Wallace, an eminently qualified city administrator, fill the city manager position. Councilman Pendergrass seconded the motion; Jubal T. called for the vote and it was, again, unanimous.

"Excuse me," Ray said, standing up to disrupt the meeting that, up until now, was going just as Jubal T. probably hoped it would. "You can't do this."

"You're out of order," Jubal T, said, pounding his gavel three times. He loved his gavel.

"Yeah, I imagine I am, but the whole council is out of order on this. The city manager position wasn't on the agenda and you can't do this without going through the legally required steps. Ask your own city attorney who, quite frankly, I'm amazed let this happen."

Jubal T.'s face turned red and he popped his gavel again. "I said you're out of order."

"Umm, he's, well, he's technically correct, you know," Jasper Dean, an attorney from Dripping Springs who moonlighted as Pleasant Valley's city attorney because the small town had no lawyers practicing within the city limits.

"Fine time to tell me that," Jubal T. growled.

"I didn't think anyone would object and that's what you wanted," Dean said barely loud enough for the city secretary to hear and record.

"I'm certainly objecting," Ray said. "It has to be posted on the agenda and it has to stand for two readings before you can vote on it."

"Well, then I guess we'll fix it," Jubal T. spat. "Meantime, Mr. Wallace will serve as acting city manager."

"I don't think you can do that either," Ray said.

"Then he will serve as an unpaid special assistant to the mayor!" Jubal T. gaveled, asked for a motion to adjourn, got it and a second, and closed the meeting. He immediately stood up and motioned for the stranger to stand beside him. Ray fumbled for the camera stuffed in his shoulder bag. Jubal T. smiled. Ray felt flustered.

"I'd like to introduce y'all to our new city manager, George J. Wallace, who has excellent credentials," Jubal T. proclaimed, waving to the woman in the front row to join them on the dais, behaving as if the previous few minutes had never happened.

Ray thought the mayor was looking at the woman with resolute lust in his heart and he wondered whether her husband noticed it, too. Jubal T. was almost drooling over her culottes.

"And this is Mr. Wallace's lovely bride Diana," the mayor said. "We know you will all want to welcome them to our fair village. He'll be moving into his office here at City Hall early tomorrow morning so remember, Mr. Wallace is the man to see." The remains of the crowd applauded anemically, then left.

Jubal T., George and Diana posed proudly as Ray walked to the table and aimed his camera. The new man did not bother to remove the Bluetooth device draped over his left ear—the one that Ray had also noticed at the Fork—and Ray wondered if perhaps he'd had it surgically attached. Implantation was the next logical step for society. Up close now, Ray realized the man shaved his head in order to hide his pattern baldness. It worked, Ray thought—the completely bald effect was bold while a fringe of hair drooping behind his ears would just look pathetic.

Ray took four quick shots, and then slung the camera over his shoulder. He asked the illegally appointed city manager, "Why would you want to come here?"

"And you are?" George asked, a wide smile on his face. Quite civilized, actually.

Ray handed him a business card. "Ray Strider. Owner and editor of the *Pleasant Valley Picayune*."

"Well, Raymond, it's — "

"I am not now nor have I ever been a Raymond," Ray said.

"His mother named him Ray because he was her little ray of sunshine when he was born," LeRoi said, smiling broadly.

Ray watched George look at the LeRoi, sizing him up, wondering if he could convince the deputy to become an ally. He saw George read the nameplate pinned above LeRoi's right uniform pocket.

"I appreciate the information — Deputy Lee Roy New Yen? I don't believe I ever ran across a surname like that previously. Is it African?" George said.

"Name is pronounced Luh-Roy Win," LeRoi said. "Nguyen is Vietnamese."

George pursed his lips together, making him look like an orangutan. "You don't look like you hail from Southeast Asia."

"My daddy did. My mom was a nurse in the Army and they got married in Nam. They got out just in time and I was born in Corpus."

"Sorry to interrupt this ancestral discourse here, but, Mr. Wallace, what about my question? Why come to Pleasant Valley?"

"Well, Ray," George said, holding on to his pleasant smile. "This seemed like an excellent opportunity for me. I've previously served as a director of public works and was an assistant city manager, so this was the next step up. Plus, when we surveyed Pleasant Valley we thought it was a most excellent small town and the perfect place to raise our children."

"So you intend on staying here a while?" Ray asked.

"Absolutely."

"Any relation to Bigfoot Wallace?" Ray asked.

"No, no relation although I sincerely hope to do justice to the great reputation of the man."

"Is that the hickory nut reputation or the pie-eating reputation?" Ray asked.

"I'm not familiar with all the various deeds of Ranger Wallace," George said, his smile fading just a little.

"Named for George Wallace the racist governor?" LeRoi asked. George rubbed his cheek. The full smile came back. "No. George Wallace the comedian."

Ray turned to the mayor. "I'd like to see his resume and whatever other paperwork in the morning."

"Go to the city manager's office, not mine," Jubal T. said.

"Ain't no city manager. Yet," Ray said.

"Official or no, he'll be in his office in the morning. You talk to him from now on. You don't have to pester me with all your time-wastin' questions. You deal with Mr. Wallace from now on." The mayor ushered the Wallaces out of the council chamber.

"You see how Mrs. Wallace looked at you?" LeRoi asked Ray as they walked to their cars.

"Was it love at first sight?"

"Oh, man, if looks could kill. If looks could kill."

CHAPTER 9:
THE OCEAN CITY, COLORADO, BLUES

At nine-thirty Wednesday morning, Ray drove to City Hall in his khaki-colored 1954 International pick-up with the name "Valdez" painted in peeling red paint on the driver's side door just below the window. He parked next to a silver blue Tesla Model X with Colorado plates. He wrote down the license plate number in his reporter's notebook before he slid out of his truck.

"What's new?" he asked Loreen Meade, the Pleasant Valley city secretary who also served as the City Hall receptionist.

She rolled her eyes. "You know what's new, hon. He's taking over Taylor's old office." Carmen Taylor had been the city's public works director before she got religion, got pregnant, got married, and got out for the greener pastures of Wimberley.

Ray walked down the hall, saw Wallace arranging items in his credenza, and tapped on the door jamb before walking in.

"Come in, come in," George Wallace said with a smile and a wave of his hand. Ray obliged. "I trust we didn't get off on a bad footing last night just because some corners were cut by the mayor because, I hope you understand, knowledge of regular procedures in matters such as these can be elusive for newcomers."

"Really?" Ray said, sporting an artificial smile of his own. "Robert's Rules of Order don't ring a bell? Texas Open Meetings Act?"

"May I offer you some coffee?"

"No thanks. I never drink coffee while I'm working, it keeps me awake."

George shifted his weight and sat on the edge of his desk that was piled with manila folders. "Mr. Strider, how may I help you?"

"OK," Ray said. "What I'd like is to get some routine information about you for the story I'll have to write on your appointment. You know, where you're from, previous positions, if you're married, have any kids, all of that routine stuff."

"You met my wife last night," George said, noticing the pen and notebook now in Ray's hands. "Diana and I will be married two years in June. Children haven't blessed our union yet, but we have hope."

"Tell me where'd y'all meet?"

"Luray Caverns," he said, then pursed his lips together in the gesture that Ray thought looked like an orangutan. "She was working there as a tour guide and I was on a tour and I asked her out and one thing led to another and we married."

"Were you working in Virginia then, too?"

"D.C. Umm, I wasn't working there, really, going to a city administration short course put on by the U.S. Chamber of Commerce."

"So where are you coming from?"

"Colorado. I was an assistant city manager for nearly three years. Very pleasant place."

"And did this pleasant place have a name?"

"Ocean City, Colorado. Wonderful views at the base of the Rockies."

Ray almost dropped his notebook. He knew Ocean City all too well. He chuckled a bit and said, "Lovely little place. I hope it hasn't changed from the last time I was there."

"Oh, you've visited? When would that have been?" George's smile was now gone.

"Long time ago," Ray's smile had returned and this time was genuine. "Late Sixties. I passed through when I was in the Navy."

"You've been there? You were in the Navy? What did you do?"

"Served from '66 to '72. Got out as a full lieutenant, then made light commander and commander when I was in the reserves until I retired back in '89. Office of Naval Intelligence. Did a tour in 'Nam at exactly the wrong time, from October '67 to November '68 and had to deal with Tet and all that. Adak, Diego Garcia, D.C. at two different facilities. One in Suitland then at Crystal City."

George flinched when Ray said "Crystal City" and his look got more serious. The illegal city manager and the weekly newspaper owner now engaged in a stare down, Ray smiling and George glaring. Without dropping the stare, George asked, "Let me ask you a question, the same as you asked me last night. What are you doing in a place like this?"

Ray blinked and shook his head just a little. "I was a reporter at the *Houston Post* from the time I got off active duty until the paper went out of business in '95. One of my ex-wives and I used to come up to this area all the time to hike in the parks and paddle the rivers and so we bought this weekly newspaper so we could move here and sort of semi-retire. City living is unnatural anyway. Life here's been nice and quiet — until this week. I may have to try to remember some of the skills I haven't used for a few years. May have to go back as far as the Navy."

George stood up and took a step toward Ray, his smile returning. "That doesn't sound like semi-retirement to me."

"Me neither," Ray scowled. "You have a resume I can use for the story?"

George turned and shuffled through the folders on his desk, found what he was looking for and snapped it to Ray, smiling. "Have at it."

•

Ray drove to his office and made two telephone calls.

The first was to the number listed on George Wallace's resume for the City of Ocean City, Colorado. It was answered on the first ring.

"Ah, Ocean City," a sweet voice said.

"Hello, city manager's office, please," Ray asked.

"Speaking," the voice said.

"Wow, a city official answering her own phone. I'm impressed," Ray said.

"We have a small staff here and we're, ah, quite busy. Is there something I can do for you?"

"I'm checking on the employment record of one of your former employees. A George Wallace who was assistant city manager?"

"Ah, yes, Mr. Wallace worked directly under me and he was a top assistant. I was sorry to have him, ah, leave. What is your inquiry in regard to?"

"I'm Ray Strider with the *Pleasant Valley Picayune*. In Texas. Your ex-assistant is in the process of becoming our first city manager.

I'm just compiling some background information on him for a story about his appointment."

"I'm afraid I can't provide you with much, Mr., ah, Strider," she said. "Personnel matters are confidential, as I'm certain you understand. I can confirm his employment and that he left here under, ah, exceptionally good circumstances and that we would hire him back."

"Can you tell me what sorts of projects he was involved in?" Ray asked.

"As I said, I'm really not at liberty to discuss such matters. But Mr. Wallace was, was involved in every aspect of the city's operation and he performed his duties well."

"I'm sure he did," Ray said. "Oh, one more thing. What's the current population of Ocean City?"

"Ah, population?"

"Yes, you know, how many people currently live in your fair city?"

"The last census said, um, it was around 10,000. I'm really uncertain of the exact number if that's what you need."

"No, that's OK. Thank you for your time."

When Ray hung up, he laughed a little and shook his head. He opened the door of the mini-fridge under his desk and got a dark Milky Way and a Vanilla Coke. He turned on his computer and checked his e-mails as he ate his mid-morning snack. He opened a new Word file and saved it as "WALLACE," typing in the last phone conversation, then his impressions of his conversation with George Wallace earlier in the morning at City Hall. He opened the file marked "COUNCIL-Apr1" and copied the paragraphs he had written about the mayor's illegal maneuver to appoint Wallace city manager, and then pasted them into the "WALLACE" file. Leaving that file open, he closed the "COUNCIL-Apr1" file, checked his Rolodex, and dialed a number in the 719 area code.

"City Desk," a familiar voice answered.

"Monica. I'm glad I got you. This is Ray."

"I know, Ray. Welcome to the Twenty-first Century—Caller ID and all that," she said. He could picture the dimples in her smile.

"How's life in the boondocks treating you?"

"Until this morning, nicely, nicely."

"*Guys and Dolls.*"

"Actor?"

"Tubby Kay. No—Stubby Kay."

"You're too good. You need to go on a quiz show and make a million bucks," he said.

"I don't think they have quiz shows based on knowledge anymore. I think it's all eating bugs and jumping into big bowls of Jello."

"Well, if you were going to jump naked into a bowl of Jello, that I'd watch."

"You wish."

"What're old Posties good for if not to make leering remarks? But you couldn't get away with hanging a rubber rooster over my boss's desk like the editor—I can't believe I've forgotten that bozo's name—did back then. Not in today's workplace."

"And Mary always kept a rubber chicken in a desk drawer that she'd whip out if the conversation lagged or got redundant."

"Yeah, but her chicken wasn't sexual," Ray said.

"True enough. Now we're all caught up, what next?"

"I have a question that relates to a story I'm working on. You've got a pretty good handle on the Rocky Mountain State after all these years on that big Colorado daily, right?"

"Not so big, but sure. And I have a state-issued road map and a big county-by-county map book," Monica said. "And by the way, the official nickname is the Centennial State."

Ray drank the last of his Coke. "I stand corrected. You ever hear of a place called Ocean City?"

"In Colorado?"

"Ocean City, Colorado."

"Ray, is this another one of your jokes? Do you know how far any of our borders are from either ocean?"

"Don't need to. I have a globe on my desk and I can see that big ol' square state planted just to the left of the middle of the U.S. of A. You have an Ocean City listed anywhere?"

Ray listened to silence for a bit, then picked up the sound of rustling papers.

"Let me check one more place," Monica said. More rustling. "Hold on." Then he heard the clicking of computer keys. Finally, she said, "I checked all the maps, checked the big state phone book we have, and I know from having driven, pedaled, or hiked over just about all Colorado's one hundred thousand square miles that there's no Ocean City here. When I Goggled it, all that came up was a blog saying the beach at Chatfield State Park was no Ocean City."

"That's what I thought," Ray said. "I just wanted to make sure someone hadn't founded one in the past couple decades."

"What's this all about?"

"Trouble is, I'm not sure. But lookit, I'm going to e-mail you the files I have so far and go ahead and look through them. This may involve the feds, I'm really not sure, but if it does you'll want the story, too. So hold on to the files. I'll add more as I get them."

"Anything for a Postie."

"Thanks, Mon."

He tossed his trash into a waste can and walked next door.

•

The Pleasant Valley Print Shop was a little bit of everything. In the front half of the building was a copy center, a store full of office supplies, and a graphic artist hiding behind two large computer screens. Custom-made T-shirts were pinned to the right wall, behind the main counter. Ray waved at Ben, one of Trey and Solange's sons. He managed the business end of things and the copy machines while his mother did all the graphic work and his father ran the old printing presses in the back half of the building. Ben just nodded as Ray walked behind the counter to Solange's computer. Her brow was knit in concentration and her left hand was busy caressing a mouse, so he knew not to disturb her. As he walked by she raised her right hand, Ray squeezed it, said, "Hi," and then walked into the back where Trey was running large sheets of paper through a folding machine.

Trey waved and held up a finger. Ray walked over to the desk in the back of the room while the rhythmic racket from the Baumfolder destroyed just a little bit more of his hearing. He watched as the machine grabbed single pieces of paper from a tray, shot them through a system of rollers and metal arms, stacking up sheets of 11-by-17-inch paper printed on both sides neatly folded into leaflets of 8.5-by-11 that, when finished, would become this week's inserts into the *Pleasant Valley Picayune*, touting the banana split special at the village's Grab and Gobble, paint discounts at Ace hardware down in Wimberley, and a car wash in San Marcos among other small businesses begging for business. Finally the machine stopped.

Trey rubbed his hands with a rag and walked over to Ray, taking a seat at his desk.

"Got a favor," Ray said. Trey answered by raising an eyebrow. "One of your sons works over at DPS, doesn't he?"

"Mike," Trey said. "He's in Human Resources."

Ray handed Trey a piece of paper with a number on it. "That's a Colorado license plate. Can he get me who it's registered to and an address?"

Trey sighed. "I don't really think that's his area."

"I know, I know. But he's got access to all the right programs. He can find out in just a couple of clicks."

"I reckon he can. Now?"

Ray answered with a shrug of his shoulders and a nod of his head. Trey held up a finger and picked up the phone. Ray went back into the front room. He saw Solange leaning back in her expensive, ergonomically proper chair, her hands behind her head.

"Anything special for this Saturday?" he asked her.

"LeRoi is supposed to get me his sauce by Friday night so we'll have all the usual. Ronny is baking a cake and he'll bring that in from his bakery in San Antone Saturday morning. I have one little appetizer surprise."

"Which is?"

"If I told you, it wouldn't be a surprise."

"All your boys be here?"

"Ray," she said. "Ray, when was the last time we ever had all the boys together?"

He shrugged.

She sucked her teeth. "Christmas nine years ago. They say children are a great comfort in your old age. I just know they'll help me get there quicker. And I have a feeling that even when I die they all won't be able to show up for the funeral."

"You shouldn't have had so many."

"Who'd've thunk I'd be so damn fertile and Trey'd make sure they all had handles on them?"

Trey waved to Ray from the back doorway, Ray ordered Solange to get back to work and then walked to the back. Trey handed him a piece of paper where he had written down in perfectly formed square letters the information his son Mike had just given him.

"Wallace, George Jefferson. 742 Evergreen Terrace, Ocean City, Colorado 80808," Ray read aloud. "Can I use your computer just a second?" he asked Trey. Trey nodded and Ray got online, went to the USPS site and typed in the zip code "80808" and read the results: "Calhan, Colorado."

"What's going on?" Trey asked.

"I wish to God I knew," Ray said, leaning back in his chair. "For one darn thing, it's all happening too fast. Lookit, in the first place, this new city manager isn't at all what or who he says he is."

"But when Mike ran his plate, it came back with his name and old address," Trey said.

"Yeah, that's one of the problems. The zip code is for a different city and when I called the number on his resume for Ocean City I got right through to the city manager there. What're the odds of that ever happening? And Ocean City, Colorado, doesn't exist. At least not on any maps. What bothers me is that the guy seems to have all his bases covered. Someone was at that dummy number ready to identify herself as being his old boss and the plate info was also ready to identify him. This isn't something you or I could pull off. This is deep spook shit."

Trey looked at him sideways. "Ghosts or are you turning racist?"

"Spooks. Gummies…gumshoes. It's what we used to call people in the various clandestine services like the CIA or DIA or NSA or, well, even us at ONI," Ray said.

"Seems like a big leap."

Ray shook his head firmly. "Not when it's about Ocean City."

"OK. I get it. You don't think Ocean City exists, but that don't mean—"

"You don't understand," Ray said, leaning forward. "Lookit, do you have any idea how the military transports nuclear weapons?"

"Never thought about it. I reckon they put 'em on a plane or in a military convoy."

"A plane is too dangerous because planes crash. In fact the oceans are littered with atom bombs," Ray explained. "Convoys attract too much attention. If you're a terrorist looking to hijack a bomb or two all you'd have to do is get the right intell, wait until you see the right convoy, hit it, and if you get lucky or have enough people, you overpower the escort and scram with the nuclear device. No, they're sneaky about it. What they do is just stick them in things like concrete culverts and slap them on a flatbed truck, or stacked carefully in the trailer of a big rig, or sometimes even in a fake cement truck. The escort is ahead and behind, in nondescript vans or SUVs, even sedans. You've probably driven right by them dozens of times on interstates and never knew it. We used to have to keep track of their movements because most of them were being taken to Navy ships, subs and guided missile frigates and cruisers, like that. Now, all those trucks were made up to look like regular vehicles, complete with Interstate Commerce permit numbers and names of companies and city headquarters, all of that stuff painted on the doors. Sometimes even a company logo. Well, somebody thought it would be funny to have the city be Ocean City, Colorado. You know, because Colorado's so far from the ocean. I'm sure not all of them were, but enough of them were for it to become an in-joke among the services. Got to be where when you got fake ID papers, half the time the city would be Ocean City, Colorado. It used to be a signature spook thing. I'm surprised they're still using it."

"Damn," Trey said.

Ben walked over. "I couldn't help hearing y'all. That address you mentioned sounds familiar to me."

"You mean it's real? How would you know?" Ray asked.

"Well, I'm not sure, but I think 742 Evergreen Terrace is where the Simpsons live," Ben said.

"The TV cartoon?" Ray said.

"Ben's a big fan," Trey said.

Ben nodded.

"Crap," Ray said, "And that's not all. Wallace could tell I knew something about Ocean City when I mentioned it and then I purposely told him I had been stationed at Crystal City, Virginia, and I thought he was going to have a heart attack."

"'nother spook thing?"

"In a different sort of way," Ray explained. "Crystal City used to be collection of high-rise office buildings, not far from the District, and one of those buildings housed all sorts of offices from various clandestine alphabet soups. All those I mentioned before, Defense Intelligence, National Security, Naval Intelligence, even Central Intelligence had a full communication station set up there even though their main offices are in McLean. There were even more, some I had no idea what they were. I don't know if the place is still there, still used the same way, but our alleged city manager recognized the place."

"So the schmuck's a spook?"

"I'm a cross-eyed snail herder if he ain't."

"What the hell is he doing in our little village?"

"Unfortunately, that's for him to know and me to find out," Ray said. "Can I use your phone?"

Trey nodded. Ray dialed City Hall, asked for Mr. Wallace and was connected.

"Mr. Wallace, this is Ray again."

"Yes, Mr. Strider."

"I was remiss when we spoke earlier. A friend of mine is having a big birthday barbecue on Saturday and the whole village'll be there and we figured it'd be a good way for you to get to know folks. So I'd like to invite you and your bride."

After a few moments of silence, George responded. "Well, yes, certainly."

"Great. Starts at noon. Ask Loreen and she'll tell you how to get there."

"Thank you."

A broad smile on his face, Ray hung up.

"What the hell?" Trey said.

Look to the Sky

Here he was, better than any Luke Skywalker, swooping out of space in his new ship. Sleek, quiet, darker than dark. The ship responded to his every whim and he pushed it believing that if everything seemed under control he just wasn't going fast enough.

He was as conscientious as most pilots, but he was as much of a show-off as most pilots. Yoda and Obiwan would chide him for flaunting his skills like he was, but Yoda would ultimately understand. Obiwan wouldn't. Obiwan didn't have any sense of humor or sense of adventure. But what did it matter? Was he part of the Rebel Alliance or the Evil Empire? What did it matter? He was piloting a wonderful craft; he was an important, integral part of an important plan. What did it matter which side you flew on as long as you got to fly like this? He pulled the ship into a loop of excitement, then a turn so sharply to the north if someone on the ground had been able to see him they simply wouldn't have believed the maneuver was possible. He was as cool as the other side of the pillow. Oh, yes, he loved this ship.

The Wright Brothers were so long ago. Could those bicycle merchants have ever envisioned craft like this? Orville Wright numbered the eggs that his chickens produced so he could eat them in the precise order in which they were laid. The average American eats 5,660 fried eggs in his lifetime.

Concentrate, he scolded himself.

He checked the holograph display. Right on target. Over Canyon Lake now headed east. He knew what the area looked liked even if he couldn't see the ground. It was the planet Endor.

The red light of his time/speed/distance indicator brought him back to reality. He switched on his microphone.

"Rat's Nest, this is Thunder Chicken. Over."

"Thunder Chicken, ah, this is Rat's Nest. Go ahead. Over."

"Rat's Nest, this is Thunder Chicken. ETA zero two minutes. Repeat. ETA is zero two minutes. Conditions are green. Over."

"Thunder Chicken, this is Rat's Nest. Ah, roger. Over."

Rat's Nest had such a sexy voice, he couldn't wait to see her again so he could listen to that melody. A touch of West Virginia twang if he wasn't mistaken.

"Rat's Nest, this is Thunder Chicken. I am going hot on my mark. Mark. Over."

"Thunder Chicken, this is, ah, Rat's Nest. Roger. You are acquired. Out."

He pushed the play button on the phone strapped to a Velcro tab on his suit. It poured out a John Williams fanfare and the pilot smiled as broadly as he could, putting the ship into a sharp dive.

The night was perfect. Dark, heavy storm clouds—some thunderous—roiled below. No one would be looking to the sky tonight.

CHAPTER 10:
THE PIRATES' DAY OUT

"You wanna do it or not, mate?"

"I don't know. That's pretty extreme, dude. I mean, we're buds and all, but, damn, what if we got caught?"

"Matey, pirates don't worry about being caught."

"I don't know, dude."

"You'll dig it."

Bass's ensemble included an old "Pride and Poise" black and silver Oakland Raiders T-shirt that he ordered off the web. He was smiling ear-to-ear. Red wore a throwback Creamsicle-colored Tampa Bay Buccaneers' T-shirt with the old logo on it, the one with the winking pirate wearing a plumed hat with a knife between his teeth. He didn't feel very cavalier at the moment because he knew Bass was going to talk him into something he really didn't want to do.

"You ever done it before?" Red asked.

"With my bud Lance a couple years back."

"I think you're just saying this 'cause you're drunk, man."

"You're drunk, too, mate. It's a defense, I mean, in case we did get caught we just say we're drunk. Nobody'd think any less of us."

"I wouldn't even know how, man."

"I'll take you by the hand and guide you through it."

"I don't know."

"Look, matey, you don't like it, we'll stop. I promise," Bass said.

"Maaaaan, the things I let you talk me into. OK, what do we do first?"

"We need some rope and a couple of boards."

•

Sam Jarnigan said, "Sit," to the two young men and they sat

on two metal folding chairs against the far wall, staring at the gray concrete floor. The room was one of only two rooms open in an underground complex that housed full-sized props like stagecoaches and covered wagons at Frontier Gulch, back when the Gulch was more popular and the owners could afford large casts and crews. Sam thought it was a shame that all those large props were just gathering dust and rotting away behind locked doors. As a boy he loved riding on them on trips to the Gulch. He limped over to his desk and placed his clipboard and flashlight on it. He balanced on the prosthesis substituting for the right leg that was blown off when he was in the Army in Baghdad. He picked up the phone, dialed a number, and brushed some dirt off his navy blue rent-a-cop uniform.

"This is Sam down at the Gulch and I'm sorry to bother you, m'am, but I've apprehended two trespassers. Out in the field not on the grounds," he said. He listened for a while, nodded, said, "Yes, m'am," and hung up.

He stepped over to the young men and thought that if they were going to be football fans they should be wearing Cowboys T-shirts. Maybe the Texans. But not teams from the right and left coasts. "ID," he said. The two detainees fished their wallets from rear pockets and offered them to Sam who told them to take their drivers licenses out of their wallets and given him just those. They did.

"Sebastian," Sam said, using one license to point to Bass. "Henry," he said, pointing with the other license to the other youngster. "I'll bet they call you Red." Red nodded a weak yes. Sam slipped the two licenses under the bar of his clipboard.

"What were y'all doing out there?" Sam asked.

Red shrugged ignorance and Bass said, "I don't know."

"You boys understand that in Texas a property owner catching anyone trespassing on his property after dark has the full right to shoot them dead?"

Red snapped a panicked expression at Bass who answered with a crooked smile. "Bullshit," Bass said to the guard.

"Oh, no, my young friend. It's very true," Sam said, limping to a chair behind his desk.

Bass and Red fidgeted. Sam sat still and stared straight ahead and didn't appear to move a muscle until Margie Gruntle arrived twenty minutes later.

"Boys," Sam said, "this is the owner of the property you have trespassed on and she will determine your fate."

Margie nodded and smiled at both of them and it seemed to Sam that she was checking them out, the way he might a pretty girl. "You handsome young men don't appear to be criminals to me," Margie said. "Why are you here at Frontier Gulch unauthorized and after hours?"

Red shrugged ignorance and Bass said, "I don't know."

"Mr. Jarnigan said he caught you out in the big field," she said.

"They had that stuff in the hallway with them," Sam said.

"I saw that," she said. "A big round board with a couple of long boards, all with ropes attached to them." With a deft flick of her wrist, she popped a Camel from its package, lit it, inhaled deeply, and blew the smoke in the boys' direction. "When I was a child we used something similar to slide down hills with, but you boys were in the field, not up on the hill."

Red shrugged ignorance and Bass said, "I don't know."

Margie turned to Sam. "Did you find anything else?"

"No, m'am. And it's too dark out there now to look around much. In the morning we'll know more."

Smiling, she asked the young men, "What am I going to do with you two?"

Red shrugged ignorance and Bass said, "I don't know."

"Sam, make copies of their IDs," she said. Sam rose, took the drivers licenses off the clipboard, took two steps to a copy machine set atop a large fire safe and copied the licenses. He then handed them back to their owners.

"Young men, I don't know what you were doing out there but I sense you're good boys at heart and so I won't be pressing charges this time." She remaindered what was left of her cigarette to an ashtray on the desk. "However, if there is a next time, we shall throw the proverbial book at you. Understand?

Red shrugged ignorance and Bass said, "Yessum."

•

"Matey, we might of hit the grandest of all hidden treasures," Bass said as he slid into the passenger side of Red's Corsair.

"What in the world are you babbling about?" Red said, starting up the car. "We nearly got hauled off to the brig. Still might be when they see the circles in the morning. They have our IDs, man."

"But we're not in irons," Bass said as they drove down County Road 666. "And didn't you see that safe?"

"Safe?"

"The safe the copier was on, mate. That was Frontier Gulch. They get thousands of tourists every weekend so the place must make hundreds of thousands of dollars and since it's all happening on week-ends and banks are closed on Sundays they keep all that booty in that safe until Monday. All we have to do is wander back in Sunday night, break it open, and we're fucking rich pirates."

"How are we going to get into a safe?"

"You didn't see it at all, did you? It's not like a big ol' bank safe. Just a kind of thick filing cabinet. It didn't have any big combination lock, just a little keyhole on a drawer. We can punch that keyhole out in two seconds with the right tools."

"And where do we find the right tools?"

"Ace is the place, matey."

As they turned south onto the paved road, they smiled and said in unison, "Pirates!"

CHAPTER 11:
MYSTERIOUS CROP CIRCLES APPEAR IN PLEASANT VALLEY

Ray was the last to arrive at the usual table at The Fork. He chose an apple muffin from the buffet while Angie brought a small glass of orange juice to their table. Trey and LeRoi were already half finished with their prodigious cinnamon rolls.

"He won't believe this one," Trey said to LeRoi.

"You have to admit, it is rather unusual," LeRoi said back.

"Well…?" Ray asked, nibbling on his muffin.

"Crop circles." Trey said.

"Crop circles?" Ray said.

"Crop circles," Trey repeated.

"Crop circles. Right here in Pleasant Valley," LeRoi said.

Ray slammed his muffin down so hard on his plate that it crumbled into 17 pieces. "Crap. Where?"

"Baldy Flats," LeRoi said after a sip of coffee. "You think these are connected to Billy's flying saucer?"

"Beats me the crap out of me. Billy could be suffering from the Martha Mitchell Effect," Ray said.

"Who is Martha Mitchell?" LeRoi said.

"And what's her Effect?" Trey said.

"Wife of Nixon's AG. The Effect is when someone is delusional but you later find out their delusions were true," Ray said.

LeRoi nodded his head. "Just because you are paranoid does not mean they are not out to get you."

"Be able to see the circles from the Observation Tower in the fort at the Gulch?" Ray asked.

"Oh, yeah," Trey said. "In fact, I did that myownself first thing this morning."

"How'd you find out so soon?" Ray asked.

"My son Rick, he's boss of the Pleasant Valley Gunslingers and he was down t' the Gulch at sunrise getting things ready for the shows when they open at ten and saw them. Called me."

"What do they look like?" Ray asked.

Trey smiled. "Check it out yourself. You're going t' want a picture for the paper anyways."

"You seen 'em?" Ray asked LeRoi.

"Nope," LeRoi said, popping the last bite of cinnamon roll into his mouth. "Do you want to roll over and see?"

"Come on up t' my place," Trey said. "I've got just as good a view up there on Bald Knob as the tower. Better 'cause it's higher. Then y'all can help me and Solange get ready for the barbecue."

Smoothing his shirt, LeRoi stood up. "Giddy-up."

Ray guzzled the last of his orange juice and grabbed his shoulder bag. He twisted his cap on his head as they left the restaurant and mumbled, "Crap."

•

Ray took several photos with his digital Nikon from the railing of Trey's deck that overlooked Baldy Flats and Frontier Gulch. If you knew where to look, and the three of them did, you could also barely make out the roof of Billy Faust's fifth-wheel in the trees beyond the Flats. Trey's house was up on a lonely hill named Baldy Knob. The house was set back thirty feet from the cliff with a thick stand of oaks and cedars in between that served as a filter for the loud sounds of weekend activities in the Gulch. Baldy Knob earned its name back in the 1930s after all the trees that grew naturally on the hill were cut down for lumber, leaving only grass, cactus, and rocks. The owner before Trey and Solange had thoughtfully planted new trees in the 1950s and now they stood tall around the top, like a reverse tonsure on the hill. On the broad deck — all built by Trey's son Carl several years ago — were long benches on two sides, four Adirondack chairs, and a six-foot-by-four grill made of brick and iron grating.

"Doesn't look like the typical work of aliens to me," Ray said, stuffing his camera back into his satchel. "That, gentlemen, is a skull and crossbones with four weather map symbols at the corners. Wind speed symbols, I'm guessing in the 25-knot range if memory serves."

"Wind speed?" Trey asked.

"Those things that look like Fs," Ray explained. "Meteorologists use them on weather maps. The more spokes the F has, the faster the wind. What's odd, though, is that symbol near the old warehouse road is coming out of a big circle."

LeRoi warmed up the end of his cigar with a butane lighter. "Circle looks like what happens to grass after a chopper lands, the blades push down the grass like that."

"I can guarantee no chopper did that. We'd a heard a chopper up here," Trey said.

"Well, it is all a puzzlement," LeRoi said.

Ray and Trey were dressed in the backyard barbecue uniform of Texas: jeans, T-shirts, and ball caps. LeRoi was dressed in a black polo shirt over khaki slacks, huaraches on his feet. Only Austinites and tourists wore shorts in the Hill Country; locals knew better than to challenge brush with bare legs.

"What's a puzzlement is why you always got t' be dressed up," Trey said.

"Something wrong in wanting to look good?" LeRoi said, savoring his smoke.

"You ever not have one of those things in your mug?" Trey asked.

"At least I never smoke two cigars at a time and never when I am sleeping, at least not that I am aware of," LeRoi said, twisting the cigar around in his mouth.

"You should at least take that turd out of your mouth every now and then," Trey said.

"Yeah," Ray agreed. "It's so phallic and with you never having been married, well, that's how rumors get started."

"How do you know I have never been married?"

"You never talk about it," Ray said.

"So?"

Ray placed his shoulder bag on one of the benches. "Have you?"

"You know, studies show that the primary cause of depression among married people is being married and that the primary cause among unmarried people is being single. Go figure. But I dodged the marriage bullet just before I was 21."

The two others stared at their friend for a bit, then Trey said, "Well…?"

"Girl Friend Number One and I were less than a week away from getting married. She had one of those big weddings planned. All the invitations sent. Then she found out about Girl Friend Number Two and that was that. At least I am not like Ray who cannot keep up with who the wife du jour is."

"Hey, I don't have enough energy to balance two or more at once. One at a time. I'm a serial monogamist," Ray said.

"And what about Girl Friend Number Two?" Trey asked.

"Oh, she dumped me when she found out about Girl Friend Number One. That is why I moved to the Hill Country. Both of them had a boatload of brothers and cousins and uncles who wanted to do me serious bodily injury and I figured that discretion being the better part of valor I needed to tuck my tail between my legs and run away."

"From where?" Trey asked.

"Rockport," LeRoi and Ray said simultaneously.

LeRoi looked at Ray. "How did you know I came from Rockport? I've only told you about being born in Corpus."

"I Googled you when you were transferred down here from the county seat in Wallaceville," Ray said.

"You what?"

"Don't get your panties in a wad. I just wanted to know if the new deputy in town had any disciplinary problems before. I found only two newspaper articles and both mentioned you lived in Rockport, Texas. One article was in the *Corpus Christi Caller-Times* and one in the *Niagara Falls Review,* both about the same event."

LeRoi leaned against the railing and rolled his eyes. "Oh, shit. No."

"That's right," Ray said to Trey. "You see, LeRoi here was the youngest Roshambo world champion in history."

"Roshambo?" Trey asked.

"Fancy name for Rock Paper Scissors," Ray explained. "Seems there's a sanctioning group and they hold tournaments all over. Like a chili cook-off except you have people standing around shaking their fists at each other for hours and hours. LeRoi won the year Canada hosted the world championship tourney. You were a junior in high school, I think."

"Summer between my junior and senior years," LeRoi said. "I am never going to hear the end of this, am I?"

Trey and Ray shook their heads no firmly. "Sin loi," Ray said.

"You refuse to believe me, but I will tell you again: I. Don't. Speak. Vietnamese," LeRoi said.

Ray smiled. "Sorry about that."

Solange and two of Trey's sons—Ronny and Robby—came out onto the deck with folding chairs and card tables. Chigger followed with bowls of sauce covered with foil that she placed on the side of the grill. Solange and the boys went to get more tables and chairs as Chigger walked over to Ray.

Chigger wore a turquoise bikini top and burgundy boy shorts—both filled to capacity. She patted Ray on the cheek. "Why are you fighting it? We're destiny." She twirled to show herself off then returned to the storage shed with the others. As she walked away Ray's eyes fell on the partial figure of a tramp stamp swirling from Chiggers shorts, its curlicue arms like the fumes of a fart wafting up her naked back. She bent over and he almost gasped.

"Why do people have to spoil perfection?" Ray mumbled.

"I do not think I have ever seen someone fight so strongly against something every other person would welcome," LeRoi said.

"What about fighting for something you'll never be able to get?" Ray snapped.

"I will get Doria to see my way of thinking," LeRoi said.

"Why you putting all your eggs in that basket anyway?" Trey asked. "She's not interested in you."

"Or any other man, far's I can tell," Ray added.

"She will come around," LeRoi said. "She and I are two of only three differently colored people in this blisteringly white county."

"Plenty of other fish in our little sea," Ray said. "And it's the Twenty-first Century. You are allowed to miscegenate these days."

LeRoi shook his head. "I have experience with this. Mixed marriages do not work. I was never accepted in the black community in Corpus and I was never accepted in the Vietnamese community on the Gulf. I do not want my children to go through what I went through. Doria is smart, she has a great sense of humor, she has a cute nose—"

"And she's a lesbian," Ray said, ready to provide his friend with a definition of the word if he needed one.

"She is just in an experimental stage. She will get over it," LeRoi said. "You will see."

"Experimental like m' boy Carl? He experimented himself right into AIDS." Trey said.

"I think women who sleep with other women may be the most immune from contracting AIDS as long as they do not share needles," LeRoi said. "I know I face a few obstacles, but for Doria, it was love at first sight for me."

Trey pushed his glasses up his nose and turned to Ray. "Look, I know you go through wives like a weasel in a hen house, but, really, have you ever been in love with any of 'em?"

Ray heaved up a sigh. "When did this conversation get so darn heavy?"

"Simple question," Trey said.

"Just one," Ray said. "Just one. The others, I guess I was just bored and wanted a little adventure."

"Which one?" Trey said.

Ray waved the question away with his hand. "You know which one."

Solange, Chigger, Robby and Ronny returned with more lawn furnishings. "Hey," Ray said, "you think we should help out a little?"

"Be easier to shlep now than get fussed at later," Trey said and the three went to the storage shed.

"Greg going to wrestle the chair again?" Ray asked.

"Wouldn't be my birthday 'less he did," Trey said.

Chapter 12:
Chair Wrestling and Fellowship at the Happy Birthday Barbecue

Trey was tending the ribs and steaks and chickens on the grill while Ray poked his nose into the various bowls nearby.

"No ketchup?" Ray asked.

"The Reverend Sylvester Graham believed that ketchup would drive a person insane," LeRoi said. "And he knew what he was talking about."

"He some TV preacher?"

"Invented the Graham Cracker."

"So tell me why you invited that Wallace schmuck to the party. We don't know 'im," Trey asked Ray. "You can just tell he's crooked's a bucket of snakes."

Ray nodded. "That's why I asked him up. I'm hoping that in an informal setting he and his bride will let down their guard. Show a little of their real selves. And I want to watch the way he interacts with people, especially strangers. Gives me insight into who he really is."

"I just hope he don't scare no people off," Trey said. Turning to LeRoi he said, "Can you do the beer honors? Put a good calf-slobber on 'em?"

"I am your huckleberry," LeRoi said.

A crowd had now gathered. LeRoi assumed the role of beer dispenser and pumped out pints from a keg of Miller Lite or a keg of Shiner Bock; take your pick. Solange facilitated choices from a long table full of salad makings, home-baked breads, and hors d'oeuvres. Rockabilly music moved the crowd, each person nodding a head or tapping a foot or finger. The driving force of the band was the dobro in the hands of Gregory Martin Burleson IV. Greg was joined by Robert Charles Burleson on accordion, Ronald Wayne Burleson on rhythm guitar, William Louis Burleson on drums, and Michael Steven Burleson on guitarrón. They called themselves Las Crias de las Chichis and got together to play at family holidays like birthdays, Easter, Thanksgiving, and Christmas.

Trey gave a sign to Robby and the band paused, allowing Trey to ring a dinner-triangle hung beside the grill and holler, "Come and get it." When people grabbed a plate and headed for the grill, the band played on.

After a while, LeRoi abandoned his beer station and joined Ray in the meat line.

"The mayor and the new guy have been talking to each other for an hour," LeRoi said, gesturing with his thumb.

"I wonder if either of them was listening?" Ray said. "You hear any of it?"

"Just a little. Apparently a significant amount of money is going to change hands soon, but I did not catch to whom or for what. I did, however, clearly hear the mayor say the word 'subdivision' twice.

"Subdivision? You didn't hear where... oh, crap," Ray said, recalling the mayor and Bubba holding up papers on the rock Monday morning. "They're going to develop all that land around the Gulch."

"Baldy Flats?"

"At least. Who knows how much more? Tear down all the trees and name the streets after them. The Gruntles own the Gulch and the Flats but Billy owns the tube business on the Dark Fork and everything from the tree line back for at least a half-mile," Ray said.

LeRoi whistled. "I did not know Billy was a member of the landed gentry."

"That land has been in his family since the Texas Rangers chased the Tonkawas off," Ray said as Trey plopped a T-bone on his plate. LeRoi opted for ribs despite the stereotype. They went to the long table. Ray chose bread and rice that was flavored with Jamaican spices and the bourbon sauce LeRoi had provided. LeRoi opted for the rice and potato salad and he drowned his ribs with some extra sauce.

"How'd you like that tube steak paté, darlin'?" Solange asked Ray.

"Is that what it was?" Ray said. When she smiled and nodded, he said, "It was remarkable. What's in it?"

"I thought you might like it. I use hot dogs and sweet relish, some olives, mayonnaise, garlic pepper then blend them all up and serve them on the wheat bread triangles."

Ray and LeRoi took seats near the deck, balanced their plates on their knees and started eating.

"Billy's sold off some of the land when he's needed money. I don't think his Marine disability or Social Security amounts to much," Ray said.

"He lives frugally enough," LeRoi said. "I would not think he needs much."

"Not these days, but he used to spend a lot of time working as an extra in movies and he'd go just about anyplace to get in a film. Extra pay wouldn't cover his expenses. These days, yeah, he's pretty much Pleasant Valley bound. I guess his nephew Orin will get it all when he dies."

"You think the mayor has bought him out?"

"I guess it's possible, but Billy's such a fanatic about family traditions that I'd have to doubt—"

The band stopped playing and put their instruments in stands. They moved away as Robby announced to the crowd, "And now ladeeez and gennelmen, the moment you've been waiting for with abated breath. For your dining entertainment, my brother Greg will wrestle the nefarious chair. For those of you keeping score, the chair has won all previous matches for a record of nine-to-none. Let's hear it for Greg." The crowd cheered its approval. "And the chair," Robby said as Solange brought out a wooden kitchen chair and placed it next to her son Greg. The crowded resoundingly booed the chair.

Guided by his mother, Greg sat on the chair. In a moment, the chair tipped over backwards and the fight was on. The chair and Greg wrestled on the grass, twisting this way and that, and at one point Greg was pinned under the legs on the chair but unlike previous battles, Greg pushed the chair off and leaped up grabbing the back of the chair and raising it over his head. He turned the chair over a few times, set it down, and quickly sat on it. The crowded roared.

"Ladeeez and gennelmen! You have witnessed history being made! Greg has pinned the chair! Let's hear it for Greg!" The crowded roared approval. Greg stood and took an elaborate bow. But as he reached the apex of his bow, he grabbed a leg of the chair and flipped it up, and then he dropped and pulled the chair on top of him again.

"One... and two... and three. Ladeeez and gennelmen, the chair has pulled off a come-from-behind victory. Let's hear it for the chair," Robby said as the crowd booed the chair.

Solange picked the chair up and Greg jumped to his feet, holding his fists in the air. "Wait'll next year," Greg hollered after the chair, then to the crowd repeated, "Wait. Until. Next. Year!" And the crowded cheered.

Chigger came by and when she leaned over to peck Ray on the cheek he was sure her bikini top would fail its assigned task. He knew she was presenting this view with purpose and as he took the sights in he thought, Crap. She sat down in the empty chair beside Ray that he had put out for Trey. Her plate was all salad and she spent more time pushing the lettuce and celery and carrots and peppers around the plate rather than eating any. Her left hand played with the tight curls of her short, strawberry blonde hair. "I hope—" she began.

She was interrupted by the looming presence of George and Diana Wallace. Diana looked around, studying the crowd. George's patented smile was carved onto his face. He laughed and said, "I must say, I've traveled far and wide and that was a first."

"We have'r small town ways," Trey said as he joined the group.

"This is the birthday boy," Ray said, introducing Trey to the Wallaces. "Trey Burleson. He's fifty-two years old today and doesn't look a day over sixty."

"Prematurely gray," Trey said. "Those were my sons in the band, that was my boy Greg wrestling that damned chair."

Ray grabbed three folded-up chairs, unfolded them and offered them to Diana, George, and Trey. The two men sat down.

"I like standing," Diana said. "Who drives that, ah, old pickup?"

"That'd be me." Ray said. "You like old pickups?"
"Naw. I just saw the sticker on the, um, windshield. It's an Area 51 pass, right? You know about the aliens at Area 51?"

"Know about 'em? Who d'you think had the chutzpah to kill 'em?" Trey said, pointing to Ray with his plastic glass of beer.
She almost smiled.

"Do you Texans not believe in bridges?" George asked.

"Hunh?" Ray said.

"The house my wife and I are renting out on Shallowford Trail, near Huth Lane, requires we cross some creek and the river to get there and I found no bridges. The road just goes over the water."

"We call them low-water crossings," LeRoi explained. "In small towns, why waste money building a bridge? You just build up the road base and you get across."

"But the key word is 'low-water'," Ray said. "Don't even think about crossing in high water. Most people don't understand just how strong water current is and if the stream is up high enough to cover the crossing, that water could be moving fast enough to take your car with it before you get to the other side."

"Six inches of water will move a sedan," LeRoi said. "The Hill Country is the most flood-prone region in the United States. We go for months with a drought then we get a flood, so do not be fooled. And when it floods, it does not kid around."

Ray gestured with his last bite of steak on his fork. "One of our recent floods, TV showed somebody's house just floating down the Guadalupe River. Heck of a thing to see if you're watching TV and that's your house."

"But if you have a drought for a few months, why would it flood when it finally rains? Wouldn't the rain just be soaked up by the ground?" George asked.

"First, this area sits on bed rock sometimes just a few inches from the surface so the rain runs off. We do not have much topsoil here. That is why you do not see large farms in the Hill Country like you do down in The Valley. Mostly just cattle, goats, and chickens." LeRoi said. "Second, when the ground has been dry for so long, it gets hard so when the rain comes the ground initially behaves as if it is made of rocks. So those first couple of days, the rain just washes right away instead of soaking in. After a few days, the ground gets loosened up enough for the rain to soak in like it should. In the meantime, it floods something fierce. We lose a couple of people a year in the Hill Country drowned. Most of them are not from around here and they do not understand those low-water crossings. So they drown."

"I guess that's what that sign means on the river crossing I go over every day," George said. "I thought it was a joke."

"One that says, 'When This Sign Is Under Water This Road Is Impassable'?" LeRoi said. George nodded.

"Native Texans understand," Trey said.

"And are you a native Texan?" George asked.

"Yup. From Bug Tussle."

"I'm being put on."

"I don't think so," Trey said.

"But… Bug Tussle?" George said, sipping beer from a large plastic cup. "That's made up."

"Nope. Up near Elm Mott. A skosh north of Waco," Trey said.

"What's a 'mott'?" George asked.

"A copse," Ray said.

"You win. What's a 'copse'?"

Ray sighed. "It's like a clump of trees."

"Bug Tussle was pert near in the middle of nowhere," Trey said. "That's why I moved to Houston and then to the Hill Country after I realized that without billboards along the freeways Houston wouldn't have any landscape at all."

"But, come on, guys. Bug Tussle?"

Now, Ray noticed, Diana was smiling.

"Welcome to Texas," Ray said. "We've got an Uncertain, a Dime Box, a Gun Barrel City and a Cut 'n' Shoot, and there's a Veal Switch someplace. Then there's Diddy Wa Diddy, but it's a ghost town. You might like Jolly or Happy or maybe Looneyville is more your speed."

LeRoi spoke up. "You do not even have to leave the state to travel all over the world—just go visit Moscow or Paris, Miami or Memphis, Atlanta or Pittsburg, Naples or Nazareth, or Italy, Scotland, Ireland, even Turkey. Hell, right here in the Hill Country you can live in Oatmeal or Comfort or Welfare or even in Utopia. Whatever floats your boat."

"And don't leave out Ding Dong," Trey said.

Ray nodded his head. "Oh, yeah. And that's in Bell County."

"Now I know I'm being put on," George said. All three of the other men shook their heads no.

"It all sounds like some Spike Jones routine," Diana said.

Ray sat up straight in his chair and stared at her. "You're too young to know Spike Jones."

She shook her head. "I watched him all the time on videos when I was growing up. One of my aunts, ah, sang in his band. Funny looking guy with weird clothes. Made fun of songs and TV shows and, ah, movies. My aunt had tapes of the TV shows she was on. She said in real life he wasn't anything like he was performing. She said he was sour and didn't have any, ah, sense of humor."

"I met him once and he didn't come across that way at all," Ray said. "I was a kid I spent summers with my Uncle Tony and Aunt Gerry in El Paso and they took me to see him when he did a show out there. I got to go backstage after because it was my birthday. He was very nice to me. Gave me a present."

She nodded with a faraway look in her eye and that almost-smile on her lips.

"And Ding Dong Bell is where you're from?" George asked Ray.

"Terlingua," Ray said, drawing the word out so he could emphasize the final syllable as "Gwah!"

George rolled his eyes. "That sounds made-up, too. Where would that be?"

"In the Big Bend. West Texas. Where they hold the World Chili Cook-off Championships every year. You have heard of the Rio Grande? Down there. I grew up next to a cinnabar mine."

"Cinnabar?" George asked.

"They make mercury from it," Ray explained. "The mines were a big deal until after World War II then they all closed down. Mine heads and shafts all over the place. Odd, really, I went from living in the largest county in Texas, Brewster County, to the smallest, Bigfoot County. Heck, Bigfoot would fit between the towns of Terlingua and Lajitas with room to spare. When I left to go off to college I doubt more than a couple dozen people lived in the entire south county area. When I was in high school I had a two hundred-mile-roundtrip on a school bus every day."

George laughed loudly. "I've always heard that Texans can tell tall tales, but the prize belongs to you guys."

"As an officer of the law, I can vouch for the veracity of everything these gentlemen have said," LeRoi said.

"Beetle Bomb," Diana said quietly, emphasizing all three syllables. Ray touched his beer glass to his forehead then saluted her with it. They both nodded.

"Fine," George said. "So why did you come to the Hill Country?"

"I went to Houston first," Ray said. "At the time, I had a lust for humidity. I loved that humidity, then it abused me. Like a marriage I once had. Or two. Over the years I did stories on insurance fraud, gubernatorial races, children murdered by their mothers, children murdering strangers to see what it felt like, eighty-year-old women being raped, the Challenger explosion, a rash of high school suicides, innocent men sent to death row for murders they didn't commit, sociopaths on death row for murders they did commit, failed savings and loans, killer bees, clandestine air strips supporting Iran/Contra stuff. I've interviewed several presidents, Gloria Swanson, A.J. Foyt, Moses Malone—which I got to tell you was not easy—the king of Norway, and a beer-drinking goat." He looked up at Diana. "I even interviewed a woman who was in town acting in a dinner theater play who used to sing with Spike Jones. I got burned out. One day I'm interviewing Lily Tomlin who was in town doing her one-woman play and she says, 'For fast-acting relief, try slowing down.' So I took it as a sign when the *Post* got sold and shuttered. I moved here and slowed down. Amazing how quickly that worked. But enough about us. Where are y'all from?"

He asked the question of Diana, but it was George who answered. "My story is boring compared to yours. I'm just a middle-class boy from a middle-class neighborhood in a middle-class town."

LeRoi finished the food on his plate and set it on the ground. "What town would that be?"

"I grew up in Baltimore. Went to school there. Public administration captured my fancy and I've worked in several other cities, most of them on the east coast. First time I've been west of the Mississippi, actually."

"Except for Colorado," Ray said as he farted. Chigger, who was enveloped in the ptomaine poison, slapped his arm playfully. "Oops, my butt sneezed."

"Well, yes," George said, folding his arms across his massive chest. "I guess I don't think of Colorado in terms of the Mississippi since it's north, you know."

"Oh, yes," Ray said. "I know."

George stood up from his chair, his smile fading. "Well, we

must go, guys."

"Buh-bye," they all said. Ray waved.

"We're about as popular with him as nipple-piercing in a nunnery," Trey said.

•

The pop-pop-pop-pop-pop of a gunfight drifted up the hill. Ray didn't need to look at his pocket watch to know it was three p.m. Every Saturday at eleven a.m., one p.m. and three p.m. the Pleasant Valley Gunslingers acted out a gunfight in Frontier Gulch using black-powder blanks. On Sundays, they performed only one show, at two p.m. Ray knew that a half-hour before each gunfight, Trey's son Rick performed as legendary Texas Ranger William "Bigfoot" Wallace, telling one of a dozen tall tales from the life of the man the county was named for. Rick had come up in his buckskin costume after the one p.m. gunfight to sing Happy Birthday to his father and have a piece of cake and would return after this last gunfight.

Ray walked up to the mayor who was accompanied by his Doberman. His wife Margie was down in the Gulch, managing things while dressed in her favorite Victorian outfit. Jubal T. had named the Doberman "Ralf" so it would be the only dog in town that could say its own name. The black Doberman couldn't have looked more German if it grew a Hitler mustache, Ray thought.

Jubal T. was talking with Father Guerrero, the pastor of St. Christina Mirabilis Catholic Church.

"October Fourth," Father Juan Ivan Guerrero said. "I realize it's a way off, but if we could get the city behind it, it would be wonderful."

"I dunno, padre. I'm not sure it'd be even legal for us declare it official Animal Baptism Day in Pleasant Valley. Church-and-state, and alla that."

Father Guerrero reached to pat Ralf on the head, but the Doberman growled softly and the priest withdrew his hand. "Why would God make such wonderful creatures if we couldn't spend eternity with them?"

"I dunno. I'll ask and see what the council thinks but I ain't promising a thing."

"That's all I ask," Father Guerrero said. "God bless you."

Jubal T. mumbled something that Ray couldn't understand but was sure wasn't a return blessing. Then, when the mayor saw Ray, he said a very dirty word very clearly.

"I got a question for you," Jubal T. said, interrupting Ray's attempt to speak. "Why's the media so full of ourchists?"

Ray was confused. "Ourchists?"

"Yeah, ourchists. Don't believe in authority—"

"You mean anarchists."

"I know what I mean. Y'all're all a product of the me generation and are only out for yourselves. All y'all think capitalism is evil. Hell, nothing really happens in the world until somebody sells something. Y'all're out to break down society."

"To what end?"

"I don't know. I'm not one of them. You are."

"No, I'm not," Ray said.

"Reporters are crazier than poets. What do you want, anyway? I got to pick up Margie."

"I was just curious about something," Ray said. "Didn't you notice the city Mr. Wallace was supposed to have come from? Where he was the assistant city manager?"

"So what's your point?"

"You weren't even a little suspicious of Ocean City, Colorado?"

"Margie wondered about that, Colorado being so far from any ocean and all, but when I made mention of it he pointed out that the city wasn't named for a body of water but for a prominent area citizen, Daniel Ocean."

"Danny Ocean?"

"Oh, you've heard of him?"

"Yeah, me and several millions of other people. *Ocean's 11*? The old Rat Pack movie and the more recent Frat Boy flick?" Ray said. "Frank Sinatra? George Clooney? Ring a bell?"

"Shit."

•

The sun was on the verge of setting and the crowd and most of Trey's sons were gone. Ray, Chigger, Trey, and LeRoi sat on the deck listening to Greg play music. Solange was inside with sons Robby and Rick, cleaning dishes and putting up food. Chigger had volunteered to help with the clean-up but Solange said she had enough help with her boys so the young woman returned to Ray's side where she continued to be ignored. Ray was conscious that she was enduring a lonely day, knew she was hanging around his side just to gain his attention, and he felt bad about paying more attention to his friends and the music, but this was her choice and not his.

Greg's fingers flew over his gypsy guitar, faster than Ray had ever seen anyone's fingers play a guitar. Trey was right; the boy was good. He finished up a Django Reinhardt composition, *Douce Ambience*, took a long breath and then went into *Dolores*, a gypsy classic and his father's favorite. When he finished, he stood up and everyone applauded. Trey went over and kissed his son on the cheek and said, "Thank ya, man. I love ya."

"Love you, too, Dad," Greg said and turned around carefully.

They watched him go down the stone walkway to the sliding door on the side of the house and go inside. They could see him touch the living room sofa and a chair with just the tips of his fingers on his way into the kitchen where his mother and brothers were.

"You've got a good kid there, Trey," Ray said.

"He's a mensch. And you know what? They're all good kids. Most of 'em men now. I don't think I ever imagined I'd be old enough t' have adults instead of children."

"Savor it. It is what life is about," LeRoi said.

"How come you don't have any kids yet?" Trey asked.

"Never been with anyone long enough, I guess. It will happen. Doria and I will make beautiful children."

"Beautiful black children," Ray said. "We don't have any of those at all in Pleasant Valley."

LeRoi sucked in on his cigar. "Funny thing about being black. I am half African and half Asian but everyone sees me as black."

"Well, you do have a certain look about you," Ray said.

"I know. I know. That is why I think of myself as black. That is what I see in the mirror. But my older brother, half-brother, he is African-American, my mother is colored and my maternal grandparents are Negroes. My great-grandparents, well, let's not go there."

"Blacks are the only group that came to America against their will," Chigger said.

"Oh, yeah, right. Spare me the liberal white guilt expressing solidarity for your darkie brethren," LeRoi said. "We would be much better off if we lived in Africa today where the average life expectancy is about 42, with your belly button kissing your backbone and you are too lethargic to swat flies eating out the fluid in your eyes, and if you belong to the wrong tribe you get your head whacked off with a machete."

"Don't go getting all serious on us," Ray said. "Is it too much beer or not enough?"

"I will know for sure when I try to stand up," LeRoi said as he rose. "Not enough. But I believe I will head home and see if I can find the bottom of a bourbon bottle."

"I reckon I better scootch in, too," Trey said, waved and left.

"Just us now," Chigger said as they stood up.
Ray sighed. "Party's over."

"Not for them," Chigger said, pointing off to the woods below where red lights and soft music emanated from around Billy Faust's trailer home. She stepped to the deck's railing with Ray.

"Imagine that," Ray said. "I've never known Billy to ever have a party."

Chigger slid her arm around his and pulled close to him. "First time for everything."

Chapter 13:
Enlightenment Arrives in Pleasant Valley

The aromas of patchouli and giggle smoke filled the air. Billy breathed in the pungent bouquet gratefully; it delighted his senses—which hadn't been delighted in longer than he could remember—and it meant he had company. Even if that company was from Austin, the blueberry in the tomato soup of Texas. He never had company.

The group of six sat around his trailer on camp chairs and beach chairs and folding chaises while Billy sat on his rocking chair that wobbled dangerously on the backstroke, something he'd been vowing for fifteen years to get fixed. The group had flashlights outfitted with red lenses that, Anita had explained, preserved night vision. The red lights enabled them to see around the field but still kept the night sky vivid and not dark the way it would seem if they used regular, full-spectrum lights that could shrink their pupils. It sounded vaguely familiar to Billy, something he might have learned a very long time ago, maybe in the Marines—Semper Fi—but he still couldn't make clear sense of it.

Someone was playing odd music from a credit-card-sized box connected to a cigarette-pack-sized speaker. At first, Billy thought the man playing it said it was called "star music" but when Billy asked him which star the man said it was "sitar music." Billy had never heard of a place called Sitar. At least the volume was low. Anita sat closest to him and she patted his arm every now and then but he couldn't figure out why.

"I sure am happy y'all came out to my little abode," Billy said to her, tipping his sweat-stained cowboy hat so old and crumpled it looked like it served as a buzzard's nest in a previous life.

"Our privilege, Billy," she said. Her Birkenstock-wearing, hemp-clothed, monthly-bathed, aging members of the lucky-sperm club fancied themselves possessed of knowledge superior to that of people who didn't believe in auras, past-life regression, fairies, karma, or flying saucers. Anita gathered them from among her friends in Austin who were anxious to see eyeball proof of the vortex ley line they were convinced emanated from the Bigfoot River in Pleasant Valley that connected all the major vortices of the world—Sedona, Roswell, Altun Ha in Belize, Tulum in Mexico, Easter Island, Stonehenge, the Egyptian pyramids, Nazca in Peru, and the Bermuda Triangle—to each other.

Billy didn't have enough parking space around the fifth wheeler—cedars and mesquite hugged it too closely—so he had them park in the Frontier Gulch lot and walk across those new circular things carved in the grass on Baldy Flats. The group seemed fascinated by those figures, conjecturing all sorts of explanations for their appearance, but since they were seeing them all cattywampus they couldn't figure out what the figures were. And it was getting dark when they walked across the field anyway.

He didn't think Jubal T. or Margie would mind these folks parking in the lot since the Gulch was closed now after dark. Plus, Margie would cut him slack since he acted in the last two of the Gulch performances on Saturday and the one on Sunday. He was, after all, the star performer of the Gunslinger Show.

Jubal T. kept trying to get him to sell his property, but Billy would never give up the Faust family heirloom. Besides, Nephew Orin deserved the land for all his hard work over the years.

Normally, Billy wouldn't have much, if anything, to do with this group and he felt uncomfortable with them around now, but he was happy to have company and delighted to be able to have other witnesses to prove to yes-siree-Ray down at the paper that he wasn't so crazy after all. Anita's odd light therapy the other day had seemed to calm his anxieties, so maybe her friends weren't so bad either.

More things in heaven and earth than are dreamt of in your philosophy, Horatio… whoever the hell Horatio was. Did he know Horatio? Horatio Caine? He knew York. Alas, poor New York, I've been there, Horatio. Didn't I? It was hell getting old. He could remember the names of all the kids and their parents on Paint Rock Road back in San Angelo when he was growing up eighty years ago, but he was stumped when he tried to remember what shows he watched on TV last night. In fact, as he caught the overcooked bouquet of marijuana, he struggled to remember why these aged hippies were here and looking to the sky.

"There!" one of them hollered, pointing up. Now he remembered. The flying saucer. He looked where the perm-haired man with the Bob Marley tie-dyed T-shirt was pointing. Nothing.

"I think that's a plane," someone else said.

"No, that can't be a plane," the man said.

"Plane," Anita said.

"I never saw a plane like that," the man countered. "Look, you can see several small disc-shaped objects all flying in a tight formation."

"I guess you've never seen a plane at night before. You're seeing the cabin lights. It's a passenger airliner," another woman said tiredly.

"Plane," Anita repeated. Billy felt their collective sigh of disappointment.

Several minutes passed and a woman leaped to her feet, her finger pointing high in the sky. "Look! Look! Don't tell me that's a plane. Look how fast it's going. Must be going at light speed. Omigawd!"

Anita shook her head. Even Billy wondered, had these people never been outside to look at the night sky before? "That's a satellite," Anita said.

"How do you know that?" the youngest man said. "You can't see a small little satellite from here, they're the size of basketballs. To see something that far away in space from the surface of Gaia, why, it'd have to be the size of, of, of—"

"Cleveland!" said an oversized woman wearing denim bib overalls with nothing on underneath so that when she moved one breast or another would threaten to slide out from the bib and she would have to tuck it back in. Billy thought that must be an irritation and an inconvenience for her, but he was glad she didn't mind. If she didn't mind, he wouldn't mind, no-siree-Boob.

"Imagine a space ship the size of Cleveland. Wow," the man said, nodding his head, sucking sweet smoke deep into his lungs.

Billy shined his red-lensed flashlight at his wrist. It was nearly two-thirty-five in the morning, the time the real UFO would arrive, and he'd been putting up with all this jabbering ignorance since dusk.

He knew that couldn't be Cleveland up there. Cleveland was north of Houston. Had one in Ohio, too, he was certain. Certainly. The Cleveland Indians and Al Rosen. Who could forget that little broken-nosed guy who hit forty-three homers in Fifty-Three? That's when Al cut off his shirt sleeves to show off his biceps and ever since the Indians wore tank tops in his honor. Didn't he become a manager or something with the Yankees? Or was it the Astros? No, no, he remembered it clearly, it was the San Franciscans. He'd better write himself a note about that. The Franciscans at Saint Christina Mirabilis hosted their Blessing of the Animals in October and Father John John had asked him to be a key speaker at the event and he needed to prepare his speech, pointing out all the wonderful things animals did for people. October was a while off, but he would need the time to chase down and corral his thoughts.

"Okay. Who's parked at the Gulch?" a voice boomed from the edge of the gathering. It came from a man large enough to be called "Tiny," dressed in a navy and Columbia blue rent-a-cop uniform, wearing a scarlet Frontier Gulch cap cocked to one side on his head.

"Who are you?" Billy asked.

The stranger posed with his hands on his hips, legs spread, looking like George Reeves as Superman, Billy thought. But didn't Superman kill himself? How was that possible? "Name is Jarnigan and I'm chief of security at the Gulch."

"Since when? I ain't never heard of you," Bill said.

"You heard about the kids who broke into the carnival games of chance and stole a bunch of stuffed animal prizes? Kids who vandalized Baldy Flats with those crop circles? Well, I'm here to prevent that sort of thing happening again. I know all about you, Billy, and you're okay, but everyone else here has no right to park on Gulch property."

"Not enough room on my place. Depty LeRoi can barely get his cruiser in here when he comes by."

"Not my problem. All you people are parked illegally. You need to get your vehicles off Frontier Gulch property immediately or I will call the sheriff and have you all cited for trespassing. And maybe you'll get a possession charge or two considering what I smell on the night breeze. Be willing to bet a few of you been arrested before. Want another charge on your record?"

Anita stood first, then the others who folded up their chairs, gathering up their Fiji waters and SoBe Lean green tea bottles. A collective sigh was so strong, Billy felt it move the air around him like a vortex. "I'm sorry, Billy, I guess we'll have to go."

"Just go park out on 666," Billy said.

"That's illegal, too," Jarnigan said. "Park there and I'll be obliged to call the sheriff's department and you'll be cited for parking on a public right of way. Might be a lower fine than trespassing on private property, but it'll still go on your record."

Anita kissed Billy on the cheek. Hell, he thought, now he'd never get the witnesses he needed to convince the paper to run a story. Maybe somebody up to the old Burleson place had seen the flying saucer. That homestead was way up on the hill that overlooked the steep gulch where the Gulch and his trailer were, and certainly would have as good or better view of the flying saucer than he did. Naw. Nobody up there would be up at no two-thirty any morning. Whole village closed down at nine, including the grocery and gas station. Everybody in bed by ten. He'd have to go by Bubba's Hardware and Lumber tomorrow and buy one of those disposable cameras.

"You be careful, now, Billy," Anita said. He nodded and sighed. The crowd walked quickly past Jarnigan who turned to limp after them.

They froze when they heard Billy yell, "See? See?"

They turned to see him pointing and jumping up and down. They looked up.

Anita and the man in the Marley T-shirt saw it: a shape darker than the sky, a sky lit by stars and a quarter-moon. The shape moved quickly and in ways they knew no airplane or helicopter could. The shape stopped and they almost lost sight of it, but it flashed a light down on them. The light flicked off immediately but they picked up the shape again when it sped off. Then it disappeared.

"Get going," Jarnigan ordered the group.

"I saw it, Billy," Anita hollered. Billy waved to them, but they had all turned and were herded to their hybrid cars.

"Asshole," the woman in the bib overalls said softly as he walked by the guard.

"Pig," Anita said. She was older.

Look to the Sky

Here he was, smoother than any Sulu, sliding in with precision and panache. He wondered why Captain Kirk got all the credit for the Enterprise when it was Sulu who was the helmsman. He was the pilot. He flew the ship.

The stars surrounded him, embraced him, made him one of them. The stars were familiar, were family, were comforting. He was at home here among the stars, piloting his ship effortlessly. A glorious trek among the stars, indeed. Somewhere below, in the darkness, was a mundane world he was happy not to be a part of. This was his dream. He flew. He flew! His ship was so instantly responsive it was more an extension of himself than a separate entity. He wore his ship like a tight-fitting sweater and it comforted him. He pulled into a tight lateral loop, a maneuver most pilots would say was impossible, especially at the speed he was traveling. He went into a vertical loop, a large one, dropping thousands of feet and gaining thousands of feet.

He loved his ship. He was proud to be its first pilot.

The blinking red light of his time/speed/distance indicator brought him back to reality. He switched on his microphone.

"Rat's Nest, this is Thunder Chicken. Over."

"Thunder Chicken this is Rat's Nest. Ah, go ahead. Over."

Yes, he decided, he loved Rat's Nest's voice. It was too bad her personality didn't match it. He pushed the play button on the phone strapped to a Velcro tab on his suit. It poured out a John Williams fanfare and the pilot smiled as broadly as he could, preparing the ship for a sharp dive. He was on the verge of giving Rat's Nest his ETA when he saw something below. "Rat's Nest, standby one. Out." He punched off the fanfare. He slowed and hovered, silently motionless. He loved his ship. He tilted a little to the left first and then to the right. Still hovering he rose a few hundred feet, flew straight about a hundred more, turned and observed.

"Rat's Nest, this is Thunder Chicken. Over."

"This is, ah, Rat's Nest. Over."

"Rat's Nest, this is Thunder Chicken. I have observed activity at or near the landing zone. I am aborting the mission. Over."

"Thunder Chicken, this is Rat's Nest. Ah, explain. Um, over."

"Rat's Nest, this is Thunder Chicken. Unauthorized activity at the LZ. Thunder Chicken returning to BSL-4 HQ. Contact landline. Out."

He pulled the controls to him, pressing the throttle to full. He was pushed back into his seat as the ship rose and flew away. He was the star of this rodeo, bareback riding a comet. His mind screamed an otherworldly Yee-ha! He wanted the feeling to continue forever.

CHAPTER 14:
A CHIGGER IS A TERRIBLE THING TO WASTE

Only one terrible thing happened in Pleasant Valley on Sunday.

Those few who were up at sunrise saw reds and golds and oranges reflected off of scattered clouds, then saw the sun chase off most of the clouds and indigo establish a plush coverlet in the sky. The greens of the grasses, the cactus, the cedars, the hackberries, the oaks, the cottonwoods, and the sycamores were too varied to count, accentuated by red and yellow and blue wildflowers.

The Catholics flocked to one of two masses at Saint Christina Mirabilis, one in Spanish at nine a.m. and one in English at eleven a.m.

The non-denominational Sanctuary of the Waters held its single service at ten a.m., with song and prayer praising God, Yahweh, Allah, the Goddess, and Gitchi Manitou led by Pastorette Sylvia Sarplaninac who had a voice like a hound and her able assistant Doria Charmeine who had a voice like an angel.

The air was clear and fresh and the village was quiet. It was a silence that frightened urbanites who had never heard such a thing. Soon the cicadas would begin their incessant thrumming, sounding like an old refrigerator, but not yet. Not yet. A dog barked somewhere distant—just one dog and just one bark. The aroma of wildflowers and fresh water tumbling over rocks in the river filled nostrils. Once taken in, the aroma was addictive and enamored people to Pleasant Valley. Love at first inhalation.

Two of the three restaurants in Pleasant Valley were closed on Sundays. The Fork in the Road had usual waiting times of an hour or more for a table, so most families gathered around their own tables for an afternoon dinner or drove the family car to nearby cities for dinner at the Wimberley Cafe or Cracker Barrel or Krause's or McDonald's. Some families drove west for a picnic at Pedernales Falls State Falls or Enchanted Rock State Natural Area, or drove north for a picnic at Inks Lake State Park, or drove east for pork and pies at Royer's in Round

Top. Some families drove just a couple of miles north to a lush field of bluebonnets in which they carefully placed their children, taking photographs that would be mailed and e-mailed and Facebooked and YouTubed to friends and relatives around the world.

Men mowed lawns then retreated to their man caves to drink beer and eat salty snacks while watching a baseball game on television. Teenagers on back porches gawked at surrounding trees, pining for friends and shunning parents—some wrote poetry. Children not forced on outings to parks or wildflower fields cowered in their bedrooms playing video games. Infants flopped around on living room floors covered with thin blankets smelling of spoiled milk and green poop, trying in vain to focus on dancing bunny rabbits on a DVD playing on the HD TV. Women knocked back a shot or two of Kahlua before dusting and sweeping up.

By late afternoon, the sun was warm enough to allow Sylvia Sarplaniac and Doria Charmeine to lounge around Sylvia's small, nicely-landscaped pool wearing their nicely-shaped birthday suits while sipping pomegranate juice. The air was nearly hot, but the water remained cold.

Father Juan Ivan Guerrero spent the afternoon on the front porch of his small cottage, drawing silly cartoons starring a randy raccoon, a crazy squirrel, and a philosophical frog that he posted regularly on his anonymous website.

After fixing his usual brunch, Bigfoot County Deputy Sheriff LeRoi Jones Nguyen called his parents in Rockport, listening to his mother tell him about her week teaching special education students and his father lying about the amount of shrimp he had brought in during the previous week.

Trey, Solange and Greg Burleson drove an hour and half to the Lone Star Bakery in Round Rock to indulge themselves in the golden, melt-in-your-mouth doughnuts the bakery was renowned for. After gorging on the doughnuts, they would find a movie and pig out on buttered popcorn and Sno-Caps and 64-ounce Coca Colas. After the movie they would return home where Greg would practice on one of his guitars while his parents retreated to their bedroom and practice an activity that, with so many sons as proof, they knew all too well. In the evening they would watch *The Amazing Race* on TV, read books, and then call it a day.

But at five minutes after eight o'clock that morning Ray Wyatt Strider woke up in his bed with a headache, blocked sinuses, and a pain in his stomach. He turned over and his hand touched something unfamiliar. He forced his eyes open to see Tiffany Melissa "Chigger" Montgomery's naked body serene in sleep next to him. This was, to him, a terrible thing.

"Crap," he said.

CHAPTER 15:
WOMAN PROBLEMS

The trio gathered at the Fork. Ray nibbled on a cranberry muffin and didn't look enviously at the Big Rolls on the other plates.

"A little surly this Monday morning," Trey said to LeRoi, pointing his roll-filled fork at Ray.

"You know how it is, surly to bed, surly to rise," LeRoi said before gulping down about a third of his coffee. "I cannot wait to hear this explanation."

"Go to hell," Ray said.

Trey put down his fork and pushed back a little from the table. "Oh, my gravy. This is as serious as squatting bareassed in a nest of rattlers."

Ray shook his bowed head. "I'm sorry. It's just... well... I did something I knew I shouldn't do and now that I did it I'm regretting it even more than I thought possible."

"Must have finally bedded down with Chigger," LeRoi said. Trey nodded agreement and went back to his roll.

After a few moments, Ray said. "Yeah. I'm a tower of strength. I can resist anything except temptation."

"Well, how bad can it be? Seems hot enough to me," Trey said. "You could do worse."

"I always do," Ray said. He ate some of his muffin. It was sweeter than he thought it should be—too sweet if you weren't used to it or weren't six years old.

Silence returned and hung around longer this time. Finally LeRoi said, "We are your friends. Did something bad happen? Failure to launch? You can tell us, you know."

Ray tossed his muffin so hard on his plate that it bounced off and flew onto the floor. "Lookit, the fact that it happened is bad enough. I guess I didn't realize it before, but she looks... Hey, I'm old enough to be her grandfather, for crying out loud. This ain't going to end well."

"Stop kvetching, grandpa," Trey said.

"Change the subject," Ray said.

"World peace? The meaning of life? What is on TV tonight?" LeRoi said.

Instead of discussing any of the proposed subjects, two of them concentrated on putting away their prodigious cinnamon rolls and Ray sipped orange juice. Finally, Ray asked Trey: "I know Rick and Will both work for the county, but which son is in the clerk's office?"

"Rick," Trey said. "Will's with the assessor/collector."

"Thanks."

"Where'd you be without my sons?" Trey asked, drinking the last of his coffee.

"Having to do his own legwork," LeRoi said.

●

When Chigger walked into the office, she smiled at Ray who was on his phone, went over and kissed him on the back of his neck. He turned as she walked away to her desk and started going through the morning mail.

Ray listened to Rick tell him, "No prob, Uncle Ray, I don't even have to look it up. Bubba came in here last week and filed the plans. I noticed because it was a huge development and it was in Pleasant Valley. You need to know the corporation name, I can get you that."

"That would be good, and if it's a corp or a DBA—"

"I know, you'd like the principals," Rick said.

"You're a treasure," Ray said. "Can I get copies of the plat?"

"Sure, regular charges apply. But I remember those places real clear. I grew up looking down on Baldy Flats and the river but after they build this, Mom and Pop'll be looking down at the tops of houses. Can't imagine."

"Change is inevitable, I guess, whether we like it or not."

"Can you do anything to stop it?"

"Well, I sure as heck can publicize the crap out of it. And I'm going to let the Pleasant Valley Historical and Cultural Preservation and Beautification Society know what's going on and I know they'll raise a stink."

"Isn't Margie the president of that?" Rick said. "Seems odd Jubal T. would be doing something like this. I'd figure she'd be pissed enough at this kind of development to kill somebody."

"Seems odd to me, too. Well, get me that info and I'll stop up later. Thanks."

Ray put the phone up and waved to Chigger. He said, "Lookit, we have to talk—" and heard a soft pop, and then a rancid smell filled his nostrils. He stood up and looked around.

Chigger was at one of the windows, trying to open it. When she failed she rushed to another window but couldn't open that one either. "O.M.G!"

Ray's voice rose. "What the heck?"

"Somebody sent a stink bomb in the mail and I can't get the windows open because they're all stuck."

Ray saw two boxes on Chigger's desk. One was a cardboard box full of plastic peanuts. The other was a four-inch square wooden box with the lid open. The smell was gushing from the wooden box. He looked over and saw the lid of the wooden box had a spring attached to it that was apparently attached to the stink bomb's fuse. When Chigger opened the wooden box, she set off the bomb. He picked it up and carried it outside.

"First thing we do is get this darn thing out of here," he said. He tossed the small, fuming pyrotechnic into the parking lot. Returning inside, he left the door open, then turned on the room's two ceiling fans.

Chigger's eyes widened. Her lips pursed together. "The windows are all stuck."

"They don't open," Ray explained, sitting back at his desk, waving his right hand to guide the fumes around him.

"Seriously? Well, that's stupid."

"Didn't have any choice. We had to prevent people from breaking in and smashing up all the computers."

"That's happened?" She stood by the door, breathing in fresh air.

"Not too long after I bought the paper," Ray said. "Came in through a window and smashed all the computers with a baseball bat.

Ripped some files up. Place was a real mess."

"If the windows don't open why do some still have screens on the outside?"

"I'm putting screens on all the windows, as I can afford them. Only two to go. They're expensive because they're not really screens. They're much stronger. Stainless steel security screens. They're designed to keep someone from throwing rocks or bricks through the windows."

"People have done that?"

"Nope. And I don't particularly want her to."

"Her," she said. It wasn't a question.

Ray shrugged and rolled his eyes. "The Ex-Wife from Hell."

"Y'all must have had a lovely relationship."

"We did for all of six months. Marriage lasted a whole nine months. I'm not sure how."

"So what in the world did you do to set her off like that?"

Ray shrugged again. "Past history. Water under the bridge. Let bygones be bygones. How many clichés would you like?"

"That's one B.A.C..."

"Hunh?"

"Bad ass chick," Chigger said. "Well, did she send the stink bomb?"

"I can't think of anyone else who would. This is right up her M.O. Childish stuff. She hasn't done anything physical, though, in a while. Worst lately has been when she calls up an advertiser and tells them the paper is going out of business—"

"Yeah, yeah, I had Bubba at the hardware store say just the other day he was sorry we were folding but I assured him we weren't. I just figured it was a simple mistake. I didn't know it was, like, malicious. Seriously."

Ray appeared lost in thought for a moment, then said, "Malicious. Oh, yeah. I'm just glad she lives in Clear Lake. That makes it a little more inconvenient for her to travel out here and do physical damage. Didn't think about the mail, though—"

"Can't you stop her? Do I have to worry about her doing something crazy... to me?"

"I don't think she'd harm a hair on your strawberry head.

Probably feels sorry for you that you have to deal with me every day. I can't prove she's the one who did any of this, so, no, I can't stop her. It'd be counter-productive to get the cops to talk to her because that would just aggravate her off more. So I've learned to live with it. As time goes by, the anger seems to dissipate. I just wish she'd get a girl friend. She needs to get laid."

Chigger came back in the office and sat on the corner of Ray's desk. "Girl friend? Your wife likes girls?"

Ray shrugged. "Let's just say she's user-friendly. When we broke up she swore I'd revealed to her just how disgusting men can be, etc. etc., and she'd never date another man again. That wasn't true. But what she needs is some woman to treat her just as badly as she thinks men do to kind of even things out."

"Maybe a woman wouldn't."

"Lookit, when we first started dating I had to listen to all sorts of war stories about how terrible this boyfriend or that boyfriend was. What's the common denominator in all of that? Her. It's how she handles relationships. Took me a few months to figure that out but by then some goofball had pronounced us husband and wife."

Chigger stood, shook her head a little, and walked back to her desk. "You've got tons of interesting stories, Ray."

"That's what happens when you're old enough to remember when snakes used to walk. Give yourself some time; you'll collect a few."

Then a brick flew through the window above Ray's desk, one of the only two windows without the security screens. Glass flew and Ray and Chigger dove for the floor as shards rained down on them. The brick crashed into the computer sitting on his desk with a sickening "tink" of metal warping and circuit boards moaning a death rattle.

CHAPTER 16:
NOBODY LIKES MONDAYS

Monday morning, Professor Doctor Farvel Jerome Perittomatopolis stood in the middle of the lab, looking at his assistant—Denise? Deborah?—who was perched on a stool, twitching it back and forth. He despised that sort of childish, nervous energy and reached out to stop it. She scowled at him.

"Listen," he said. "This is unacceptable. That second dose of KP 2761 was essential. I cannot adequately continue in my research if I'm not provided with the proper supplies in a timely manner. You understand how important this is so I don't feel as if I must lecture you on those aspects, but one of your jobs is to facilitate the delivery of supplies and I'm disappointed that you have failed."

"One missed delivery isn't, ah, going to—"

He waved a finger across her face. He could tell from the narrowing of her eyes and sucking in of her cheeks that she didn't like that one bit and he didn't care one bit. She wasn't supposed to like it. "No excuses. One failure is one failure too many. The work I had scheduled for today must now be delayed. It is, I will repeat, unacceptable. This will not happen again."

"No, Doctor Perittomatopolis, it will not," she said.

"We understand one another," he said. What passed for a smile settled on his lips as he turned to the Clean Room.

•

Monday afternoon, Diana and George ate lunch at The Fork. George had the Moroccan Bean Soup of the Day and a small salad. Diana had the Jalapeño Chicken Fried Steak special with a salsa sauce drowning both the steak and her french fries.

George said, "The mayor is acting odd lately. Seems a little on edge and asking questions he doesn't need to know the answers to. You need to bug him."

"Got it," Diana said, savoring a french fry.

"How's Sam?"

"Oh, the big lug's just fine. Why wouldn't he be? He gets to draw his regular salary from the Gulch and, ah, gets twice as much from us just for not being around at certain times and for ignoring the warehouse."

"And the doc?"

"That's a different matter. The herr professor doktor is being uppity and I don't like it, ah, one bit," she said, stabbing her steak with a knife and fork. She quickly cut a piece and gestured with it. "We had to abort a delivery and he's all weepy." She jabbed the meat into her mouth.

"Can you fix it?" he asked.

"I have. It'll solve the, um, problem and should make the mayor happy, too."

"That's good, that's good. Now I just have to calm the mayor down."

"Being uppity, too?"

"Thinks he's in charge."

"Same as the nutty professor. What's the mayor's problem? He's got wads of cash and the doc did him a favor."

"He thinks this paper guy is going to make trouble," he said, dipping a sweet roll into the soup. "The mayor's getting cold feet but his inflated bank account should keep him in line. The paper guy does know too much. I mean, what are the odds? We chose this podunk town specifically because we figured everybody here would be... I don't know..."

"Rubes," she said, setting down her iced tea with lime. He was telling her that "rubes" was the right word, and was going on about how carefully the village was chosen and how it was well off the beaten path and gave the agency plausible deniability this far outside The Beltway, but Diana Slingerland didn't really hear it all.

Her mind marched off into the past when she grew up in the King Steed Shows and Midway, her mother and aunt, twins, working in the carnival's strip show. Everyone thought she would follow in their sequined g-strings, but she had unfortunately inherited her physiology from her father—an alcoholic who drove his car over the side of a mountain when she was four—and she became tall and lean with willowy muscles and baseball-sized breasts that few would pay to see. Her aunt suggested surgery, but she would have none of that.

She craved excitement ever since the first of many times she climbed out her crib and roamed around her parents' modest trailer home while they were fast asleep.

She rode her bicycle into strange woods every place they camped.

She mastered the toughest routes on the show's climbing wall before she was ten.

She stole money from her mother's purse when she was twelve and bought a plane ticket from Baltimore to New York City just so she could see the Empire State Building for herself after watching *King Kong* on TV the night before.

She returned home before her mother ever knew she was gone.

She saw a television show one day about women with breast cancer climbing Mount Everest and thought she would become a mountain climber, but then discovered she needed an independent source of income or corporate sponsors to do that.

She took a job as a tour guide at Luray Caverns when she was seventeen because it seemed exciting and that was where she met George Frass. He gave her all the thrills she wanted.

She went to work for the Office and became an Expeditor, her official job title.

She had loved going through the Office's Expeditor School where she became *kunoichi*, an invisible assassin and spy.

She learned how to handle every firearm manufactured, learned hand-to-hand combat, learned how to kill with makeshift weapons such as pencils or coat hangers.

She learned how to merge with the shadows, how to move without being seen.

She learned free climbing and parkour.

She learned high speed chasing and evading.

She didn't much like the Office's Med School where she learned about first aid, how to set broken bones, how to break bones, about biological and chemical warfare, and about various venoms and poisons. Too much book learning for her. She liked action. But the knowledge was useful. And here she was now, sitting across from this short, chubby, bald man with the infectious smile.

She tuned back in to the conversation as George was saying, "Turns out this guy's worked as a bigshot reporter for a bigshot daily, even has a military intelligence background."

"Yeah, but he's, ah, nearly retired," she said, then chuckled. "Hah, he doesn't even have his computer files anymore. That was the best toss I've ever made. He's not really going to get in the way, do you think? I mean, when push comes to shove?"

"We shall see. This should have all gone smooth and quiet, like planned. Now everything is unsettled and getting complicated. I don't like it."

"I'm getting the distinct feeling that this project is, ah, becoming a cluster-fuck," she said.

"Not as long as I have you as a troubleshooter, babe."

•

Monday evening, Ray returned to his office from Austin. He drove to Austin through Wallaceville so he could pick up a copy of Jubal T. and Bubba's proposed subdivision and was saddened when he learned his guess was right—the development was planned to be adjacent to the Gulch, out on Baldy Flats, with homes planned right up to the banks of the Dark Fork of the Bigfoot River, some of it on land he knew was currently owned by Billy Faust. Billy didn't own much along the river, just enough for Orin to run the weekend tubing business that consisted of a gravel parking lot and a wood shack with the sign "On the Sixth Day God Created the Bigfoot River and on the Seventh Day He Went Toobing" over the door, and a pen for inflated inner tubes behind the shack. That building was not on the plans.

Once he finished up in Wallaceville, Ray went to the Apple Store at Barton Creek Mall in Austin to buy a new computer. Since his insurance was paying for it, Ray spared no expense and got the top model with a metric buttload of memory and a 42-inch screen.

When he returned to the office, he saw that Chigger had done as he requested—gotten the window repaired and the two remaining steel screens installed. He also saw a car parked by the front door. He carried the first of the two bulky boxes from his truck to the door, set it down, returned for the second box as two people got out of the car and walked to the door. It was Chicken Charley and her mother Sarah.

"What's up?" he said in greeting. They said hello but neither looked happy. He unlocked the door, kicked it open with his left foot, invited the visitors inside, then scooted the two boxes just inside the office and closed the door. He pulled a chair up to his usual visitor's chair, sat down in his own chair, and said, "What's new?"

"Gertrude's back," Charley said. "She was back this morning when I went to let the hens out of their pen."

"I figured she'd show up," Ray said with a smile.

"You *don't* understand," she said, nodding her head down firmly. "She was in the coop. She didn't open up the door and walk in and close and latch the door behind her. Whoever took her put her back. But that's not all. When I found Gertrude back this morning, I found that Ursula and Zelda were gone."

"I think somebody's playing around with you," Ray said.

Charley scowled and shook her head no once, firmly. "Why? What's the joke? I don't get it."

"This has been going on for a while, I think," Sarah said. "I didn't think anything of it before, but I noticed one of the hens was missing last Saturday. Charley was off on a Girl Scout outing and I was looking after the chickens and when I did a count Saturday it came up one missing. I think it was one of the reds. I didn't worry too much because I thought maybe it flew over the fence or something and would come back. I just hoped it would come back before Charley got home or I'd catch it."

"Flew over the fence? I didn't think chickens could fly," Ray said.

Charley leaned forward and pointed at him with two hands clasped together. "Yeah, most people think that, but they can. It varies with the breed, but they can get up to maybe five or six feet, not too far. Not too long, either. Maybe ten seconds at a time. Last summer Roger the rooster got up in an oak tree and he kept going higher and higher until he was way out on a top branch and crowing like nobody's business. I think he was ascared. My Uncle Melson came up with a big ladder to get him down. That didn't work, but he scared Roger enough to get him to go back down. But anyway, you're not going to see them migrate."

"Excuse *me*." Sarah coughed a little and suppressed a sneeze. "And on Monday morning that hen that was missing was back. In her pen. Then I thought that I had just miscounted them, so I didn't pay it any more attention until all of this…"

"Well—" Ray started to say.

Charley interrupted him with a finger in the air. "Last night I saw who's taking the chickens."

"You saw somebody?"

"My bedroom is in the back of the house upstairs and I have two windows and they both overlook the back yard. I heard some fussing early this morning. Before the sun was out. And I looked out the window that's over my bed and I saw a spaceman stealing Ursula and Zelda. I didn't know they were Ursula and Zelda then. Not until it got light out and I went down and looked."

Crap, Ray thought, but said, "Charley, are you sure—"

"I know what I saw, Mr. Strider. It was a spaceman. In a spacesuit."

"Charley isn't given to making things up," Sarah said. "She's a very down-to-earth young woman and she's never had a wild imagination."

"I'm not doubting you saw something, Charley, but help me figure out what," Ray said.

Charley did her head nod. "It was a spaceman."

Ray didn't reply. He tried to think of what to say, but was at a loss.

"We came by earlier, Mr. Strider, but you weren't here," Sarah said.

"I had to go to Wallaceville and Austin. I'm sorry I wasn't here," he said, his eyes falling to Charley's T-shirt. "Charley, you can draw really well—"

"I know. What has that got to do—"

He pushed a legal pad toward her and handed her a pen. "Draw me the spaceman."

She smiled, nodded, and drew a perfectly proportioned person dressed in what was clearly a spacesuit, although Ray thought the helmet looked more like one from a Star Trek movie than the bubble-headed NASA helmets that were directly descended from deep-sea diving helmets.

"Thanks, guys. I'll put something in the paper. Maybe somebody will recognize something or if someone is playing a joke maybe they'll take credit.'

"Thank you, Mr. Strider," Charley said as she and her mother rose to leave. He walked them out.

Returning to his desk, Ray felt a sharp pain in his abdomen. He belched several times and the pain seemed to go away a little. He walked around the office, trying to encourage more gas to escape. It worked but he still felt sore from the forced burps.

He got a bottle of water from his mini-fridge, took a long swig then went to the boxes. He opened one box, pulled out the computer and its assortment of cables and manual and disc and warranty card.

He pushed his chair to one side, turned his desk around and shoved it against the wall. He hated facing the wall with his back to the door but this way no one could toss a brick through the window and hit the computer. Inconvenient but necessary. He arranged the cables and connected the computer to his surge protector, then connected his Internet modem and printer cable to the computer. He was tempted to turn the system on to see how it worked but he knew if he did that he would also install all the software he needed, both for the Mac's operating system and for word processing and graphics design and manipulation of photographs and he really didn't want to get into doing all of that now. It was nearly nine o'clock. He was exhausted. He was going to go home, hope Chigger didn't call or show up, and go to bed.

And the phone rang. "Crap," he said. He just knew it was Chigger, but it wasn't.

"You sitting down?" LeRoi asked.

"Yeah," Ray said.

"Well, you are going to want to come out here to Billy's place."

"Hunh?"

"Billy is dead."

CHAPTER 17:
AT HOME WITH JUBAL T. AND MARGIE

Her shoulders back and smelling of Jasmine and Camels, Margie strolled into the living room. She watched Jubal T. turn to look at her. His only acknowledgement was to frown when he saw the cigarette between her fingers, languishing at her side. He stood barefoot and bare-chested, his paunch slouching over the waistband of his flower-print Bermuda shorts. He returned to looking at himself in the mirror, studying his nose. She watched the man she'd spent the last thirty-three years of her life with push his nose first to one side then the other, then push up the tip. He seemed satisfied.

"Just because you got your snout fixed doesn't mean everyone in town has forgotten what it used to look like," she said. She snatched a quick drag from the cigarette, and then used it as a pointer toward him. "You grew up in this town. The furthest away you've ever lived in your whole life was when you went to Southwest Texas down in San Marcos—"

"Texas State University!"

"Yes, well, it was Southwest Texas when you went there and sending away for a new diploma that says 'Texas State' on it doesn't mean it wasn't."

He walked towards her. "Just what is your problem?"

Margie wanted to say, "You are," but she didn't.

She *liked* being a wealthy woman. Before the Civil War, her great-great grandparents Siegfried and Ursula Moellering came to the Hill Country as newlyweds from Germany but when they helped found the village they didn't give it a Teutonic name like Boerne or Fredericksburg or New Braunfels like the other German settlements in the area. They called their new home Pleasant Valley after Homer Pleasant, the man who had befriended them after coming to this valley in the midst of the Texas Hill Country.

They had refused to speak German ever again and, unlike most of the other German immigrants, never taught their children their mother tongue. Siegfried and Ursula had left Germany behind and they declared they were Americans and they would speak American.

Her grandmother told her all sorts of tales about her ancestors, about how Siegfried was smart enough to test the soil before buying farm implements so when he discovered the limestone bedrock that lay just a foot under the topsoil all across the Edwards Plateau that made up the Central Texas Hill Country, he knew farming was out of the question. He spent the couple's savings on several breeds of goats and a few sheep.

Siegfried and Ursula made a small fortune before and during the Civil War.

Their son Bertram made even more money selling wool and bat guano to the U.S. Army after the turn of the century. But he lost everything except the family's 24,000 acres of land in the Great Depression after a local banker friend talked him into investing his profits.

Her grandmother never ceased warning Margie about putting money into the stock market and about never trusting banks and never trusting outsiders and never trusting change. She told her the only people to trust were family.

Margie's heart broke when her grandmother told her of owning only two dresses: a light gray cotton dress for summers and a heavy navy blue dress for winters—hand-me-downs from two older sisters, dresses she would later hand down to a younger cousin.

Margie listened with tears in her eyes every time her grandmother told her about each parcel of land she had to sell off to pay medical bills that grew and grew as her husband fell ill, then all three of her children. Margie's own mother died in childbirth from complications of a heart murmur she acquired when she had measles when she was younger and that's how Margie had come to live with her grandmother on what was left of the family ranch once her father was killed fighting Germans in World War II.

Margie hated riding a horse to school every day, a peanut butter and butter sandwich lunch tucked away in a saddlebag. Many others had to do the same, but those students who had mothers that could afford the time to bring them to school in automobiles looked down on the horsebackers.

Jubal T. was one of only three students who had their own cars to drive—his a 1959 Jaguar that he complained was a hand-me-down from his mother who'd bought an Oldsmobile. Margie tutored Jubal T. through math classes and he took her to the prom. They married a month after graduation, combining his parents' money from real estate investments and her family's still extensive goat ranch. She was certain she loved him back then.

She *liked* being the mayor's wife and one of the most prominent ladies in Bigfoot County. She founded the Pleasant Valley Historical and Cultural Preservation and Beautification Society 25 years ago—the driving political force in the valley until the village incorporated itself 13 years back and Jubal became its first mayor. She had assumed getting Jubal elected would cement the Society's influence over the valley, but with each passing year he paid more and more attention to people who wanted to change Pleasant Valley into something her great-great grandparents would never recognize. He was more worried about appearances than tradition. But their bank account had certainly been engorged, especially in the past month.

She *liked* running Frontier Gulch. It was like stepping into the past and every time she put on her Victorian garb and twirled her parasol while walking down the Gulch's boardwalks, she felt like she was channeling her grandmother. The Gulch was one way of preserving her past, Pleasant Valley's past, and now her own husband was threatening that if what Ray Strider told her was true. Jubal T. didn't deny it when she confronted him. He just snapped at her, asking her if she thought money grew on trees and saying that money grew out of concrete and wood frames and field stones and vinyl siding. How could he have hidden this from her?

She *liked* being liked. Her ten o'clock routine trip to the post office always took her at least an hour because of all the people she knew that she would meet there. They all knew they could find out what was going on in the village quicker and with more accurate detail by gossiping with her than by reading the paper. The same thing happened at the grocery store. If she didn't love all the attention, she'd stop going out to eat because her food always got cold before she could finish it since town folks came up to her all through the meal to say hello, to drop a piece of news, to ask a favor, to say thank you for a favor she had done. All that would end if she filed for divorce and shuffled off this gelatinous mound of ego walking toward her.

Margie sucked in the candy taste of the Camel, deeply this time. Sometimes smoking these new butts was like sucking air through a straw.

Jubal T. glared at her, his stomach touching hers. "Well? What's your problem?"

"Nothing," she said. He rolled his eyes and shook his head as he walked by her and out of the room.

CHAPTER 18:
PLEASANT VALLEY'S FAVORITE LITTLE DEVIL IS DEAD

When Ray arrived at the dilapidated fifth-wheeler, the EMTs were loading Billy's body into the back of their ambulance. Ray stood there as one of the medics latched the door, a move and sound just as final as a preacher tossing a handful of dirt onto a casket. The ambulance drove away, no need for speed or a siren.

Four other cars were parked one behind the other on the grass beside the driveway—two tan and green sheriff's patrol SUVs, one white pick-up with "Bigfoot County" painted in green on the door, and one dark blue Jeep with massive tires. Justice of the Peace Steve Clement wrote notes on a small pad at the foot of the stairs. LeRoi stood in the doorway.

"Don is taking a leak out back," LeRoi said as Ray walked up. Ray nodded.

"What the hell happened?" Ray asked at the doorway.

"Looks like an accident," LeRoi said, stepping down to let Ray up. "Ask the Evidence Chick for the gory details."

Ray stood in the doorway, careful not to step inside, and looked around. From the door he could see all of the small fifth-wheeler. The dining and living area was directly opposite him, a narrow table and one chair with a television on another table just to the left of the door and a humming refrigerator to left of that. The bedroom was just a mattress, blankets and pillows on the overhang of the trailer to the right of the door. At the far left were a closet and a closet-sized bathroom. To the near left was the kitchen with a small sink below a wall cabinet, a short counter, an electric stove with untold layers of grease piled on top, and barely enough room for the Evidence Chick to kneel down and take photographs of the floor and front of the stove.

The Evidence Chick's real name was Ginger Tovar, but no one ever called her that, and she was the county's entire forensics unit. She was short and muscular in a burnt orange Longhorn polo shirt, her black hair pulled back in a tight bun, and she had dimples that rivaled the Grand Canyon when she smiled.

"What can you tell me?" Ray asked her.

"Oh, hi, Ray," she said, propping her hand on the refrigerator to help herself stand up. He could hear her knees pop. "This isn't official yet, and you can't quote me anyway, that has to come from the high sheriff hisownself and the J.P., of course, but it looks like one of those chains of disastrous events."

Ray scribbled in his notebook.

The Evidence Chick pointed to the stove that dripped several years of grease down its front. "Pan of bacon on the front burner says he was making breakfast. There's two eggs on the counter so it looks like Billy was going to fry up the bacon and crack the eggs into the grease. The bacon's burnt to a crisp. That smell led the Gulch's security guard out here to check and he's the one who found the body."

"I got a preliminary statement from him and he will be down to make an official one tomorrow," LeRoi said.

The Evidence Chick pointed at the floor. "I don't know how you single guys can live like this, but I've seen it way too much. This floor hasn't been cleaned probably since he moved in. Stove neither. The floor is covered in dirt and grease, the top and front of the stove are covered in grease. It's early in the morning, an eighty-year-old man probably hasn't got his sea legs yet and it looks like he slips on some grease, reaches out to grab something and misses." She indicated a handprint in a smear of grease on the front of the stove, then the handle to the oven. "When he falls, it looks like his head cracks on the handle. Got blood and skin and hair on it. Head had a deep gash in it on that side. Looks like he falls flat on the floor and knocks himself unconscious."

"That what killed him?" Ray asked.

The Evidence Chick took a step forward and pointed to a hole in the floor, just to the right of the stove. "This trailer's got a lot of holes in it. Some on the walls, one in the ceiling, and a few on the floor. Some of the holes have paper towels or toilet paper stuffed in them. I found a mouse nest under the floor in the closet and snakes like their mice. This is the Hill Country and we've got more than a few snakes out here and this trailer is just at the edge of the woods and, well, it looks like a rattler came in through one of the holes and while

Billy was blacked out it bit him on the neck."

"He died from a snake bite?" Ray said.

The Evidence Chick pointed to a cardboard box on top of the dining table. "Looks that way. Bite marks directly on his carotid on the right side of his neck are consistent with a snake bite. The area around the bite was swollen, his lips were purple and he had a frothy white fluid in his mouth and nostrils. It may be that the venom didn't kill him directly, it seldom does despite what you see in the movies, but at his age and pumped straight into the artery, it might have led to cardiac arrest. And a lot quicker than if you or I were bitten."

"I found the snake sitting under the table," LeRoi said. "Jarnigan warned me about it so had my stick and the box when I came in. It rattled at me a little, but I slapped the stick on its neck and put the box over it. Me and Don flipped the box upright and closed up the flaps. Snake was pretty pissed for a while, but he has calmed down some. He will likely start shaking that rattle again when we move the box."

"What're the odds?" Ray said.

The Evidence Chick put her camera down beside the box with the rattlesnake in it and picked up a bag of swabs, knelt back down and began taking samples from the floor. "Shit happens."

"Too much lately," Ray said, shaking his head. He stepped back into the front yard, quietly singing words from a Mexican song, "*el trabajo no está amigo mio...*"

Sheriff's Sergeant Dan Germaine returned from the woods and stood beside Ray. "Walked around a bit and didn't see no sign of anyone coming in through there or the field. Somebody coulda come in from the road, I guess. Can't tell much on that caliche. But why? Who'd wanna do Billy no harm?"

•

"I was driving by and saw the lights on," Chigger said as she walked into the office. Ray was staring blankly at his blank computer screen.

"Go home," he said.

"Something wrong?"

"Billy's dead for one thing."

"Seriously?... What happened?"

Ray gave her all the details, his voice rising with each sentence.

"What are you mad at?" she asked.

"Life," he answered. "Go home."

"I'll be happy to stay."

"Go home."

"Why don't I go home with you? You look like you could use some sympathy. We..."

"There is no 'we.' You need to get that through your pretty little head. I'm old enough—"

"I know, you're old enough to be my father."

"No. I'm old enough to be your *grand*father. It happened once. It won't happen again. I'm not ready to take our relationship to the next level."

Her eyebrows snapped together as she looked at him. "Marriage?"

"Counseling. Now, go home."

"I'm sorry, Ray. I understand you want to be alone and I understand you're angry at what happened and that you're grieving for a friend. I'll be here for you when you need me." She left.

Ray threw a magazine at the door after she closed it. "Crap!"

He longed for the days when he worked at the *Post* in a real newsroom. One huge, open room with windows everywhere. No cubicles. Only a couple of glass offices. Only the darkroom was closed off. More than a hundred people pecking away on typewriters, then on computer keyboards, or talking on the phone, or talking to each other. That's what he really missed, that ability to get up when you were having trouble thinking a thing through and wander over to another person's desk and talk. Talk about the problem, talk about your day, bitch about the boss or your spouse. It didn't matter. More often than not, just talking to someone familiar with your job was enough and your brain figured things out subconsciously during the conversation. He could always talk it out with Monica or Tom or Leslie or George or Mary. Reporters he liked and trusted.

He had none of that here. Even talking to his friends wouldn't work. It needed to be someone with that reporter's outlook, reporter's fame of mind, reporter's background. He was feeling lonely and old and slow-witted and his stomach hurt.

What was going on? What did he know? Know for sure? Actually, he thought, nothing had happened but a couple of accidents that wouldn't get more than a graph or two in a Houston paper. No crisis loomed. That he knew of. Oh, yeah, his stomach really hurt.

He rubbed his face, grabbed a legal tablet and a pen, and made a list.

Fred dead
        —space footprints?
        —loose chicken made Fred swerve?
Flying saucers
        —sighted by Billy others near Canyon Lake
Charley
        —chickens missing
        —chickens returned
        —spaceman?
New subdivision
        —where did Jubal get money?
        (said 2 months ago Gulch reno emptied bank acct)
        —did Billy sell his prop?
New C.M.
        —fraud
        —fed?
Crop circles
Billy dead
        —rattlesnake?

He thought about the first and last notations together. The official cause of death for Fred was multiple traumas resulting from a vehicular accident. In Billy's case, the preliminary ruling, pending toxicology, was that Billy died "of unnatural causes: rattlesnake bite."

Snakes lived all over the Hill Country and it was a good bet they routinely slithered into Billy's trailer to feed on his mice. But why would a snake bite Billy? Critters only kill for food or to protect themselves. Billy was too big for a snake to eat and he certainly wasn't a threat if he was lying unconscious on the floor. Maybe he fell next to the snake and frightened it. Could a rattlesnake bite be faked? Could you train a snake to bite on cue? Had Billy sold his property? He wrote a note on the pad to check with Rick at the county clerk's office about that.

Oh, yeah, that pain was spreading up into his chest now. He tried to belch and failed. He sat up straighter in his chair and that seemed to help.

What would a spook want in Pleasant Valley? Was he active or maybe fired looking for a job? If he was no longer a fed, quit or fired, he couldn't use his real résumé. Why here? This was no place. Could that be the reason, because it was no place?

Oh, crap, this hurt. He stood up and walked around a bit with the legal pad in his hand.

Pirate crop circles? What sense did that make? Were they connected to the spaceman and the flying sau—

Crap. This pain was ridiculous. He dropped the legal pad and reached for the phone, dialing Chigger's cell phone. Before she had a chance to say hello, he said, "I need you right away. Hurry up. Back to the office. Now."

He locked up and waited for her outside. Why had he called her instead of Trey or LeRoi or the EMS for that matter?

Before her car came to a complete stop, Ray got in and told her, "Hospital. Now."

Her voice quavered and her hands had a death grip on the steering wheel. "Which one? CTMC? Seaton? Hill Country?"

"Hill Country. It's the smallest but the closest. Put your flashers on and get there."

She did. Hill Country Regional Medical Center was in Wallaceville and as she sped north he watched the countryside flash by. He wanted the pain to go away.

He tried to concentrate on the change he was seeing and how much he hated it. He moved to this place because he thought it was immune to change. It was once all goat farms and cattle ranches, but the old farmers and ranchers were dying off and farming or ranching was the last thing on the minds of the kids who inherited those huge tracts of land. So the land got sold to developers who built fake Tuscan towers on the driveways into the new subdivisions. Like that one, he thought as they passed one. Why Tuscany? Had every architect in Texas gone to that same movie a few years back?

He tried to focus on being angry at all the changes he'd seen in the past few years but the pain in his chest kept interrupting. The pain was so strong he couldn't focus enough to be angry at that.

When they arrived, the emergency room was empty. He told the admitting nurse he was having chest pains, she gave him a form to fill out and told him to sit down but before he could sit another nurse came out of the ER and brought him into a curtained-off cubicle full of machines and tubes and tables with sharp looking objects on them.

"Male over seventy with chest pains? Take this. Put it under your tongue," she ordered. He did so. He guessed it was a nitrogylcerin tablet but she never said so.

She asked him questions about the pain, having him rate it on a one-to-ten scale and frowned when he said, "It goes to eleven."

She had him describe how the pain radiated from his abdomen. She asked him if the pain had subsided at all and he shook his head negatively but she asked him again so he said aloud, "No."

She ordered him to open his shirt and lie down on the examination table. She wheeled over one of the machines, stuck electrodes on his chest, turned the machine on and ran out a narrow strip of paper that Ray recognized as an electrocardiogram. She turned the machine off, pulled off the electrodes and smiled at him for the first time. "EKG looks OK, but I'll let the doctor read it to you. You can button up now."

"That was fast," he said.

"Don't need much anymore to see if something serious is going on. Try to relax and he'll be in soon." Then she took blood.

The on-duty physician came in with a clipboard in his hand, reading it over as he walked to Ray who sat up on the table. Without looking up from the clipboard, the physician extended his hand and said, "Mr. Strider, I'm Doctor Razu. ECG is fine, but you're having some pains?" He finally looked up. "Show me where."

Ray did so as the reporter in him wondered what the difference was between an EKG and an ECG. The intern, recalling recent medical training, said, "Hmmm."

Chigger cowered in the corner of the cubicle.

"Have you done or experienced anything out of the ordinary lately, Mr. Strider? How long have you had these pains? Have you ever been diagnosed with heart problems?" the doctor asked.

"No heart problems that I know of," Ray said. "My mouth tastes like I've been drinking water hot dogs were boiled in. I've been constipated a lot lately, I don't know if that's related but it's been a problem..."

"Experiencing a lot of gas, bloating?"

"Oh, yeah."

"Give me a couple of deep breaths. Hold it for a second then let it out slowly," the doctor said as he placed a stethoscope against Ray's chest, abdomen, then his back.

"Lie back down," the doctor said. He poked around Ray's side and abdomen and stomach. "Did that hurt? Did that hurt? Did that hurt?"

"No. Well, it did when you let up."

The physician nodded. "Let's get you an ultra sound," he said and left before Ray could ask a question. In a few minutes, a tall man wearing a lab coat came in pushing a wheelchair, asked Ray to get in it, told Chigger they would be right back and took him to a dank room with equipment that looked like something straight out of a 1930s' Universal monster movie.

The technician, who didn't look a day over 16, pulled Ray's shirt up and jeans and underwear down a little, glopped some goop over his abdomen and ran what looked like a Magic 8-Ball on a cable over it. The tech looked at a screen that Ray couldn't see. He finished, toweled Ray off and wheeled him back to the exam cubicle. The physician returned in about twenty minutes.

"Mr. Strider, it appears you have acute cholecystitis with cholelithiasis and choledocholithiasis. You'll need a cholecystecomy. I've notified the on-called surgeon," Doctor Razu said. "She's quite good. Doctor Paula Cornet. We'll get you all prepped and ready to go by the time she gets here."

"Hey, for what?" Ray said.

"Oh, your gall bladder quit on you. It's going to have to be removed. Looks like it hasn't functioned in a long while."

"Well, what does that mean? How do I function without a gall bladder?"

"No problem," the doctor said. "You won't miss it."

"I don't need one?" Ray was on the verge of panic and wanted a tranquilizer quickly.

"You'll get by without it just fine."

"Then why do I have one?" Ray said to the intern's back as he left.

CHAPTER 19:
DELIBERATIONS

The Pleasant Valley City Council meeting was one of the shortest on record. Mayor Jubal T. Gruntle called the meeting to order promptly at seven o'clock and opened the floor to public comments but none of the nine people in attendance cared enough about any issue to speak. Then the Council approved the minutes of the last meeting and took reports from the City Secretary/Treasurer, the Public Works Director, and the City Inspector (personally chosen by Margie Gruntle and known affectionately as the "Sign Nazi") but none of them had anything to report. The Council authorized the City Secretary/Treasurer to disperse funds to pay bills. The Council then approved, on first reading, the hiring of George Jefferson Wallace to be City Manager. They then adjourned. No one mentioned the empty seat that was usually occupied by *Pleasant Valley Picayune* Editor Ray Strider.

The mayor retired to his office, followed by Mr. And Mrs. Wallace. They shut the door behind them and took chairs across the expansive, custom-made cypresswood desk that Jubal T. settled behind.

"I'm going to need more money," Jubal T. announced without pleasantries.

"An agreement has been reached previously and we've met our part," George said. Diana fidgeted in her chair.

"My situation has changed," the mayor said. "I now have an opportunity to purchase the remaining land for my new development and I can't let that opportunity slip through my fingers. Get my drift?"

"A problem on your part does not constitute an emergency on my part," George said.

Jubal T. leaned forward and the ridge over his eyes seemed to grown in prominence as he did so. He smiled. "Nevertheless. If you wish to continue, I'm going to need more funds. Maybe more later. Who knows?"

"You can't, ah, do this," Diana said.

"Don't you worry your pretty little head over what I can and cannot do," Jubal T. said. He turned to George. "Bottom line is that I don't have to put a final reading on the agenda next week to confirm you as City Manager. Bottom line is that I can evict you from the premises you are, shall we say, renting." He put finger quotes around the last word. "Bottom line is you need me more than I need you."

"Don't be—" Diana began. She was interrupted by George's hand touching her lightly on her forearm. She would have continued anyway, but she noticed the mayor almost drooling as he watched George touch her golden skin and she smiled inside. She would handle the mayor.

"Beyond the abrogation of our agreement by you, budget constraints limit what can be done," George said. "X amount of dollars just can't be handed over on a moment's notice. That sort of expenditure requires approval, approval at several levels. Work moves exceedingly slow in governments and the higher the level, the slower it works."

"Bottom line is in addition to that original amount you've already paid, I need half of that again."

"That's outrageous. A few more thousand more might be found lying about in petty cash, but nothing like that."

"Too bad," Jubal T. said. "I'll need it before the next council meeting or, well, as I said, you might not be approved and that means packing your bags—all of you—and going elsewhere."

George stood and Diana followed. "I'll see what can be done."

•

"Well?" she said. They were driving home in George's sleek Tesla and he hadn't said a word since they left the mayor's office. The headlamps of the Tesla lit up the darkness in a flat cone of artificial light that made Diana uneasy. She was used to streetlights and traffic. They hadn't passed another car, in either direction, since they left City Hall two miles ago. She tried to relax by imagining herself back in Luray, but it didn't work. Caverns were supposed to be dark, city streets weren't.

"It's just an incomplete success so far. Certainly, mistakes were made in the planning process," he answered.

She rolled her eyes. "I can just see the mistakes waking up one morning and figuring they'd wander over and, ah, foul us up because they didn't have nothing else to do. You were wrong."

"Don't you think if I were wrong, I would be aware of it?" he said. "Besides, alternate choices are non-existent."

"We always have a choice."

"Pull the plug? The doc is set up and great progress is being made. The importance of this cannot be overstated and it'd be a major set-back to be forced to start over somewhere else. Any future man-caused bio disasters will be fewer in number, perhaps even prevented, by this contingency program. My life is dedicated to this."

"Mmm-hmm," she said. She really didn't care if what he said was true or whether he was just angling for a promotion, she was just happy to be by his side. Doing what she loved.

The Tesla's tires made low, rhythmic thumping noises as the car moved over the low-water crossing.

"He's getting pressured from the missus, what I hear on the, ah, bug," she said. "He's worried about the paper guy, if I read him right. And if we give in, where does it, um, stop? You know the deal with extortionists, they keep coming back for more and more and more, until, you know, something gives."

He spoke softly. "That I am aware of. I am totally aware. But what can be done? He owns the place."

"Ah, no," she said. "He and the missus do and she might be won over if we promise her funds for that beautification gang she runs. Preserve paradise and stop the parking lot?"

"That's a contingency that hasn't been adequately analyzed..." They arrived at their one-story, one-bedroom rental cabin painted tan and purple. Inside, she flipped on the living room/kitchen light while he walked directly to the bedroom. She followed, grabbing a bottle of single malt scotch from the coffee table by the sofa, and then turned off the living room light when he turned on the bedroom light. He took the bottle from her and poured them both drinks as she shrugged off her clothes—she never wore underwear so it was a quick strip. He sipped his scotch. She gulped down half of hers, set the glass on the end table, pulled back the covers and slid into bed.

"I don't like the way he looks at me," she said as George

tugged off his clothes, his short, chubby fingers fumbling over the buttons on his starched shirt the way they always did. He put his Glock on his end table by the glass of scotch. He lay down next to her, propping himself up on an elbow.

"Who?"

"That paper guy."

"He wasn't even there tonight."

"I guess that's why I was thinking about him. The way he looks gives me the creepies."

"What's not to look at? You're a beautiful woman."

Beautiful was what her mother and aunt were, she thought. Not her. She knew she was attractive for some reason, but she also knew she wasn't beautiful. "Slighted in the mammary department."

He cupped the breast nearest to him, leaned over and tasted her. "Anything more than a mouthful is wasted."

"That's not how he looks at me," she said. "I'm used to that look. It's like he *knows* me."

His hand was now caressing her side, along her hip, across her thigh. "*I* know you and I think you're the most beautiful woman I ever saw."

She looked at him. He was average in every category she could think of and yet she thought she might be in love with him. Her first and only love. Why? Because of what he just said and what he was now doing. He was focused on her and only her. He was attentive to her. He savored her. But right now she was distracted.

"Like I said before, this operation is teetering on becoming a cluster fuck," she said, unsure if he was listening. "We can salvage the mayor but we can't this paper guy. We thought he'd be, um, a rube like the rest, but he's got connections. We do him and all his former colleagues get involved. They're scattered all over the country now, some even in TV. They'd do stories for, ah, months. For him we need leverage. Every other operation we've ever worked on has gone smooth as silk, but, ah, you know, the best swordsman in the world has nothing to fear from the second best swordsman in the world."

He rose from her other breast to look into her eyes. "What does that mean?"

"A saying my *kunoichi* instructor used to quote all the time.

Ah, Mark Twain, I think. When you're the best, you know how all the other folks who are, you know, second best or worse, are going to, ah, behave. But you come out among the rubes and the rubes don't know the rules. It's how all those amateurs beat all those pros in the big poker tournaments. What's happening here. We're playing with amateurs. They don't know who's in charge or when they're, um, beat."

"I guess we'll have to show them."

She patted his arm. She wriggled to face him, pulling him toward her, engulfing him in her arms, her hands on his hips. They kissed.

She'd find leverage on the paper guy. And she loved salvage.

CHAPTER 20:
THE ADVENTURE OF RAY AT THE HOSPITAL

He was watching a movie in his head about it happening to someone who looked like him. Dressed in a negligible hospital gown and lying on a gurney, Ray half-listened as Doctor Cornet showed him printouts from his ultrasound exam and explained how his gall bladder was malfunctioning and how, if it wasn't removed soon, a body part he had never thought of before might kill him.

She explained how she would take out the offending organ laparoscopically, a minimally invasive procedure that involved a couple of inch-long incisions and inserting a special camera. He didn't understand how a camera could roam around his innards and he didn't understand how a body part could be pulled through a one-inch cut but he didn't bother asking. He signed a surgical consent form. An anesthesiologist arrived, introduced himself in a lilting accent that tagged him from the sub-continent, and watched as a nurse jabbed a gigantic needle into the top of Ray's hand to set up an IV tube. The anesthesiologist told him things but none of it registered. He was wheeled into the surgery anteroom and as he looked up at the beige ceiling was, suddenly, gone.

He woke in another beige room with Chigger sitting beside him. A nurse hovered next to his bed, taking his blood pressure. "Everything went just fine," the nurse said in mellifluous tones. "We'll take you to your room in just a few moments."

Chigger got out of her chair, moved to his side, and said something that he didn't hear. The rest was a fog.

Somewhere in the fog, the surgeon told him how the surgery went and he recalled her telling him about the drainage tube that hung from his right side. She also said something about the gall bladder itself and something about a second surgery and he didn't want to hear that but she smiled and assured him that was over. He didn't understand.

He slept. He dreamed music—music he hadn't heard in several

decades, perhaps not since he was a child: *Canadian Sunset, Stranger on the Shore, Autumn Leaves*. He loved that music. When he got home he was going to have to find some of it online and listen to for real instead of just in his head-head-head. Jungle birds chirped. *Quiet Village*.

The next day, the fog lifted a little. The metallic sounds and raspy announcements over the hospital's public address system, along with the antiseptic smells that surrounded him, made Ray pay more attention.

His day nurse was a tall, barrel-chested man about the same age as Ray with fat fingers and a kind manner. His nametag said he was Bartholomew but Ray thought of him as a gentle Bluto because of the way he waddled when he walked. He checked Ray's incisions—the first time Ray saw them. One was at his belly button, another was maybe eight inches above that while a third was a few inches to the right. Hanging from a fourth cut was a plastic tube and bag.

"Looking good, my man," Bluto said.

Ray ran his fingers over the red scars. "I don't see any stitches."

"Naw, they use super glue now," the nurse said. Ray didn't know whether Bluto was kidding or not, but he could neither see nor feel any stitches. Super glue—what'll they think of next?

"Hey," Chigger said when she arrived at mid-morning. "You look a lot better. How do you feel?"

"I used to use my hands," he said. The joke flew miles over her head so he added, "I'm OK, I guess."

"Doctor Paula told me it took her four times as long to do your surgery as normal because your gall bladder had calcified," Chigger said. "She said she had to chisel it out. Said it'd probably been bad for ten years. She said you were lucky."

He nodded and tried to smile.

"She said while she was going in through your tummy to get the gall bladder another doctor was going down your throat to scoop out all the stones that had piled up in there. She said your insides were a real mess."

That was the second surgery Doctor Cornet had mentioned, he thought. He was glad it'd been done at the same time. He really didn't want to go through another ordeal like this. He didn't like the fogginess and hated not being in control.

He felt comfortable in the routine—the day nurse came in at regular times to take his blood pressure and pulse, every now and then checking on his scars and little green bag. Chigger jabbered on about something or another. She finally left to get dinner for herself and Ray hoped she wouldn't come back.

The night nurse said her name was Jeannette. She was built like a porn star with blonde, wavy hair that Ray knew would be beautiful when released from the loose bun it was pulled into. She gave off a lilac aroma when she moved. Her smile and light green eyes would significantly increase global warming and Ray thought of her as Naughty Night Nurse.

Solange and Trey returned with Chigger.

"Look who I met in the lobby," Chigger announced.

"How you doin', man?" Trey asked. Solange walked over to his bedside.

"Fine, I guess," Ray said. "Everything went OK, they got me super glued up. Doc says I'll never have to worry about constipation again, so I don't see any down side."

"We were worried about you, darlin'," Solange said softly.

Ray swallowed and nodded. "Thanks," he whispered.

"LeRoi says he hates hospitals so 'less you're ready to croak he's not goin' to be by," Trey said. "Chigger says the doctor says you'd be out in a day anyway."

His three visitors sat—Solange and Ray on a thickly padded bench near the window and Chigger in a chair on the other side of his bedstand.

Ray prided himself on his memory. It was a prized skill among journalists and he'd tested it many times, comparing what he remembered someone saying to a recording, and he was always precise. It came in handy when skittish interviewees balked at the sight of a tape recorder or a notebook.

But this day, the only thing he could remember his friends talking about was that Chicken Charley and her mother Sarah were in the same hospital being treated for the flu. Charley was in a room just a few doors down from his; her mother was in ICU. He blamed his lack of memory and focus on the after effects of general anesthesia. At some point Trey and Solange left and Chigger curled up on the bench under a blanket that Naughty Night Nurse provided.

Naughty Night Nurse turned into Nurse Mildred Ratched at eleven-twenty-seven p.m.

"I'm OK," Ray insisted.

"You're not. You have to be able to urinate completely."

"I'll be fine once I can get up. I can't pee into that plastic bottle while I'm lying down."

"I have the catheter right here. Just relax." She even smiled.

"I don't need a catheter." He realized he was protesting not from any fear of pain but from modesty. "Really. I'm OK."

"This will just take a moment and you'll feel much, much better." She pulled back the covers on his bed and lifted his gown while he rolled his eyes and sighed. He shivered a little feeling the cold every hospital seemed to love.

He knew it was inevitable. He tilted his head back on his pillow, took a deep breath, closed his eyes. Lubricant? Antiseptic? He couldn't place the smell but refused to look. She grabbed him—he barely felt her hand—and she guided the catheter in quickly with less pain than he thought he would feel. But, really, if a woman was going to grab him there he expected friendlier activity than her shoving a tube up it. And, really, if another woman was going to handle his privates then he really didn't need his current almost girlfriend standing by the side of his bed.

"Eeyeeew," Chigger said.

That was it. Just like when he saw Chigger bend over in front of him at the birthday party and her round ass stretched the fabric of her boy shorts well up her butt cheeks and he knew at that moment they would become lovers, this was the opposite moment. He knew their relationship was absolutely over, at any level. It was over anyway because she looked so much like— Who? What? The fog was functioning as a steel curtain. But he distinctly heard her say, "Eeyeeew." Certainly anyone not a medical professional who witnessed a catheter being shoved into a penis might have thought "Eeyeeew," but no one over the age of 25 would have actually said it out loud. To her, oldies music was Hootie and the Blowfish and he didn't even know what a Hootie was. Hell, he'd slept more hours than she'd been alive. How could they ever have an intelligent conversation? The landmarks of his life were liking Ike; watching Princess Summerfall Winterspring and Hoppy and J. Fred Muggs and Fulton J. Sheen and Maynard G. Krebs; watching Annette's breasts develop; listening to Ray Charles and the Beatles; being shocked when Kennedy was shot; arguing over Ted Williams and Mickey Mantle; Vietnam and anti-war protests; Joe Namath backing up his Super Bowl guarantee; watching men on the moon on TV; following Watergate; be amazed as smiling and up-beat Jimmy Carter morphed into rabbit-fighting President James Earl Carter, Jr. and fell into a malaise 52 hostages paid for with 444 days of their lives; the Challenger explosion; 9/11. What were the landmarks of her life? Justin Timberlake, Brad Pitt, Snoop Dog, Paris Hilton, Beyoncé, OJ, Gennifer/Kathleen/Juanita/Elizabeth/ Sally/Dolly/Paula/ Hillary, Lindsay Lohan, Britney Spears, Michelle, Lady GaGa, the Black Eyed Peas, American Idol, maybe 9/11. Reagan? No, she was born while he was president and wouldn't have remembered a thing about him or Iran/Contra. Obama?

"Hey," he called to Chigger once Nurse Ratched left with her tools of torture.

"Yeah?" She leaned over the siderail of his bed.

"What do you think of the Iraq war?"

"What?" she said, using three syllables.

"You know, the war in Iraq. What did you think about it?"
"I don't know," she said, looking like she thought the painkiller dripping into his IV was scrambling his brain a little. "I guess I didn't much. I know whatever they showed on TV. Cars burning in the streets and someone saying some soldiers got blown up. I don't know. I don't know anyone who's over there or who's been. It really doesn't affect me."

He felt the drug wrap around him like a thick quilt on a cold evening. He thought, America's not at war. The Marines are at war. America's on their cell phones, and he floated off into a deep sleep.

Ray was a passenger in a flying saucer driven by José Jimenez. The saucer was flying an erratic flight, like a drunken bumble bee if a bumble bee could get drunk. The pilot from the planet Tyvek was dressed in a spacesuit and instead of keeping his eyes on the sky kept turning around and saying to Ray, "My name… José Jimenez. I yam…

an astro-note." That stereotypical creation of comedian Bill Dana would not fly in modern politically-correct America, and he'd only been marginally funny back in the Sixties, a one-note joke that became a career because of José's believable sincerity.

Ray remembered seeing José Jimenez for the first time on the *Steve Allen Show*, interviewed by the great Steverino himself. José had been dressed in a spacesuit then, as he was now. But somehow this spacesuit was different.

Ray woke from his dream focused on José's spacesuit. Something about it was not right. He couldn't put his finger on it. It seemed now, in his drug-induced, post-operative fog that it wasn't really a spacesuit. But it was. No. It looked more like the plastic bee suit he wore when he covered the killer bee stories in Central and South America in the Eighties, the stories that almost won him a Pulitzer. But no. It wasn't a bee suit. What was it? It was a spacesuit from the planet Tyvek. Ray tried to focus but he was dragged back into the darkness.

"You were sleeping well," Nurse Bluto said the next morning as Ray woke to the pressure tightening on his arm. "We could hear you snoring all the way down the hall at the nurses' station."

"Didn't mean to disturb you," Ray said, trying to smile.

"No problemo," Bluto said. "But, you know, they got surgeries now that'll fix that snoring."

"I think I'm done with surgeries for a while."

"I understand," the nurse said. When he left, Ray was alone for only a few minutes until Chigger returned. She was wearing an old woolen, navy blue shirt with a black and gold "All Navy Champion 1966 Judo" patch on the left shoulder.

Ray pushed one of the bed's remote control buttons to move himself up into a sitting position. "Where'd you get my shirt?"

"Your place. I hope you don't mind. I went home to change earlier and I thought you might like to shave and everything before you leave here so I stopped by your place and picked up a few things." She held up a paper bag and opened it showing him his shaving cream, razor, toothbrush, toothpaste, and shampoo. "I got cold and this was hanging over a chair in the bedroom and I put it on and I forgot to take it off."

"How'd you get in my house?"

"You gave me your keys when you checked in here. Your keys and your wallet and watch."

"Oh," he said.

She pointed to the patch. Its gold bullion threads hadn't faded over the decades. "I didn't know you were so famous."

"I won in '67, too, but it was just the Navy. Maybe I could have gone to the Olympic trails and maybe gone to Mexico City. Who knows?"

"Why didn't you?"

"I volunteered for Vietnam instead."

"You volunteered?"

"My duty. All other generations fought for their country, this was my fight and I wasn't going to miss it."

She shook her head, patted his hand, put the bag on his bed stand and sat down in the chair. "I want to learn everything about you, especially considering the life you've lived. You've met four or five presidents…"

Ray held up five fingers.

"Well, you met five but you interviewed only four from what you said."

"Why would you want to know everything?"

"Cause I'm nosy."

"Hunh?"

"What?" Chigger said.

"That's why I became a reporter. I'm a nosy guy."

"I know."

"Now, how could you know that?"

"You told me," Chigger said. "Us. I was in a class you spoke to at TSU a couple of years ago and that's why you said you became a journalist. You told us about the time you were six inches from Ronald Reagan's crotch and showed us that picture, the one you took when you were knocked down during a press conference and you ended up so close to the president's waist but he didn't bat an eye and kept on talking and you couldn't get up because all the other reporters had leaned in with their microphones so you took your pictures and one, one with Reagan's head in a halo of microphones taken from way down there, won you an AP prize. Epic. You have such great stories."

"You need to go off and create your own stories," Ray said.

"That's what I'm doing. When I'm an old woman of 40 I want to be able to say that I slept with the man who had the last interview with that teacher who died on the Challenger space mission and who chased Africanized bees all over Brazil and Venezuela and Panama and Costa Rica. The man some woman rock star propositioned and your wife was standing right beside you—"

"Ex-wife number two." Ray nodded.

"The man who sat on a wooden bench for a week in some rural courthouse covering a trial about a gang rape that happened at a cock fight," she continued. "The man who's done stories from Coast Guard planes flying fifty feet over Gulf beaches to chart the extent of an oil spill and in gliders and with Sky King—whoever Sky King was— and in hot air balloons and in World War II fighters and in blimps. And the man Tom Seaver threatened to punch out in a locker room, even though I don't have a clue who Tom Seaver was, either, except he was a famous pitcher."

"You put it like that and I sound like Baron Munchausen."

"Who's that?"

"Before your time. Waaaay before your time," he said.

•

The next day, Doctor Cornet came in to inspect her handiwork, asked Ray a few questions, read over his chart, and told him he could go home. She went to his side, untaped the tube leading to the small bag on his side and slid the tube out. When he saw what she was going to do, he expected pain but felt none. She covered the incision with a pad loaded with antiseptic cream and taped that down

She told him not to get it wet for a couple of days. She said he should rest for a few days, then could return to work when he felt comfortable doing so. She told him to avoid food high in fats. She told him not to do any heavy lifting for about eight weeks. He thought of a joke, but kept his mouth shut.

Chigger left to bring her car around to the front entrance while Nurse Bluto pushed Ray in a wheelchair toward the elevator. Ray told him he was fine to walk, but the nurse said hospital regulations required he be wheeled out—probably a legal issue, Ray guessed.

"Wait. Stop," Ray said as they passed a room with "Colvin, Charlene M." written on the tag by the door.

"Something wrong?" the nurse said.

"No. I know the little girl in here. I want to stop in and say hello."

"Charley's a fine young woman," Bluto said. "Everybody who works the floor loves her. She's not contagious anymore, so let's go visit."

Ray rose from the wheelchair as soon as he was in the room. Bluto wheeled the chair to the side and told Ray to give him a buzz when he was ready to leave.

"What's up?" Ray said.

Her eyes and nose were red and her voice sounded raw. "Not a pretty sight, am I?"

"You're lovely. How do you feel?"

"Like all my hens have been scratching around inside my head and down my throat. I thought they were down in my chest yesterday."

"What happened?"

"They say I got the flu. It came on real quick. Mom, too. Mom's really bad off, they tell me, but I haven't seen her since we came in. I talked to her yesterday on the phone. She sounded terrible." She shook her head firmly. "It's not even flu season."

"I'm sorry, Charley. I'm sure she'll be OK. Is there anything I can do to help? Feed the chickens?"

"My Uncle Melson is doing that. I'd tell you to ask Mom, but they won't let anyone in to see her. They say she's real contagious."

Ray wrote both his work and cell phone numbers on a small pad on her bed stand. "If you do need anything—anything at all—you just call me. OK?"

"Thanks, Mr. Strider."

"You get some rest now," he said. He turned around and pushed the wheelchair out of Charley's room, figuring to push it down to the nurses' station. Immediately outside the room, a physician stopped him. "Dr. T. Barlett, M.D." was embroidered on his white coat and Ray thought calling yourself both a doctor and an M.D. was a little redundant.

"Are you family?" the doctor asked.

"No," Ray said. "Friend of the family."

"Close?"

"I suppose. I've known Charley for several years."

The doctor touched Ray's arm and moved him a few feet from the doorway and lowered his voice. "I was just on my way in to tell Ms. Colvin that her mother has expired. The young woman might respond to that news better if it came from someone she knows."

Ray sighed. "I'll tell her. What happened?"

"She got pneumonia yesterday and it progressed quickly. This morning she suffered congestive heart failure and we couldn't save her. She was too weak. Her heart just gave out. The flu precipitated everything. Ms. Colvin is lucky that she's younger and much stronger."

"The flu…"

"We're running tests now and we've sent samples off to the CDC as well, but I've been around flu cases all my days as a doctor and I've never seen a strain this virulent and fast."

"My lord… Charley'll be OK?"

"Every indication we have says so. She has no fever now and the symptoms have abated. I'd like to keep her longer than we otherwise might, for observation. We'll probably discharge her in a couple of days." The doctor extended his hand to Ray. "Thank you for telling her."

Ray returned to Charley's room, sat on the edge of her bed, held her hand, and told her the news.

Charley exploded into tears, burying herself in Ray's shoulder. He held her tightly. She cried so hard she started to cough and gasp. He patted her back. She cried so much, Ray felt the shoulder of his shirt getting soaked with the tears but he wasn't about to let her go. He felt more like a father than he ever had before in his life, understanding her pain and knowing he could do nothing about it, couldn't fix it, that all he could do was hold her and let her cry and that would, ultimately, be enough.

Exhausted, Charley fell asleep and he settled her back on the bed, covering her. As he rose, he saw Chigger at the door and wondered how long she'd been there. He'd forgotten all about her.

"You didn't come down and I got worried," she whispered to

him as he took her outside the room.

"Sarah died. I had to tell Charley."

"Oh, I'm so, so sorry."

"I know. Lookit, I'm staying here tonight. You go home and come back in the morning. I'm not leaving her alone."

"I'll stay—"

He pushed her away. "Go. Don't argue."

She nodded and left. He returned to Charley's side, pulled a chair up next to the bed, and watched the little girl sleep. He felt protective and wanted to fight for her, but had no one to fight. He felt nurturing, but had no experience. He felt angry, but had no target. Tears filled his own eyes and he drifted off to sleep even though it was the middle of the morning.

He slept fitfully, but Charley never moved. She didn't wake when lunch was delivered, so he nibbled a little of it and even drank some tea even though he thought all tea tasted like dishwater. She woke in time for dinner. She tried to eat, but couldn't. He ate water. They never spoke to each other, but he held her hand until she drifted off to sleep again. He followed.

The next morning, Nurse Bluto woke Ray with a gentle nudge after taking Charley's vital signs.

"Oh, I had the most terrible dream…" Charley said to Ray after the nurse left, tears welling up in her eyes. "It wasn't a dream, was it?"

Ray shook his head and said softly, "No."

Charley nodded her head in a firm yes, making it so, and squeezed a couple of tears from the corners of her eyes.

"Do you have anyone you can stay with?" Ray asked.

"My grandparents and my Daddy have all passed and my mother didn't have any brothers or sisters. I guess my Uncle Melson in Wimberley is my only relative now. He's a nice man. He'll let me stay with him."

"Charley," he said. "Charley. I'm going to have to go, but I'll be back later today. I wrote my phone numbers down for you in case you need anything. And I mean anything, you understand?"

She nodded and smiled just a little, holding out her hand. "Thank you, Mr. Strider."

"Call me Ray."

She nodded and squeezed his hand as he reached over and kissed her on the forehead.

Doctor Bartlett came into the room looking over a chart.

"Any more details on that flu strain?" Ray said.

"I'm sorry, Mr. Strider, there isn't much I can tell you officially," the physician said.

"Somebody told you who I am?"

The doctor nodded. "We have privacy issues and you would have to get specifics from the hospital's public information officer who is—"

"I know who she is," Ray said. "I'm not here as a reporter. I'm here for that young woman. Whatever you say to me I can guaran-darn-tee you won't ever read in my paper."

"I understand, I understand. But even then I don't have much information. It's the flu, but we knew that. One of the co-agents in the tests we ran also found traces of anthrax."

"Anthrax?"

"Yes. I guess it's not that unusual since the Colvins live on a farm."

"It's not really a farm. Charley just raises chickens. Chickens don't carry anthrax do they?"

"I'm no expert. I know it's carried by livestock and by deer. Some chickens will carry flu. So even if they didn't raise cows, they could have picked something up from deer or maybe her chickens. We do have more than a few deer in the Hill Country. They're so plentiful I have to shoo them off my front porch when I go to work every morning."

Doctor Bartlett listened to Charley's breathing through his stethoscope, looked up her nose and down her throat, and told her that she was much better today. He told her he was sorry about her mother, then left.

"It was the spaceman," Charley said to Ray. Before he could protest, she nodded her head and repeated. "It was the spaceman's fault. He did something to the chickens and we got this nasty bug from them."

The phrase "bird flu" immediately snapped into Ray's mind.

"It was the spaceman, Mr. Strider."

And then Ray recognized the suit José Jimenez wore in his dream. It wasn't a spacesuit. It wasn't a bee suit. It was a HazMat suit.

.

LOOK TO THE SKY

Here he was, more skillful than any young Anakin Skywalker, his ship more responsive than any E3 Ve01 Starfighter. He could dance in the sky. He was a whirling dervish of flight. He touched the controls—lightly, lightly—and his ship rose, banking to the right then back to the left, and dove.

Once he thought himself lucky to be the first to pilot this exquisite ship in action, but now he knew it was not a matter of good fortune. He was the only pilot good enough to command this ship. They were made for each other. In the hands of a lesser pilot, the ship would have dominated or the lesser pilot would have tried to dominate the ship and disaster would follow in either scenario. He was good enough—the best—to keep pace with the capabilities of this ship and knew better than to try to dominate. He became one with the ship, like a grand horseman and his steed. Indeed, he was akin to Anakin himself, piloting his repulsocraft in the pod races on Tatooine, darting this way and that, sailing around obstacles at deadly speeds. He laughed in exhilaration, then sneezed.

Concentrate, he scolded himself.

He checked the holograph display. Right on target. Over Canyon Lake now headed east. He knew what the area looked liked even if he couldn't see the ground. It was the planet Geonosis with its labyrinthine catacombs.

The red light of his time/speed/distance indicator brought him back to reality. He switched on his microphone.

"Rat's Nest, this is Thunder Chicken. Over."

"Thunder Chicken, ah, this is Rat's Nest. Go ahead. Over."

"Rat's Nest, this is Thunder Chicken. ETA zero two minutes. Repeat. ETA is zero two minutes. Conditions are green. Over."

"Thunder Chicken, this is Rat's Nest. Ah, roger. Out."

He smiled. He was a basan, the fire-breathing ghost chicken that frightened Japanese city dwellers at night. Concentrate, he com-

manded himself. He was more cautious now, hovering the ship a few moments before heading in for the landing zone, tilting to one side then the other, scanning the earth for signs of movement. None.

"Rat's Nest, this is Thunder Chicken. I am going hot on my mark. Mark. Over."

"Thunder Chicken, this is, ah, Rat's Nest. Roger. You are acquired. Out."

He pushed the play button on the phone strapped to a Velcro tab on his suit. It poured out a John Williams fanfare and the pilot smiled as broadly as he could, putting the ship into a sharp dive.

The night was perfect—overcast thick enough to mask the moonshine. No one was looking to the sky tonight.

CHAPTER 21:
THE PIRATES WALK THE PLANK

They parked the Corsair far off the shoulder on County Road 666, under some cedars. It was eleven o'clock and Pleasant Valley was quiet and dark. They got out of the car, closing the doors quietly behind them and jogged down the road, keeping a wary eye out for car lights so they could duck into the trees.

Bass's particular ensemble this evening was a black Raiders hoodie fleece sweatshirt with the silver and black crest on the chest showing the one-eyed pirate quarterback backed by crossed sabers. He wore a black do-rag and black cargo trousers that rattled when he walked. Red wore a black Pittsburgh Pirates pullover with a small Pirates logo featuring a rugged one-eyed buccaneer backed with crossed bats. He wore a black knit cap with the same Pirate logo in dark grey on the side and black cargo trousers that didn't rattle.

In a matter of minutes they were at the door to the administrative offices of Frontier Gulch with no sight of any vehicles or the guard who had apprehended them the last time they were here stomping out piratey crop circles.

Bass removed a crowbar from one of his large trouser pockets and easily popped the door open. They waited a moment to hear if any alarm went off. Hearing nothing, they went in. Another quick jab with the crowbar opened the office door inside. They closed the door behind them and while Red held a flashlight on the safe, Bass took a large screwdriver and hammer out of his cargo pockets and placed the screwdriver over the fire safe's lock and hit it smartly with the hammer. He expected it to pop out as easily as the doors had opened, but it didn't. So he hit it again. And again. And again. The fifth time was the charm—the lock dropped back into the safe, the office door opened, the lights came on, and the large security guard stood blocking the doorway.

"And just what're you boys up to?" Sam asked, his hand resting on his holstered Taser.

Red shrugged ignorance and Bass said, "I don't know."

"Y'all ain't too smart, are you?"

Red shrugged ignorance and Bass said, "I don't know."

Sam's shirt pocket played the Caisson Song. He pulled out the cell phone and answered. "Yes, m'am.... A break-in at the office... Those same boys... Caught them banging away at the safe... No, m'am, they hadn't taken anything yet, but they was close... Yes, m'am." He put the phone away and motioned with a finger for the boys to follow him. He stepped across the hall and opened Margie's office door, turned on the light, and told the boys to have a seat. They sat on two metal chairs against the wall near Margie's desk and next to her day bed.

Sam stood in the doorway until Margie arrived ten minutes later.

"Boys, boys, boys," she said. "What am I going to do with you?"

Red shrugged ignorance and Bass said, "I don't know."

"Sam, I'll handle them from here," she said.

"Might not be wise to be alone with these two," he said.

She shook her head and smiled, taking a rather large Bond Arms derringer loaded with .410 shotshells from her purse. She held it lightly without pointing it at anyone. "Oh, I don't think they'll be any trouble. Will you, boys?"

Red shrugged ignorance and Bass said, "No'am."

"I'll turn the silent alarm back on when I leave, then," Sam said. "You need help, you hit the button and I'll come running and bust they heads wide fuckin' open."

"Thank you," she said. The boys sat with heads hung low, not knowing what to expect. She placed the pistol in a skirt pocket, sat on the edge of her desk, legs crossed in front of her. Lighting a Camel, she inhaled the sweet smoke deeply and exhaled slowly. "Boys, you've gone from simple trespassing to a felony. That safe has several thousands of dollars in it, so you're looking at some serious prison time. I think perhaps that might be too severe for such young, good-looking lads. Being behind bars would be such a waste. Such a waste."

They looked at each other, sat up more, and looked at Margie.

"I see by your outfits that you are pirates," she said.

Red shrugged ignorance and Bass said, "Aye."

Margie chuckled. "You ever done anything piratey? I mean, other than this?"

Red shrugged ignorance and Bass said, "Aye, of course we have."

"Such as...?"

Bass held his head high. "If we told you. We'd have to make you walk the plank." Then he looked back down at the floor. "You know, just in case you were an informant for the Crown."

"Walking the plank wouldn't be much of a punishment right now with the river so low. Might come a flood soon, though," she said.

"Well," Bass said, keeping his head down but looking up at her. "I guess we could be off with your head."

Margie chuckled again and thought for a moment. "Ever do something like that?"

The pirates looked confused. Red shrugged ignorance and Bass said, "Arrr, if we told you—"

"OK," she said. "You haven't. So how about ravishing wenches? You've done that haven't you?"

Red shrugged ignorance and Bass said, "Aye, we've ravaged many a wench."

"Am I a wench?"

The boys looked at each other and Red said to Bass, "I'm thinking Deborah McCoy the Buccaneer's Girl."

Bass shook his head no. "I think more Mistress Spitfire Stevens. A pirate wench with balls."

"Stand up," she ordered. They did.

"Strip down," she ordered, motioning with her cigarette. They looked at each other and shrugged and did as she had ordered, stopping at their underwear. Bass wore black and silver boxer shorts. Red wore a red thong. Bass looked Margie in the eye while Red looked at his feet.

"The rest," she ordered. Bass did.

Red still didn't look up but said, "M'am, I don't think—"

"That's right," she said, standing up. "Don't think. Just get naked, lad." He did and she looked them up and down. "I would say you were both up for it right now. Oh, look, you're both blushing.

You're pirates and I can see you're obviously up for some ravishing, but you're still boys."

Bass spoke up quickly. "Now, you just—"

"Hush," she said.

Margie stubbed her cigarette out in the desk ashtray, stepped to the day bed and pulled it forward so the portion of the mattress that formed the back of the sofa dropped flat to form a double bed. "Hop up," she said. They did, sitting Indian style on the bed.

Margie kicked off her sandals, stepped out of her skirt, and pulled her sweater over her head. "I think I shall call you Captain Long and Captain Wide." She stepped to the bed, unfastened her bra and stepped out of her panties, and then Margied on the mattress in front of the boys.

"Instead of sending you off to prison, which would surely be a waste, let's have a little party instead," she said. "It's going to be a long and bumpy ride."

Red shrugged and Bass said, "Let's get some booty."

•

Margie dressed as the boys watched her from the bed. They had no idea what to make of what had just happened to them, but neither felt like complaining.

"I trust you had an interesting evening. I apologize for it not being as profitable as you might have wanted, but I won't let you go away without car fare," she said. She fished a stack of hundred-dollar bills from her purse, removed the band, and counted out five to each of them. "It was worth every penny," she said. They smiled.

"Now, boys, perhaps you'd like to earn even more than that. You being pirates and all."

Red shrugged ignorance and Bass smiled, "Maybe. How much?"

"How does ten thousand dollars apiece sound?"

Red shrugged ignorance and Bass, absent-mindedly playing with himself, said, "Who do we have to kill?"

CHAPTER 22:
RAY'S FIRST DAY BACK AT WORK

Ray leaned back in his chair, propping his feet up on his desk. The Fork was still closed—three days now, according to Trey—while Tom tried to solve his septic problem, a problem that sent sewage fumes into the restaurant. Not a very appetizing situation.

Ray missed his friends. He missed being able to clear his head before starting work each day. He belched the Shiner Bock and Newman's Own Crème-Filled Chocolate Cookies he'd had for breakfast and made a mental note to go by the grocery store on his way home because now both his refrigerator and pantry were officially bare. Chigger came in the office and Ray stood up to face her.

"So we didn't have a paper last week?" Ray said.

Chigger's eyes got wide, surprised at the anger in Ray's voice. "What could I do? I couldn't put it all together myself. I don't know how. I couldn't cover the council meeting, I don't know how to do that, same for the county commissioners' meeting or the school board, I can't do any of that, I'd mess it all up. And even if I did, where does the other stuff for the paper come from? How do I get that? And even if I could find enough to fill it all up, I don't know how to do that, I don't know how all that gets laid out in your computer and I wouldn't know how to send it to the printer if I got that far. It's all like magic, as far as I can tell."

"Solange and Trey could have helped," Ray said.

"I didn't know. I didn't know."

Ray slammed his butt down in his chair and said, "Crap."

He rubbed his face with both of his hands and she backed away to her own desk, trying to avoid the daggers he was staring at her. He was being unfair, he knew. She was right. Anyone who had never worked as an editor or reporter did think of a paper appearing on their front lawn as magic. They had no clue how news was gathered—from press releases and letters and attending public meetings and calling people who might have news or interviewing people who had made news, bits and pieces coming in from stringers who got paid next to nothing but loved seeing their names in print, then writing and rewriting it all up, scrambling for fillers from the wire, using photos proud parents or coaches or teachers or event chairs had sent in, using photos taken by staff reporters and photographers.

And it was his own darn fault, trying to do everything on his own with just an advertising sales person as the lone employee. He *was* the news staff. He was reporter and editor and photographer and layout person and manager. And owner. He was responsible for this, not her. He and the ex-wife from hell knew they couldn't make a profit if they had a staff so they had done everything themselves. They both knew how. When he bought her out, he kept on that same path. It *was* his own darn fault.

"I'm sorry," he said.

"Don't worry about it," she said without turning around. She picked up her phone to call someone or pretend to, he didn't care which.

He went through his e-mail then his real mail.

The e-mail was all junk except for a long one from Trey that Ray figured Trey had copied from a web site. It was a story from the April 19, 1897, edition of the *Dallas Morning News* about an airship that many citizens had seen speeding around the countryside. Ray recalled reading about the event, but not the details. He read about the UFO having mechanical problems and crashing near a Fort Worth suburb on the property of a local judge. The flying saucer collided with a windmill and exploded, scattering debris across several acres and destroying the judge's flower garden. The Army was called in to investigate and they found the pilot of the craft inside. The pilot was dead but the chief investigator confidently proclaimed that the saucer pilot "was not an inhabitant of this world." The officer thought the creature was from Mars.

Now he remembered the story—the Martian was buried in the Aurora, Texas, cemetery. One of the other *Post* reporters was sent up to do a story on the incident, but couldn't find a tombstone for the creature or any verification that there had ever been a grave dug for a spaceman. Was that Olive? Yeah, and she never did file a story on it. At least he would have come back with something, even if it were all smoke and mirrors. He could always find a story.

He didn't know what Trey expected him to do with the e-mail. Maybe he could work it into whatever story he did on the Pleasant Valley flying saucer, showing that Texas has been a hotbed of UFO activity for more than a hundred years.

Most of the real mail was junk, too. He sorted out three press releases he would use in the next edition: The Fork was hosting a free bluegrass music jam now every Friday evening from seven to nine o'clock, the Bigfoot Rangers Cowboy Action Shooting Club was holding their annual shoot this Saturday beginning at nine in the morning at their range northwest of the village, and a ground-breaking ceremony was scheduled for noon a week from Saturday for the Pleasant Valley Botanical Conservatory.

He hoped Tom's septic problem was fixed by Friday otherwise the musicians would be playing *Soggy Mountain Breakdown.*

He'd forgotten all about his own club having their annual match this week; it was only the biggest event of the year for them.

Margie Gruntle and her Pleasant Valley Historical and Cultural Preservation and Beautification Society had been trying to raise money for this pet conservatory project of hers for the past five years and Ray was surprised they finally had enough money because the last time she mentioned it to him they were short nearly $100,000. The release said the two buildings, one a 46,000-square-foot museum and the other a two-acre greenhouse, would be located adjacent to Frontier Gulch providing the village with yet another venue to part tourists from their money. Ray thought for a moment, trying to remember if Jubal T.'s new development included this project. He didn't think it did. He wasn't certain.

He looked at the two While You Were Out notes, both from people who wanted to report seeing a UFO. He should have never run that story in the paper because now he was getting several of these a day since then—people looking for their fifteen inches of fame.

Unable to concentrate fully, he sighed, got up and left the office. He drove fifteen minutes to the Hill Country Regional Medical Center.

Standing in front of Chicken Charley's room, he was greeted by a sign that ordered, "No Visitors."

At least she wasn't in ICU, he thought as he walked to the nurses' station. "Why is Charley's room off-limits?"

One nurse looked up, smiled and asked him, "Charley who?"

"He means Charlene Colvin," Nurse Bluto said, walking up and placing a clipboard on the semi-circular counter. "Are you doing well, Ray?"

"Getting by," Ray said.

"Good. Listen, since you're not family I can't give you a whole lot of details about Charley's condition right now but it's worsened and she's contagious again."

"Is her doctor around? That Doctor Bartlett?"

"Do I hear my name?" the doctor said from behind Ray.

Ray turned and extended his hand to Doctor Bartlett who shook it and smiled an artificial physician's smile.

"I was hoping to learn about Charley's progress," Ray said.

"I'm afraid it's bad news."

"Don't tell me—"

"No. No. Not that bad. But we thought we had knocked the pneumonia out of her system and we were ready to release her yesterday but it came back and came back very hard. We've been able to control it and she should be able to leave the hospital in a week, maybe a day or two less than that, but I'm afraid she's going to have a rough time of it from now on."

"What's the problem?"

"The particular bacterial pneumonia she has is an odd strain we haven't seen before. It not only causes respiratory illness but, well, some rare strains can also prompt an immune system response to myelin, which is the sheathing on nerves."

Ray leaned back against the nurses' station counter. "So, what does that mean?"

"Over time the pneumonia will pass, but the impact on the nervous system resembles multiple sclerosis, for which there is no cure," the doctor said. He paused a bit, then added, "She's already exhibiting early symptoms. Tingling and numbness, a lack of balance, her vision is blurry, her right leg is weak when she tries to walk. The symptoms helped us figure it out. I'm afraid this young woman is facing a difficult life. She's young and full of energy and spunk, so we can hope she will cope with this as well as anyone can but make no mistake, she *will* have to cope."

"Thanks for the information," Ray said.

"I'm sorry I couldn't have better news," the doctor said and walked off down a corridor.

Ray turned around to Nurse Bluto. "Any idea when I'll be able to see her?"

"It'd be a guess, maybe a couple of days. Give us a call in the morning and we can tell you," Bluto said.

"Thanks, man."

"Be cool."

Ray left the hospital and returned to his office. Chigger was gone. The morning's beer and cookies were now in Ray's throat. He grabbed a bottle of water from the mini-fridge and guzzled it down as he walked around the office. Back at his desk, he picked up the legal pad with the list he'd written down the day he went to the hospital. He looked it over and over. He picked up a pen and walked to a window. He added to the list.

Crashed computer
Charley flu
Sarah dead
    —flu?
    —bird flu?

He looked at the first entry on the original list, crossed it out and wrote in:

Fred dead
    —footprints from HazMat suit?
    —chicken or person in suit made Fred swerve?

He stared at the list and felt he was still in a medicated fog. He noticed the While You Were Out pink slip on his desk with a familiar name and number on it and he smiled as he punched up the number.

"The man on a horse on the beach," the answering voice said.

"*El Cid*," he replied quickly. "What's new, Monica?"

"I knew you'd know that. I've been trying to think of that for two days now."

"You could've just Googled it."

"I finally did this morning and got nothing. First search was ten items, none related. When I added the word 'movie' I got no matches whatsoever. People are much better at processing this sort of trivia than computers."

"I'm smarter than a computer!"

"I didn't say that, Ray, old man."

"Yeah, OK. What can I do for you, Mon?"

"I'm going to e-mail you a few files that I got from our D.C. Bureau that I think you'll be interested in. Maybe there's a connection, maybe not."

Swinging upright in his chair, Ray said, "*Colorado Springs Today* is large enough to have a Washington bureau?"

"Our *chain* is," Monica said. "One guy—Tony Bonavita—and he serves nine papers including our sister paper in Denver, but he's excellent. Thinks he's Woodward and Bernstein wrapped together. He's got great sources. One of these drinking buddy confidential informants tells him the other day about a little program going on in the Office of Biological and Chemical Weapons Operations and Investigations which is a sub-agency of the Majority Agency for Joint Intelligence."

"Never heard of it."

"These new intelligence agencies are cropping up faster than Starbucks. I'd never heard of this one. Neither had Bonavita. Not listed on any data base we have. His CI says it's one of those super clandestine sub-agencies that no one ever hears of that's attached to another clandestine agency almost no one ever hears of so the agents can get paid but the big agency doesn't know anything about them either."

"Yeah, we had one of those at ONI. My second ex-wife worked in it and she wouldn't even tell me what she was doing. All I ever saw her do was read Israeli newspapers and magazines," Ray said. "So what's this OBCWOI do?"

"Beats us. But Bonavita's source says the OBCWOI is hard at work on developing vaccines for a variety of flus—"

"Not the CDC?"

"Wait for it. They're working on these vaccines with the intent of weaponizing a virus. The idea is that the bad guys are doing it, so we'd better do it and figure out a vaccine for the weaponized version."

"OK. I'm following you so far."

"This OBCWOI is apparently trying to take it all a step further, by mutating the H5N1 virus. And, of course, they're going to want tests to confirm it works, not on lab rats."

"Which one's the H5N1?"

"Bird flu."

"Bird flu," Ray said. He was quiet for a bit, then repeated, "Bird flu. Crap. You don't suppose…?"

"We don't have a clue, Ray, but Bonavita says his CI tells him what they're working on is what the CI called a "chimera," mutating the H5N1 with anthrax to make it more potent and more contagious and easier to weaponize."

"Is that even possible?"

"Well… that's one of the interesting things in this. Bonavita's asked around and can't get a straight answer to that. No matter which expert he asks, he gets a level of equivocation that would make a presidential candidate proud. Even when he promises it's all off the record, they won't commit one way or the other. Bonavita said one research doc's eyes lit up as if he was contemplating the possibility, but the guy refused to say anything. Here's the bottom line. You've got a fed in deep cover in your little town, you've got questionable deaths including one by an odd strain of the flu, we've got tips that some feds are trying to do scary stuff that, realistically, would be easier to pull off well out of the Beltway spotlight. We need way more information and I don't have a remote idea if these are connected, Ray, but if they are we've got a Pulitzer in our futures."

"Maybe yours," he said. "The flu death was the one recent death I thought was legit. Instead of going varoom-varoom my synapses have been going clunkity-clunk lately."

"We'll help you through it, old man."

"I miss a newsroom full of colleagues. Hey, the best movie about writing?"

"*Wonder Boys.*"

"Absolutely. Best flick about reporting?"

"*The Front Page*."

"Adolphe Menjou or Cary Grant?" Ray asked.

"Are you kidding me? The Cary Grant-Roz Russell version, of course. Come to think of it, it had a different title. *His Girl Friday*. Same story, though. It's the only one that captures all the sexual tension newsrooms are filled with. Menjou and Pat O'Brien not so much."

"How'd we ever get anything done?"

"By not giving in to temptation. The tension kept us all alert and sharp," Monica said, and then hung up without saying goodbye.

Crap, Ray thought as he checked his e-mail for Monica's files. I do miss a newsroom full of colleagues. He sat up straight in his chair and blinked his eyes.

When he began work as a reporter, newspapers wouldn't print everything they knew, only what they could prove. That was still the way he thought and he knew that he couldn't prove anything right now, and didn't really even know much.

Things had changed. Today, newspapers got around proof by printing rumors and discussing poll results. Television got around proof by having talking heads give opinions.

Even in his good old days, a reporter rarely got the full story. It was just the first draft of history in bits and pieces. It was like being in Plato's cave where you can only observe shadows of reality. Right now, Ray felt he was as much a shadow as what was happening around him. He breathed in deeply and exhaled slowly. He didn't believe in coincidences and more people had died in Pleasant Valley in the past couple of weeks under what now looked like questionable circumstances than had died in the previous couple of years. He couldn't purge that memory out of his mind—Chicken Charley lying in that hospital bed, crying herself to sleep on his shoulder. One way or another, he would find out what was going on. And he would make those responsible pay.

CHAPTER 23:
THE PIRATES AT HOME

Sebastian Teach and Henry Haught had showered, shaved, and had breakfasts of apple sauce mixed in Cap'n Crunch and a half a coffee cup of Captain Morgan rum each but they didn't have a class for another two hours.

"I finished that English homework. I think I did good," Red said.

"Did well," Bass said.

"What difference does that make?"

"It is an English class."

"Curses, matey, you wanna hear it or not?"

"Proclaim it to the world."

Red shook his head. Bass had been sailing high since their hook-up with the broad who owned the Gulch. "It's called '*Never Invite a Pirate to Dinner*,'" and he recited it.

Never invite a pirate to dinner.

He might be a true, Bluebearded sinner.

She may be like the likes of Anne Bonney.

She will steal with a "Hey nony nony."

You know that the usual buccaneer,

Given half the chance, will drink all your beer.

A protegée rogue of famed Edward Teach

Would bury you, head first, in desert beach.

The scurvy sea-farers will make you glum

When you find them all sunk, drunk from your rum.

Though romanticized by Robert Louis,

They rape—no matter Christian or Jewess.

Then after the laughter and rounds of toasts,

The bloody mateys will murder their hosts.

So, never offer a pirate a meal,

Or it's ship ahoy and over you'll keel!

"Captures us quite well," Bass said.

"Quite good," Red said.

Bass rolled his eyes, sitting down on the living room floor of their small frame house on Hopkins Street. "You wanna play or not? We've got a lot of time to kill, yo-ho-ho," He'd already opened up their favorite video game—*Pirates of the Purple Seas: Booty 8.* "We can go head-to-head or I can play with myself."

Without consulting each other, the ensembles they had chosen that day were Pittsburg Pirate game jerseys. Bass wore a black batting practice jersey with the cool red and yellow inserts on the sides and the fierce one-eyed pirate over the heart. Red favored a black retro road jersey with the gold and white stripes and "PIRATES" written in large gold letters across the chest. The number on the back of each was zero—Oh-Oh when seen together.

"So what'd you think of last night?" Red asked as his avatar—Captain Jack— slashes open a curtain behind a bar in a portside tavern to reveal several men and a scantily-clad woman playing dice.

"Hot and juicy," Bass said, his avatar—Captain Black— stepping in front of Captain Jack and drawing it's sword.

"That's not what I meant, although that was sweet. Old broads know how to work it better than young chicks. I never knew that."

Captain Black lunges at Captain Jack with his cutlass, but Captain Jack parries with his sword and the fight commences. "Tells you what she wants and how you should do it."

"In good shape for an old broad. Kinda thick around the middle but nice big boobs. How old you figure she is?"

"Got me. Old. Forties. Maybe as old as fifty. I can't tell once they get past thirty and they stop showing off their belly buttons."

"Arrr, you're right. That's a telltale for certain. You can get work done on your face and boobs but wrinkles around your belly button are always going to show."

Captain Jack ducks one slash, thrusting his sword upwards as Captain Black barely jumps away in time. "Hey, me bucco, why you going after my jewels?"

"So I can get the real ones." Captain Jack reaches out and snags a jeweled necklace around the neck of the wench playing dice and cuts it off her with his sword. As it slides into his hand the green box in the left corner that was his registers an additional five hundred points.

Captain Black turns toward the wench and one of the men stands to defend her but Captain Black dispatches him easily by shooting him with a pistol in one hand and then slashes at the skimpy dress of the woman with the cutlass in his other hand. "Wonder if she's got *more* hidden away?" The dress falls and the buxom woman tries to cover up her nakedness by turning around.

"That's some booty for a computer-generated wench," Red said.

"Great booty. Hey, you wonder why a broad's butt is called booty and plunder is, too."

"Kinda obvious, isn't it."

"Cause they're both treasures?"

Red twisted his wrists holding his controller, trying to get his avatar to dodge a thrust. "Aye-aye."

"The same way jewels are treasure and your nuts, too."

"Aye. It's like what we learned in English class."

"A play on words," Bass said.

"A what-you-call a homonim."

"Now, how can a word be queer?"

"I don't make up the rules for that English, chum. Hey, what's the rule for rape?"

"Worth 100 points if she's fetching, 50 if she's a hag."

"This one's real fetchin'."

"Aye-aye."

Red began punching the button on his controller. "Well, I'm commencing the rape." Captain Jack grabs the naked wench and tosses her behind a large chest.

"That was my rape, man," Bass said, tossing his controller at the TV screen that showed Captain Jack's naked butt going up and down behind the chest.

"You snooze, you loose," Red said. "You'd think they'd make these things X-rated, you know, so you could actually see stuff."

"We got plenty of the real stuff last night."

"Arrr, that's right. Best ever."

"You think so?"

"What wasn't to like? I came *three* times," Red said. "Never did that before."

"Me twice. Can't complain. How many times you think she did?"

Red put down his controller and put the game on save then turned off the TV. "Man, I couldn't tell. She seemed like she was coming all night, even when we weren't touching her."

"Probably deprived. She certainly seemed grateful as all hell."

"And you weren't?"

"Aye-aye. Always am," Bass said.

"How many people have you had sex with anyway?"
"You mean how many women?"

"Of course women."

Bass sat back and closed his eyes and nodded his head. "Three. Gloria. Well, everybody screwed Gloria back in high school, then Nicole then Shontay."

"You did Shontay? Oh, man. I did not know that. I'm jealous."

"Oh, then there was that Margie broad last night, so I guess four. I don't count the chicks that just gave me blowjobs over the years. Blowjobs don't count as sex. One of the presidents said so himself clearing all that up. Blowjobs don't count."

"Aye. Remember that," Red said.

"So how many for you, stud?"

"Counting last night, six."

"Bull*shit* six. Who?"

"Well, Gloria, of course — "

"Of course. That's a given."

"So Gloria and Margie last night makes two. Nicole because of that time we did her together even though you were the one dating her."

"OK. I wasn't figuring that one, but OK, that's three."

Red looked off to his left. "Bridget, Hannah, and, damn, I don't remember that other chick's name."

"What chick?"

"One I hooked up with when we were down in Galveston last Spring Break."

"Oh, yeah, the one kept flashing her boobs every time someone offered her beer. What was her name?"

"I don't even think I heard her say a word all night. Hell, she might have been a *foreigner* for all we know."

"She was kinda dark," Bass said. "Probably Honduran or something. So, what did you think about last night?"

"You talking about Margie's proposition?"

"Aye-aye. Sounded good to me then. Still does. A perfect piratical expedition. She's got it figured out real slick. We slit hubby's throat, dump him in the shrub shredder out by the Gulch, spread him out as mulch, and all that loot is ours."

"I know one thing I'd do with the money for sure."

"Get us a big screen HD TV."

"Aye-aye. Get one of them cables you can hook it up to your computer," Red said.

"Aye-aye indeed. Download some pornos and watch them on a 72-inch plasma. Man."

"*Five foot* boobs, man."

"Let's go earn our keep. Weigh anchor, matey."

They smiled and said in unison, "Pirates!"

CHAPTER 24:
PERSPECTIVES

What Jubal T. Gruntle saw was the most perfectly formed naked female body he'd ever seen—in pictures, on film, in person. She had blonde hair up and down. He didn't see an ounce of fat on her and he was eyeballing her carefully. She wasn't anwhorexic like some of the thin ones. She was tall, lean and muscular. Even her small titties that stood up and looked right at you seemed to have muscles. Hell, even the nipples looked like they could lift weights.

He was a little surprised when she showed up at his front door, but only a little. He knew he wasn't some young stud with a swimmer's abs but he'd discovered over the years that power was a powerful aphrodisiac and since he was mayor and on the board of several policy-making boards in this end of the Hill Country, and owned the largest real estate company outside of Austin, and had the top tourist attraction outside of San Antonio, women were easy to come by. All she'd said was that she wanted him. Well, who was going to argue with that logic? She'd shed her clothes faster than a state rep snapping up a lobbyist's check. She hadn't been wearing any underwear so the strip show was faster than he might have otherwise liked but the end result was anything but a disappointment. He dropped his Bermudas and boxers, jerked the polo shirt over his head, and felt for a moment—just a moment—that he couldn't possibly measure up to her. He stepped toward her, ready to do more, but she said to wait a moment and went to the table where she had set her fanny pack, tank top, and shorts. She took a round case out of the pack and put in a pair of contacts.

"I guess you like to see what's happening, hunh?" he said, feeling witty.

When she turned around and moved to him, swinging her hips, she said, "I like for the other person to see what's going to happen." He looked into her eyes even though it was difficult to pull his stare away from her body, and saw that her irises were now red, with a vertical slit. Cat's eyes. Like the eyes of a mountain lion he'd shot on a hunting trip to his lease down near Del Rio a few years ago. The sight sent a chill from the back of his neck to his groin and he got even more excited, which he didn't think was possible. She walked up to him, just close enough for their genitals to touch and he felt her hard abs touching his hairy, sweaty fat belly. She smiled. Oh, this was going to be the time of his life, he thought.

•

What Diana Slingerland saw was an inflated ego in a bloated body, pasty white, not a single muscle in tone, wearing the kind of smirk she used to slap off with alacrity when she visited bars. He moved like he was in slow motion, every ounce of flab following a second behind his skeleton. His eyelids were heavy but he kept forcing them up.

This honeypot salvage work was what she was destined for. She didn't know it growing up, but she delighted in her discovery while in Office schools. She had never imagined she could get paid for this sort of excitement — it was a pleasure beyond imagination.

His smirk turned arrogant as he said, "You tall drink of water, I've been lusting after you since the minute I ever laid eyes on you. I've been wishing for this moment forever seems like."

Their genitals brushed against each other, which was kind of nice, she thought. She looked down at his round face. "Be careful what you wish for." She took his head between her hands like she was going to kiss him and she felt him twitch in excitement, his eyes closing.

•

What the pirates saw took their breath away. Their ensembles consisted of identical black Pittsburgh Pirates T-shirts, black trousers, and black do-rags with a skull and crossbones in dark blue on the cloth right at their foreheads. They lurked outside the mayor's home, peering in a window, blending in with the night and the dark shrubs behind them. They'd come to fulfill their contract with Margie, but someone else was with Margie's husband and it appeared they were going to get a show. They had never seen strangers do it before. Not right here in front of them. Not in person. They couldn't understand what this fine-looking wench saw in this fat man, but each to his own they guessed.

They watched as she rubbed herself up against him. They watched as she took his head in her hands in a soft caress then moved her left hand to the back of his head, low and to the left, while her right hand gently moved to his right temple. They watched as she snapped her hands together and his neck twisted sharply and they heard the satisfying little crack that announced his spine had been severed cleanly, even though they didn't know a thing about what they had just seen. They watched as she stepped back and the mayor's body crumpled to the carpet, ejaculating.

"Matey, did that wench just do what I think she did?" Red whispered.

"Hell, yes," Bass whispered back.

"Arrr, did you see what he did?"

"Hell, yes."

"Matey, he came when he went, how's that possible?"

They suppressed giggles.

They watched as she moved the body to the bottom of the stairs, positioning it so that it was face down, its feet askew a couple of steps above it. She gathered up his clothes and ran up the stairs, found his bedroom and tossed the clothing on the king-sized bed. Back downstairs, she plucked a couple of Kleenexes out of a box and wiped up the wet spot on the mesquite hardwood flooring, tucking the Kleenex into her fanny pack, and then put her clothes on. She paused and looked around. The pirates moved back from the window. She left.

When they heard her car drive away, Red said, "What do we do now?"

"Haul ass out of here."

"But what now?"

"What d'ya mean? She just did our job for us, me bucco. We beat it and collect our booty. It's like the perfect crime and we didn't even have to do anything."

They laughed as they walked down the road to the Corsair saying, just before they got into the car, "Pirates!"

CHAPTER 25:
WHAT ARE THE ODDS?

Ray and Trey were enjoying a Big Roll at their favorite table at the Fork. Ray rolled his eyes at the first bite—a sweet taste of heaven. No more high-fiber muffins for him.

Trey shoveled some of his own roll into his mouth. "How's Charley?"

"Better," Ray said, sipping some orange juice. "They say she may be home in the middle of next week. Poor kid. She's been practicing using a cane to walk and she says she's getting pretty good at it. I believe that. I think that kid can do any darn thing she sets her mind to. Pneumonia is gone. But when she gets to go home and walks into her house for the first time, I think it'll really hit her about Sarah."

"Poor kid."

"Poor kid? Talking about my sex life?" LeRoi said, walking over to the table.

"Could be, but no. Chicken Charley," Ray said.

LeRoi set down his own Big Roll and poured himself a cup of coffee from the carafe on the table. "Oh, yeah. Poor kid."

"I had tears in my eyes when I wrote up Sarah's obit. First time that ever happened," Ray said. "I wanted to write up more but I couldn't. I mean, with Billy it was easy. He had this long life, did lots of things, was the village character. It was a tribute. This is going to come out wrong, but Sarah was just a middle-aged widow doing a good job of raising her kid. Born this date, died that date. Too soon. Her whole life comes down to a couple of short paragraphs and I guess that's why I teared up. She was better than I can give her. She was everything in the world to Charley. And she was cremated. She lives on through Charley, I guess."

LeRoi sat back and sighed. "You cannot change the world. You can only learn how to survive it."

"Yeah, but nobody gets out alive," Ray said. "Y'all going to the memorial service for her at Saint Christina's?"

"We'll be there," Trey said.

"If work allows, I will be there," LeRoi said. He sniffed the air. "Tom got the problem solved."

"Angie said the sewer line can't get run up here soon enough. They're guessing July," Ray said. "It's next to impossible to run a decent septic system along the banks of a river."

"You feel up to shooting Saturday?"

"I'm going, but I probably won't shoot. I don't feel a hundred percent yet so I don't want to endanger anyone with a loaded weapon in my hands. But I'll run the timer for our posse." Ray turned to Trey. "Come on out. Chigger told me she and Solange are doing a ladies' day out at the mall Saturday so you've got nothing better to do."

"Know what? Believe I will," Trey said, adjusting his glasses.

Ray's eyebrows went up. "Great."

LeRoi began digging into his own prodigious cinnamon roll, then gestured to Ray with a piece of roll on his fork. "You do not want to endanger anyone with a loaded weapon in your hand, why you packing?"

"How do you know that?" Ray said.

"I am a trained professional," LeRoi said before eating the piece of roll. "You have it stuck in the back of your waistband and you are sitting down bent over that plate and it is sticking out from your shirt like you have a broom stuck up your ass. That .45 Colt Commander you have had since the Navy?"

"Oops." Ray said.

Trey looked with concern at Ray. "Are you meshugeh? He's a cop, but you've got no reason t'carry a gun. Is that even legal?"

"I've had a concealed-carry permit since it was signed into law," Ray said. "I just haven't seen any reason to actually carry it before now."

Trey pushed himself away from the table. "But why? Damn, man, you eaten up with the dumbass? What if it goes off by accident? What if there's some sort of backfire? Jesus."

"Know all those tools you use every day?" LeRoi said. "No different from any of them. A firearm is a tool, is all. Ray knows how to use them, and even if he drops that sucker on the deck it will not go off by accident and I have never heard of a pistol backfiring, whatever that would be."

"I still don't like it," Trey said.

"Forget about it and you'll be fine," Ray said.

"He has a point. However," LeRoi said. "Why are you packing? You get a threat?"

"Not directly. But I don't think any of these recent deaths are what they seem."

LeRoi put down his coffee cup. "Murders? We do not have any evidence whatsoever that is even remotely the case."

"We'll see…"

UB40's reggae version of *Red Red Wine* played on LeRoi's belt. He pulled out his cell phone and answered. He scowled. "When?... I am on my way."

"The way people are dying around here, Ray may have good reason to pack," LeRoi said, standing up.

"What now?" Ray said.

"Margie found Jubal T. dead. You might want to come along."

•

Ray and LeRoi arrived in their own cars. An ambulance was parked by the front door of the house, its lights flashing. LeRoi told Ray to wait outside and he went in the mayor's house. Within a few minutes, the Evidence Chick arrived with Sheriff's Sergeant Shannon Fischer and Ray knew the J.P. wouldn't be far behind. The Evidence Chick pushed a collapsible dolly with her evidence gear stacked on it. As she passed Ray, they each said hello. She added, "Give me a few minutes to see the situation and I'll let LeRoi let you in. Gloves and booties, though." He thanked her, and then checked his camera to make sure the battery was charged. He dropped it back into his shoulder bag. LeRoi came out just as Judge Clement drove up in his Jeep.

LeRoi waited until the Justice of the Peace joined them. "Margie was out of town visiting a friend in Austin last night and when she returned this morning she found Jubal T. on the stairs. My guess is he has been dead several hours, but the Evidence Chick will tell us for certain. It appears he fell down the stairs."

The J.P. thanked LeRoi and went to the house, stopping at the doorway to put paper booties over his cowboy boots and pull purple crime-scene gloves on his hands from a small box the Evidence Chick had left by the door.

"Jubal T.'s really dead?" Ray said.

"Dead enough to convince the average coroner," LeRoi said.

"You don't really believe he killed himself falling?"

"Accidents are the fifth leading cause of death and most of those are from falls."

Ray shook his head as they walked to the house. "No way this is an accident."

"Margie has an ironclad alibi," LeRoi said. "The spouse is always the number one suspect. Number two is the one who calls in to say they found the dead guy. She is both. But with her eliminated, who else is there? You? And, Ray, I have seen several deaths from falls and this looks exactly like it should. He was overweight, he was middle-aged, he was nude. It would have been very easy for him to slip at the top of the stairs and fall."

"Naked?"

"It is his home, Ray. He is allowed to be naked in his own home."

Ray shook his head again. They put on booties and gloves and went inside. Margie was sitting on a small leather loveseat in the hallway by the living room, talking softly with Sergeant Shannon who was writing in her small notebook, nodding sympathetically at regular intervals. Ray stood at the entrance to the expansive living room, watching the Evidence Chick poke and prod the body sprawled on the bottom stairs. Two EMTs hovered nearby. She took several photographs of the body and said something to the EMTs who picked up what once had been Jubal T. Gruntle and zipped him into a heavy plastic bag. They carried him to the waiting, flashing, silent ambulance.

Ray walked over to the Evidence Chick and LeRoi.

"TOD is eleven p.m.," she said. "Seems pretty simple. He gets undressed for bed and maybe decides he wants a drink or a snack and goes downstairs to get one. Looks like he slips at the top, falls and can't stop, hits exactly the wrong way and breaks his neck. The stairs are same as the floor, some kind of hardwood. Highly polished, slick. If the stairs were carpeted, he might still be alive."

Ray shook his head. "This isn't right."

"How?" Judge Clement asked.

"I don't know, Steve," Ray said. "Don't you think you've been a little busy lately? I mean, what're the odds?"

"Ever take a math course in college?" the J.P. said. "The odds of any individual event happening may be high but that don't mean you can't have a series of events happen back to back to back, seeming to defy the odds but odds only work over a very large sample. You know. You flip a coin and it's fifty-fifty each time you flip it, but you might get ten tails after one heads."

Ray shook his head. "This isn't right."

The Evidence Chick stowed her camera and retrieved some other gear. "The evidence will tell us, Ray," she said.

"Unless you've got film from a camera that was running when it happened, the evidence isn't going to tell us enough," Ray said. "You find anything at all unusual?"

"Not really unusual," she said.

"What?"

The Evidence Chick lowered her voice. "Looks like he ejaculated as he died. You write that and I'll claw your eyes out, Ray, I promise."

"Was he having sex?" LeRoi asked.

"No. No," she said. "It's not common but it's also not that unusual. It can happen. You get even more people who relieve themselves as they die or immediately after. Everything in the body relaxes. If you're packing a load, it can blow."

Ray shook his head and walked over to Margie. He waited for Sergeant Shannon to finish her questioning, and then sat down opposite the sofa in a rocking chair.

"I'm so sorry," Ray said.

Margie fumbled her pack of cigarettes over and over in her hands, wanting one but having to wait until the police left. "It happens."

"Mind if I ask you a few questions?"

"Oh, Ray, why? I told it all to the sergeant. Can't you get it from her?"

"Nope, I have access only to the incident report. None of the investigation until it goes to court, if it does."

"There's an investigation?"

"Always. The cops assume every death is a homicide until proven otherwise. They also assume every one they talk to is lying to them."

"Why in heaven would I lie about this?"

"I'm not saying you are. That's just the way cops think. Reporters now, we just want a good story, some way to tell people just who your husband was, how special he was to you."

"Now you're blowing smoke up my skirt, Ray," Margie said, smiling. "Jubal T. was a conniving, fat bastard and most people who knew him thought exactly that. You can't write anything in the paper that'll make them change their minds."

"*You* didn't think he was a conniving, fat bastard?"

Margie settled back into the leather, scrunching her shoulders as if to draw the padding in around her. She couldn't wait. She lit a Camel, blowing the smoke over her shoulder into the wall in the hope that the police in the other room wouldn't notice.

"People change," she said quietly. "You put up with more than you think you can."

"Well, I guess I can get all his background information from our files. Tell me about today."

"I was staying with a friend in Austin overnight. I got home at about eight this morning and found him like that. I called 9-1-1 and they sent EMS and the deputy. You know the rest."

"What can you tell me about that new development he was building with Bubba?"

Margie sat up. "I can tell you it's not going to happen, that's what I can tell you."

Ray closed his notebook and dropped it and his pen into his shoulder bag, standing up. He extended his hand and she took it.

"Again, I'm very sorry for your loss."

She nodded and sank back into the sofa.

Ray walked to the front door and as he was taking his booties and gloves off, LeRoi walked over.

"Where you headed?" LeRoi asked.

"See our wannabe City Manager."

"You want to leave your Colt with me?"
"Not a snowball's chance in Hell."

CHAPTER 26:
A SNOWBALL IN HELL

Ray's jeans played the theme from *The Good, the Bad, and the Ugly*. He pulled his pickup to the shoulder of Ranch Road 666 and answered his phone.

"Name the *Magnificent Seven*," the voice said.

"Monica, I really don't have time—"

"Play the game and win a prize."

He sighed, paused a bit, and twisted his mouth around. Finally, he said, "Yul Brynner, Steve McQueen, James Coburn, Charles Bronson, Robert Vaughn, Horst Buckholtz, and Eli Wallach."

Monica made a noise like a loud buzzer. "I can't believe you missed one. You must be off your game today."

"Way off," he said. He thought for a moment, going over the names again. "No, they're all correct."

"Sorry. Eli Wallach played Calvera, the Mexican bandit leader. He wasn't one of the Seven. Usually people miss Horst Buckholtz—"

"Yeah, why pick a German actor to play a Mexican peasant?"

"Anyway, the guy you missed—"

"Yeah, you're right. Eli Wallach was the bad guy. The one I missed was Harry Luck. What the heck was that actor's name? Brad? Yeah. Brad Dexter."

"Finally got it," she said.

"What'd I win?"

"Your bad guy's real name. Bonavita's CI said the guy was at some seminar a few months back and Bonavita tracked down a group shot of the class and gave the photo to a different CI who was able to ID the guy after matching it up with the photo you sent me. Name is George Jefferson Frass. Born in Warrenton, Virginia, lives in Upper Marlboro, Maryland, works at Fort Meade."

"He's NSA?"

"Who knows? That's where he works... an office at Fort Meade. Bonavita's offering a case of Scot's whiskey to whoever can get him more details, but his primary CI on this says that may be next to impossible. Been around for about six, seven years, though."

Ray was scribbling all of this into his reporter's notebook as quickly as he could. "What kind of name is Frass?"

"Sissy says it's Czech. She's on the society page."

"Kafka."

"Gesundheit."

"No, I mean that's only other Czech I ever heard of. Guy who wrote about turning into a cockroach."

"Well, these spooks are all like cockroaches. They don't like light being turned on them."

"I'd like to squish him like one."

"Give you a bonus for the Seven characters' names."

"I already said Harry Luck, so the rest are Chico, Lee... Bernardo... Britt, Vin, and, of course, Chris."

"Didn't hesitate much. See, you've still got it. Frass's significant other is a Diana Slingerland. Don't have background on her at all, but Bonavita's secondary CI says the rumor is she does wet work. I'm guessing you know what that means."

Ray took a deep breath and ran his palm over the top of his head. "Yeah, I know what that is. Thanks, Mon, you and this Bonavita dude are doing great work."

"Just keep us posted on what's happening out there in the boondocks."

•

Ray sat in his pick-up in the City Hall parking lot for more than a half-hour running several variations of conversations with the would-be city manager over in his mind. Clever banter didn't seem sufficient and a violent confrontation would be counter-productive. Once he went in and said something, the dice, as Caesar said, were thrown. No turning back. Things would be out in the open. But right now he felt more like Sid Caesar than Julius Caesar. If Wallace—Frass—was responsible for the recent deaths in Pleasant Valley, Ray knew he could be putting himself and others, like Chigger, in danger. The last time he'd been seriously threatened was when a honey producer in McAllen called to tell him that if he didn't stop writing his dire killer bee stories his body would be found in a ditch alongside the road. He brushed that off, thinking that bullies like that were just cowards, but he also knew cowards could kill, too. In a cowardly fashion perhaps, but if you were the victim you'd still be just as dead. What he did back then was to call a Texas Ranger friend and tell him all about the phone call. Ray couldn't prove who the caller was, but he was certain he recognized the voice. He knew the Ranger couldn't do anything, but at least if he were killed the cops would know who to go after. Precious little consolation. His friend gave him the same advice other cops had over the years: start carrying a weapon.

"When seconds count, the police are just minutes away," Joaquin said.

Maybe that's why he had his Colt auto stuck in the waistband of his jeans. He knew how to use it. But would he? Could he? He pulled it out and looked at it, breathing in its pungent, oiled aroma. He thought about jacking a round into the chamber and going in to see Wallace—Frass—cocked and locked. But he didn't. Stupid, he thought. Without a round in the chamber, the pistol was nearly useless. He shoved the pistol into his shoulder bag and got out of the truck pulling the bag with him. The Colt gave him comfort.

He walked directly to the office and didn't knock.

"What may I do for you, Mr. Strider?" George said smiling. Ray paused, shook his head, entered the office, closed the door behind him.

"Mr. Strider?"

"Mr. Frass."

George's head snapped back and he cocked an eyebrow. "I can assure you I don't know who this Mr. Frass is."

"Yeah, just like you don't know anything about the Office of Biological and Chemical Weapons Operations and Investigations of the Majority Agency for Joint Intelligence."

George lost his smile. He sat backed and folded his arms over his chest.

"Just like you don't know anything about Fred or Billy or Sarah or even Jubal T.'s death."

"I admit I know the mayor, obviously, but those other people are completely unknown to me."

"Weaponizing a flu virus is also completely unknown to you, I suppose."

George stood and walked to the front of his desk. He sat on the edge of the desk, nearly within arm's reach of Ray, and folded his arms again. Ray fought back the taste of copper and a feeling of vertigo as if he were balancing on Kevin Costner Point at Big Hill in Big Bend. They stared at each other in silence. Silence was a tool in Ray's business. You had to know the right questions to ask, but you also had to know when to remain quiet because most people cannot stand silence and will continue talking past the answer they might have just given and, usually, that jabbering had more information than the initial answer. A vintage memory flashed through his mind.

His first day in Vietnam. He has checked in to the BOQ at the Annapolis Hotel in Saigon and a car sputters to a stop on the street in front of the lobby door. Ray and others watch out the window, violating one of the primary directives they'd learned back in the States: stay away from doors and windows. They watch and listen as one of the two armed guards in front of the hotel, speaking English, order the driver to move on. The car has stopped at a large sign that proclaimed "CAM DAU XE." The driver jabbers away in Vietnamese, pointing to the hood of the car, ignoring the No Parking sign. The guard again orders the driver to move on. The driver steps out of the car, opens the hood, and pokes his head in toward the engine. While one guard warns the driver a third time, the other guard is on his radio. Ray is fresh from language school and can make out most of the Vietnamese the driver is hollering, so he walks outside to reason with the guard. It's obvious the man is just having car troubles and doesn't understand English—why be so rude?—and Ray tells the guard he might be able to help the driver get the car running again and, if not, he can at least help push it down the street. Ray says he knows he can get others inside the hotel to help out as well. The guard orders Ray back inside and to stay away from the door and windows. Ray starts to argue when the second guard points a grenade launcher and, before Ray can react, fires at the car. The car explodes. Ray watches as the driver's right arm and left leg are torn from his body. The car burns. The driver burns. Ray ducks back inside the hotel and hears several small explosions start popping in the car. Then two larger explosions. Ray and the others inside watch as the car fire burns itself out. Four other armed Marines wait until the car cools, then walk over to it, poking around the burned, bent metal and still smoking seats and tires. One kicks the crispy critter curled up by the front tire and the Marine's boot breaks the body's rib cage as if the charred remains were nothing but papier mâché. Ray goes out to look. One Marine warns him away, but Ray pulls rank and the Marine shrugs his shoulders and points at the back seat. Ray sees another burned body, curled up in a fetal position, a large automatic weapon grasped in its hands. The Marine explains this was an ambush, that the second man was waiting to draw a crowd, then he would have popped up and popped off. The car exploded when two grenades on the back floor went off. The heat cooked off rounds on the body's ammunition belt. The Marine tells Ray he should be thankful the guards followed procedure and kept him from helping the stranded motorist. "No good deed goes unpunished," the Marine tells Ray.

Ray hadn't thought about the incident in more than fifty years, but he felt the same way now. Confused. Overwhelmed.

George blinked. "Speaking hypothetically, and I hasten to remind you it would be just a hypothetical, a biological being weaponized would be a result of this country being at war, Mr. Strider. Information or details of any nature for such a project would, of course, be of the highest security." He laughed a little, without humor. "Miles above your paygrade. So, hypothetically again, even if I were involved in such an enterprise it wouldn't be anything I could speak to you about."

"People have died here."

"The purpose of any such project would be to protect people, Mr. Strider. To be honest, if we had intelligence leading us to believe terrorists were weaponizing biological agents for an attack on this country, we would have to act promptly. Antigens would have to be developed. Our own biological agents would have to be developed. Immediately."

"People are dead."

George stood up. "Such a project would only be to protect

millions of people. Sometimes, Mr. Strider, collateral damage occurs. You've served in the military—Air Force I believe, in Vietnam—you know what bombings are like. Bombs can't pick and choose. Honestly, how many innocent Vietnamese died in the bombings of Hanoi?"

"I wasn't in the Air Force and that happened after I left 'Nam."

"Oh, I understand, but the concept is one you understand, I'm certain. War is hell, as they say, but it is a war we're in, Mr. Strider."

"You think we're all *Ma and Pa Kettle Back on the Farm* out here, but we're not."

Ray felt the heaviness of his pistol in the bag, cushioned from his camera by his notebook. He thought this was like a showdown scene from a Western movie and those always ended in a shootout. He wanted to use the Colt, but he knew he wouldn't. That's not what journalists did. Other people took action. Journalists were like cops—they were just around to write up a report once all the action was over. He reached into his bag.

"If you won't give me an official statement, who can I call?" Ray said, pulling out his reporter's notebook and opening it. He poised his pen over a page.

"Don't be absurd," George said. "There is no one to call because there is nothing to call anyone about. You've been out in the boondocks too long, Mr. Strider, and you're letting your imagination get the better of you."

"People are *dead*."

"Honestly, Mr. Strider, people die all the time and that's a fact you certainly must be aware of and not all of them are done in by nefarious means as a result of some vast government conspiracy."

"You don't get it," Ray said, gesturing with his pen. "People are dead, and you're responsible, and you don't care."

George returned to the other side of his desk and sat down, shaking his head. Ray now felt like he was in a Monty Python skit but that would end only when a giant animated foot came down from the heavens and squished everyone. He folded up his notebook and returned it and the pen to his bag and when he did his fingers touched the handle of the automatic. They lingered.

"Your imagination is getting the better of you," George said. "Even if what you say was happening, you have no proof, no proof at all. And you are baffled by it all. But confusion on your part doesn't constitute a deadly conspiracy on my part."

Someone knocked on the office door and opened it without waiting for a reply. Ray's hand jumped out of his shoulder bag. Sheriff's Sergeant Dan Germaine filled the doorway but remained in the hall.

"What may I do for you, deputy?" George asked.

Germain scanned the room quickly. "Deputy Nguyen asked me to check in on y'all. See if y'all were OK."

"Why would LeRoi do that?" Ray said.

Germaine shrugged his shoulders. "Didn't say. Just knew I was going to be around. Asked me to check in so I did. Everything OK?"

George rose from his chair and stepped toward the door. "Why wouldn't it be?"

"I don't know," the sergeant said. "I did hear what sounded like a heated argument. Maybe he was concerned that argument might, well, escalate."

"I was just leaving, sarge," Ray said.

Germaine nodded and walked slowly down the hallway but left the door open behind him.

"You can't do this," Ray said.

George moved to within a few inches of Ray and said quietly, "I can do anything I'm big enough to get away with. Be careful. I am your worst nightmare."

"Naw," Ray said, stepping into the hallway. "My worst nightmare is my fourth ex-wife."

CHAPTER 27:
LOOKING FOR LEVERAGE IN ALL THE RIGHT PLACES

Diana stepped into the kitchen of Ray's house, using the back door that led to a breezeway and detached garage. She looked around, opened cupboards, opened the oven door, opened the refrigerator, opened the doors under the double sink. She reached in and picked up a can of cleaner, shook it, returned it and chose another then another. They were all what they appeared to be.

She opened the refrigerator door. It was empty except for a large bottle of orange juice, seven Vanilla Cokes, three Shiner Bock beers, and six dark chocolate Milky Way bars. Only one tray of ice cubes in the freezer. She looked in the pantry. Macaroni and cheese mixes, tomato paste, spaghetti, crackers, spices, two cans of tomato rice soup, one can of beef barley soup, canned beans, a box of beef-flavored Rice-A-Roni, instant oatmeal, a box of Cherrios, a box of Ritz crackers. Like he's still in college, she thought.

She walked into the living room. She was *kunoichi*; she was invisible. The room was furnished with a brown leather recliner and a small sofa that looked fragile enough to carry an IKEA brand. The recliner showed significant wear. A 60-inch HD television hung on the wall above a stereo system that looked several decades old with imposing speakers on either side. She sat in the chair. The chair was flanked by two end tables. Two remote controls shared space on the one to the right with a coaster that looked like a small Navajo rug. The other thing on the table was a small ceramic jar with the word "snot" etched in the front of it. She lifted the top of the jar and looked inside to see several peppermint candies. Stacked on the table to the left were some books and magazines. She shuffled through the magazines — *Sports Illustrated*, *Smithsonian*, and *True West*. She read the book titles — *True Tales and Amazing Legends of the Old West, Baseball's Best 1,000, 200 Texas Outlaws and Lawmen: 1835-1935, Traveling the Lone Star State, The Five-Thousand-Year Leap, The Complete Western Stories of Elmore Leonard, Shell Clams Up, Rainbows Wait For Rain,*

I Was Tortured by The Pygmy Love Queen, and Aristotle's *Poetics*. She noticed that the author of *Traveling the Lone Star State* and of *Shell Clams Up* was Ray W. Strider and wondered how many other books he had written. On a coffee table in front of the sofa was an antique camera setting atop two large books. She got up, went over and read the writing on the camera: "Graflex Speed Graphic." The books were *Peanuts, A Golden Celebration* and *Everest, Mountain without Mercy*.

The bedroom was divided into two areas. One area was for the queen-size bed and a large dresser. The bed was made. The dresser top was hidden by a crumpled up pair of jeans and a black T-shirt draped over them. She read the word "Terlingua" above four chili peppers embroidered on the T-shirt.

The other area was a sort of office, with a small desk, filing cabinet, and computer. On the chair in front of the computer was a navy blue woolen shirt with a patch on the shoulder. She nodded her head as she read aloud, "All Navy Champion 1966 Judo." Diana sat at the desk, turned on the computer, and looked around while it booted up. In the filing cabinet were a health insurance policy and a collection of clippings from newspapers and magazines, all with Ray's byline. To the left on the desk was a landline telephone. Behind the phone was a cardboard fish bowl. Near the fake fish bowl were three small figurines: one of Mark Twain, one of Edgar Allan Poe, and one of the character she always thought of as The Babe on The Bridge from the old *Star Trek: The Next Generation* TV show. To the right of the computer was a framed photograph of a naked Jennifer Aniston—not the famous paparazzi shot of her topless on a beach but a crisp, posed photograph. Either the picture was a fake or he knew the actress very well. She picked up the photo and examined it carefully, trying to see where it might have been Photoshopped and realized that it wasn't a photo of Aniston but of someone who looked very much like her except for her nose.

The computer screen came up. The desktop photo was of some desert mountains with a dusting of snow on their summits. Diana inserted her thumb drive into a USB port then roamed around with the mouse. He kept very little on his hard drive. Several folders were labeled with numbers: 1, 2, 3, 4, 5, and so forth. She opened each one. Inside were photographs and some had more than others. Some were formal portraits, some were candids, some were at parties, several were taken around a Christmas tree. Wives? Friends? Some had wedding pictures. She shut down the computer.

She swiveled around in the chair. On the wall to the left of the computer were photos of people in old-fashioned cowboy costumes. She stood to examine them. Ray was in all of them. The black sheriff's deputy was in several. In two of the photos, the deputy was holding up plaques but she couldn't make out what was written on them.

She opened the closet door and was surprised to find it was a walk-in. Her hand picked through the clothing. He had just as many of those old cowboy clothes as modern ones. She smiled when she saw the gun cabinet. It wasn't a gun safe, but an old wood cabinet with a glass front. It was empty. She opened it to pick up the manila folder on the bottom of the cabinet. In it were documentations for the weapons that would normally be in the cabinet, she guessed. Bills of sale, index cards with serial numbers, and photographs of each. She noted that all the weapons but one for a Colt Commander semi-automatic pistol were also old cowboy weapons like the ones in the wall pictures—two double-barreled shotguns, one lever-action rifle with a brass receiver and one lever-action in deep blue with a case-hardened receiver, four single-action revolvers with four-and-a-half-inch barrels. Two of the revolvers had wood grips and two had staghorn grips. Hanging on pegs near the cabinet was a gunbelt and two holsters. He must be wearing the other set, she thought.

Diana smiled. The only difference between men and boys, her mama always said, was the cost of their toys.

She stepped back into the bedroom and saw something she had missed before because it was hanging on the wall to the left of the doorway. She got close to it, trying to determine if it was what it seemed—a toilet seat strung like a harp. It was enclosed in a plastic box. On a plaque at the bottom of the box was the word, "LATRINO-PHONE." She leaned in to read what was written on one side of the seat. "Happy Birthday, Ray—practice, practice, practice and one day you can be a latrinophone virtuoso and take your seat in my orchestra. Your pal, Spike Jones. July 7, 1961."

"I could really like this guy," Diana said aloud.

The phone rang. She listened as Ray's recorded voice said,

"You know the drill," then a beep, then to the caller.

"Ray, this is Chigger. Solange and I are going to the outlet mall this afternoon. Well, you know that, but I was just wondering if there was something I could pick up for you while we were in San Marcos. If so, call me on my cell. Love you, bye."

Diana beamed. Ah… leverage.

Chapter 28:
Home on the Range

LeRoi smiled and reached over the registration table to shake the hand of one of the cowboys standing behind the table. "You have saved the life of an unworthy man, Nada."

Nada Chance smiled back and lifted the box of Round Rock Donuts so LeRoi could reach in for as many as he wanted. "Anything for our esteemed state champion."

LeRoi—better known on the Bigfoot Rangers' range as Sergeant Rutledge—and Ray—known as the Terlingua Kid—decided to be pigs and grabbed three of the golden-glazed doughnuts each. Trey took one.

Every cowboy shooter had an alias. It was part of the game and it was the only name used on the range; for most of the shooters it was the only name they knew each other by.

They stood by a bonfire eating their breakfast, looking up and down the range.

"I gotta admit this is not what I was picturing," Trey said. "This is more like a recreation of an Old West town than a shooting range. More like Frontier Gulch than a gun club. You've got everything here, like maybe we're on a movie set. You've got a homesteader's cabin, a saloon, a stagecoach, a livery stable, a jail, a buckboard, a cavalry fort, and a railway car. I see the targets, but they're not those bullseyes I was picturing. What're they made of?"

"Steel," Ray, the Terlingua Kid, said. Downrange from each stage were several steel targets at varying distances. Some of the targets were painted red, some blue, some silver. Some of the targets were simple shapes—squares, diamonds, circles, but some were silhouettes of a squat cowboy.

Trey shook his head. "This is some shtik, downright elaborate." His two friends smiled.

"I can't believe all the outfits."

"I see by your outfit that you are a cowboy," the Kid sang, gesturing broadly.

"Everything has to be correct to the period from just after the Civil War to the turn of that century. Clothes, weapons, the whole thing," Sergeant Rutledge said, taking the cigar out of his mouth for a moment. "They are all reproductions, but the accuracy has gotten so good over the years you would have a hard time telling a group photo of us taken today and one from, say, 1885."

Trey shook his head again. "I reckon this ain't like playing Cowboys and Indians when I was a kid. Y'all spend a lot of money on this little game."

"Not as much as some do on golf," the Sarge said. "But, yeah, we do."

At nine a.m., Kettleman, the Range Officer for the club, called the crowd of 84 men, women and children together and led them in the Pledge of Allegiance and a prayer. He explained that the day's scenarios would be based on the 1935 Gene Autry movie *The Phantom Empire*. Kettleman then rattled off a series of safety tips, cautioned them about wearing "eyes and ears," repeated the word "downrange" three times, and then read posse assignments. The group broke up into smaller groups, each posse heading out to their respective stations to begin shooting.

The Terlingua Kid and Sergeant Rutledge shared a gun cart that carried all of their weapons, spare weapons, ammunition, and canteens.

The Terlingua Kid handed Trey a set of earplugs. "You're wearing glasses, so you don't have to worry about your eyes, but you need to put the plugs in to save your ears. It gets loud out here."

Trey squished the soft plastic plugs into his ears. "What was the deal with the guy saying 'downrange' over and over?"

"Muzzle direction," Sergeant Rutledge said. "No group is more safety conscious than cowboy shooters. If the muzzle of any weapon is ever pointed at another shooter, you are tossed off the range. The best practice is to always remember to keep the muzzle of your weapon, loaded or not, pointed downrange."

"And you don't get backsplash? You know, bullets bouncing off the steel targets?"

Sergeant Rutledge lit a wooden match by snapping it on an edge of the bronze "US" buckle of his military gunbelt and warmed up the tip of his cigar with it. "Our cartridges are loaded for low velocities and we use only lead bullets. Lead is softer than steel so the bullets pretty much disintegrate. Sometimes, though, you might get a piece ricochet back at you or one of the other shooters. It might sting but that is all. That is why you wear eye protection out here. Cheaper to replace the lens in your glasses than replace your eyeball."

Trey turned pale at the thought and the Sarge grinned. They approached their first stage.

"Why in the world pick *The Phantom Empire*?" the Terlingua Kid asked. "It doesn't have a single shoot-out in the whole movie. I don't think ol' Gene ever even gets his pistol out of its holster."

"Your brain is too cluttered with movie trivia," Sergeant Rutledge said.

"You're right about that. I can remember worthless information like Gene having to get back to his ranch by two o'clock every afternoon for his radio broadcast or he was going to lose his contract, but I can't figure out what's going on in my own backyard."

"If there is a clandestine lab, it has to be someplace. Pleasant Valley is not that big a place."

The two men took their weapons to the loading table to the left of the stage then walked over to listen to Kettleman read the scenario. Trey followed at a short distance.

"Ten pistol, five in each holstered. Ten rifle, staged on table to left of doorway. Four-plus shotgun, staged on rack to right of doorway. Start in doorway looking through the spyglass. You are Frankie, president of the Thunder Riders Club and you've just discovered Gene is missing and you are using the spyglass to scan the hills from your club house. You spy him lying in the prairie grass. You see strange riders emerge from a rock in the cliff near Gene and they are riding toward him. Your line is 'Thunder Riders to the rescue!' At the buzzer, step to the table, set down the spyglass and retrieve your rifle, sweep rifle targets R1 through R10. Return your empty rifle to the table and engage pistols targets P1 through P5 left to right. Holster your pistol and with your second pistol engage targets P1 through P5 right to left. Reholster your pistol and retrieve your shotgun engaging targets S1 through S4 in any order. All shotgun targets must go down or count as a miss. You may continue firing on the clock until they do."

Sergeant Rutledge shot first. He was quick and clean. No misses. No one on the posse expected any different from him. He was the state champion two years running and had the distinction of not missing a single target at the championship match and held the record for an entire year of no misses at the Bigfoot Rangers' range.

The Terlingua Kid shot next, a series of BANG/clinks with one BANG followed by no clink followed by the Kid mumbling, "Crap." He missed his third pistol target. Another BANG-no clink when he missed his fifth pistol target. Forty-point-seven-five seconds, which wasn't bad for him, plus ten seconds for the total misses.

As the Kid watched the Sarge clear his weapons at the unloading table, he said, "It's not fair that you get to use the county shooting range without cost to practice as much as you like and folks like me get to shoot only once or twice a month at a match."

"Sounds like sour grapes to me," Sergeant Rutledge said. They picked up their weapons and set them in the gun cart they shared.

"Do you *ever* miss?" Bronco Birnbaum asked the Sarge, who was dressed in an Indian Wars first sergeant's blue army uniform, his kepi pulled low and canted to one side.

"I did once last year at Comancheria Days in Fredericksburg but the timer malfunctioned and I got to reshoot and I didn't miss the second time around," the Sarge said. "My only trouble is that I am slower than I believe I can be. Kettleman there is real fast but he is not so accurate. If Kettleman dressed up in chaps and stuff that would slow him down. He barely dresses cowboy."

"Talk about the pot calling the kettle.... Aw, never mind," Kettleman said.

The friends laughed, then were joined by Vaquero Jorge who was scowling.

"Bad day?" the Kid asked.

"Starting out that way. I came out straight from work and those twelve-hour shifts at the hospital will take the edge off your concentration."

"We appreciate you thinking so much of us to come shoot rather than go home to bed," Bronco said.

"Can't think of anything I'd rather do after dealing with sick patients all night than kill lots of steel targets," Jorge said, putting up his weapons.

"You didn't kill too many just now," Ray said.

"They ducked," Jorge said.

Trey continued to watch all this from a short distance.

"Hey, pistolero, do you remember this movie?" Jorge asked.

"Yeah, if my memory serves, it was about the second worst movie ever made. Cheap special effects, worse costumes. Kids riding around with buckets on their heads," Bronco said.

"Buckets on their heads?" Jorge said.

"You'd have to see it to understand," the Kid said. "It had these robots who had metal hats and ears like Alfred E. Neuman."

"Who is Alfred E. Neuman?" the Sarge asked. "And who are these Muranians that captured Frankie and Betsy? Indians?"

"What—me worry? No, never mind, Alfred's not important," the Kid said. "The Muranians were an advanced civilization who lived in a city underground, right under Gene's Radio Ranch and they tried to get rid of him because the radio broadcasts were getting too popular and attracting tourists so they were afraid their city would be discovered."

"And don't forget the evil scientists trying to steal uranium," Bronco said.

"And somehow, despite being captured a couple times and all sorts of tribulations, Gene never missed an afternoon broadcast. He didn't want to lose his contract," the Kid said.

"How do you guys remember all this detail from a film so old?" Jorge asked.

"Was on the Westerns Channel last week," Kettleman told him.

"I have got to get a television just for that," the Sarge said.

"You'd need a lot of space for a med lab, right?" the Terlingua Kid said. "I mean, you'd need safe areas, lots of equipment, right?" Sergeant Rutledge nodded.

"Ain't no place big enough around here. You'd need a warehouse. We don't even have those small storage facilities up here. San Marcos makes more sense, or Austin or San Antonio more likely," the Terlingua Kid said, holding up a finger indicating the current shooter had one miss.

"It is a puzzlement," Sergeant Rutledge said. "Of course, you are assuming there is a lab hidden in our fair village. Your assumption may not be correct."

They finished the stage and moved on to the second one, a third, a fourth. Sergeant Rutledge continued to have a clean match while the Terlingua Kid seemed determined to miss two targets, always pistol targets, on each stage.

"What do you think?" the Kid asked.

"About the lab?" the Sarge replied.

"Of *course* the lab."

"I do not have an opinion. I find I do my job better if I do not have opinions or make assumptions. I go where I am told and I do my job once I am there and everything else is bullshit. You can speculate all day long but thinking a thing does not make it so and not thinking it does not make it not so."

"You shoot better than you think."

"Thinking only gets you into trouble. I will bet you thought you were going to hit each of the targets, did you not? Where did that get you? Thinking slows you down. Allows you to make mistakes."

"Leave my exes out of this."

They moved on to the fifth stage, then the sixth. The last of the day.

Bronco Birnbaum read the stage's scenario. "Ten rifle, staged on the rack to the left of the window. Ten pistol, five in each holstered. Four shotgun, staged on the same rack. You are Gene Autry and you have been captured by Queen Tika and you're being held in her underground city of Murania. The queen believes if you die, Radio Ranch will lose its popularity and her city 25,000 feet under the ranch will once again be safe. Say your line, 'This place is fit only for rats and moles.' Begin with both hands on the bottom of the window. At the beep, engage pistol targets P1 through P5 with your first pistol. Safely reholster the pistol and with your second pistol engage targets P6 through P10. Safely reholster your pistol, retrieve your rifle and engage targets R1, R2, R3, R4, R5, R5, R4, R3, R2, R1. Replace your rifle on the rack and retrieve your shotgun, return to the window and engage targets S1, S4, S2, S3."

"A city 25,000 feet underground. Is that even possible?" the Kid said.

"Naw," Trey said. "Isn't it 25,000 feet smack dab to the center of the Earth?"

"Can't be. Heck, the deepest part of the ocean is the Mariana Trench and that's around 35,000 feet so getting to the center of the Earth's got to be much more than that," the Kid said.

"Closer to 25 million feet I would think. So why not have a city at 25,000? Be hot and the pressure might be unbearable, though," Travelin' Jones said.

"Now, how would you know some figure like that?" the Sarge asked.

Travelin' smiled and tipped his hat. "I'm a real estate professional. It's my job to know such things."

"You'd think somebody would have noticed a whole city under the ranch," the Kid said.

"Damn, dude, it is only a movie," the Sarge said.

The Terlingua Kid nodded his head. "I know, I know, but if your premise is too outlandish viewers can't suspend their disbelief long enough to enjoy the movie."

"Been done before," Jorge said. "They put a whole hospital underground."

The Kid and the Sarge said at once: "A hospital?"

"Sure. You were in 'Nam, Pistolero. Don't you remember all those stories about some sort of terrible strain of incurable and highly contagious venereal disease that was in 'Nam and the government was afraid to let the guys who contracted it go back to the States so they shipped them off to some secret place where they would all die in peace and the VD strain with them? That was underground in 'Nam. Up near Cam Ranh Bay, if I remember right."

"I do remember the stories, but I figured they were just to keep us from screwing the baby-sans in the villes," the Kid said.

"Sure, but, you see, what with all the health scares we've had recently like anthrax and bird and swine flus and ebola and mad cow, maybe the government could have a secret hospital to care for people who've got it so they don't panic the general population," Jorge said.

"We could have a hospital underground right here, right under our range and we'd never know it."

"Under the range…?"

"Next shooter!" Kettleman hollered. That was the Terlingua Kid. The Kid staged his rifle and shotgun and stepped back while Bronco positioned the timer so the Kid could hear the beep when the starter began. The Kid said his line, stepped up and pulled his left pistol from its holster, shifting it to his right hand. He fired. He fired his second pistol. His rifle. He was clean as he picked up his shotgun, broke it open and slid two shells into the barrels. He paused. He looked back at Sergeant Rutledge.

"You OK, Kid?" Kettleman asked when the Terlingua Kid hadn't fired after a couple of seconds.

"Oh, yeah, fine," the Kid said, slamming the shotgun closed and firing two quick shots at the nearest targets. He broke the shotgun open and with a quick jerk of his hands the empty shells went flying out. He dropped in two loaded shells, snapped the weapon shut, leaned forward and fired hitting both targets. He had no misses. He waited for Sergeant Rutledge at the unloading table.

"It's obvious," the Kid said to the Sarge.

"What? How to clean a stage?"

"Where the lab is. It's underground. Like Phantom Empire's Murania. The city was right under Radio Ranch. Frontier Gulch has a huge garage and warehouse area—underground."

"That old firetrap?" the Sarge said.

The Terlingua Kid nodded. "Hasn't been used in a lot of years—before I ever moved here."

"What Rickie tells me, they keep the old stagecoach and covered wagon they used t'use down there. Locked up tight. Store fertilizer and cleaning supplies and that's about it," Trey said.

"It's the only place large enough in Pleasant Valley and it's perfectly hidden. It's huge. The Gruntles own it. Who is one of our dead people? Jubal T. Who is another of our dead people? Billy. Lives within walking distance across the field from the Gulch. Has to be a connection." The Kid said, still nodding.

"W.W.G.A.D.?" the Sarge asked.

"Hunh?"

"What would Gene Autry do?"

"Get to his microphone before two p.m. for the radio broadcast so he wouldn't lose his contract."

Trey interrupted. "So what did he do? He's the star. How'd he save the day?"

"I don't think he did anything," the Kid said. "If I remember right, some Muranian rebels screwed with some nasty weapon and the underground city melted. One scene I still can see clearly is the evil queen melting away."

"Just like the wicked witch in *Wizard of Oz*..." Trey said. "You think ol' Gene stole that idea?"

"Don't see how. *Empire* was melting evil women a few years before Dorothy did in *Oz*," the Kid said.

"Think we can get the lab to melt?" the Sarge said.

"Piece of cake. All we need is a disintegrator ray. Doubt if it would be period-correct, though."

CHAPTER 29:
THE ADVENTURE OF CHIGGER AND SOLANGE AT THE MALL

The sky was indigo, serrated by the fluffy white clouds everyone loves. The 75-degree weather, with no wind, couldn't have been any better for a day at an outdoor mall. Chigger and Solange had their walking shoes firmly tied to their feet and assorted credit cards firmly tucked into their wallets tucked into out-of-date but secure fanny packs bouncing on their tummies as they strode purposely onward.

The outlet mall in San Marcos was actually two separate malls on either side of Centerpoint Road, just off Interstate 35. Having more than a million square feet of shopping, it was one of the top tourist destinations in the entire state—after more typical places like the Alamo and the San Antonio Riverwalk—and was internationally renowned. On any given weekend, shoppers could overhear other shoppers speaking Spanish, French, German, Aramaic, Mandarin, or Farsi. It was the largest outlet mall in all of Texas and third largest in the world. It also held the distinction of being voted third best shopping mecca on the globe after New York and Dubai.

Chigger and Solange, like most of the women at the mall this particular Saturday, were seeking retail therapy. They didn't know which products they were after; the goal was to save money. And, of course, the more they spent, the more they saved.

When others paid attention to them—and few beyond cashiers did—people assumed they were mother and daughter because they were both short, both pleasingly plump, and both were dyed strawberry blondes. Solange's color mimicked the hair she used to have. Chigger's was the color she liked best to cover the natural mousy brown that she hated. They even looked somewhat alike. They went to the outlets on the south side first. Solange bought forest green hiking socks and a salmon-colored V-neck pullover, a dozen dark chocolate raspberry jelly-filled candies, and a new plastic spatula set. Chigger bought four milk chocolate covered orange peels. She looked seriously at clothing in four different shops but nothing suited her fancy.

Finished on the south side, they drove across the street to the north shops, parked and continued on their shopping safari.

All Solange found was a pair of black Wrangler jeans. Chigger found a lovely pair of black faux suede booties, a new red and gold wallet/checkbook cover, charming black high-heeled T-strap dress sandals, an exquisite red Burberry Brit metallic twill baby bomber jacket, a stunning emerald green silk blouse, a divine pair of gray pleated and cropped leg pants, a striking blue and gold Hawaiian shirt featuring precious little hula girls dancing in grass skirts, and a lovely raspberry-colored terry cloth robe with a shawl collar.

The four hours they spent took them well past lunch time and they discovered they had worked up a good appetite. They walked to a gourmet burger joint next to a pottery outlet.

Solange bought a chili cheese hamburger with peppers and onions with a side of cheese fries along with a chocolate milk shake while Chigger chose the grilled chicken club salad and an iced tea. They sat at a table on the restaurant's patio since the weather was so perfect.

"How do you like working at the paper?" Solange asked, vigorously stirring her shake to make it more drinkable. "Six months now?"

"Six months," Chigger said. "It's OK. Less work than I'd figured. Almost all the businesses in town already advertise. What I do mostly is go around or call and see if they want to run the same ad or what changes they want. I've been trying to talk Ray into letting me get more from other cities. I can see restaurants in Wimberley wanting to let people in Pleasant Valley know they're there. You know they have a great restaurant place down there? The Cafe? The owner's weapons-grade drooly. Hell, the outlet mall here should advertise."

"A small weekly in such a small town isn't much of a challenge is it?"

"Well, it's a good learning opportunity."

"How long before you figure you'll want to move up? Bigger weekly, maybe a small daily?"

Chigger mumbled through a mouthful of salad. "Not another weekly. When I go, it'll be to a daily. Sorry, too big a bite." She paused to munch a little then swallow. "Even a larger weekly is just a lateral move and I can probably learn more from Ray than most editors of weeklies. Have you and Trey known him long?"

"I've known him since I was a freshman in high school."

"Seriously? Cool beans."

Solange smiled. "Before you were born."

"Where was that? Houston?"

"Alpine."

"Alpine? That's West Texas, right?"

"It's at the northern edge of the Big Bend country," Solange said. "I was a freshman and Ray was a junior. He lived in Terlingua and back then there was no high school down there so he had to make that terrible school bus drive every day. A hundred miles up north then after school was out a hundred miles back down south."

Chigger looked up with wide eyes. "You're kidding. How could anybody do that day after day?"

"Kids did it. But when Ray got to be sixteen, his mother rented an apartment up in Alpine and she'd come up a couple days during the week, he'd stay there alone a couple days, then they'd both go home on the weekends. A lot of parents in South County did that to save on that bus ride."

"South County?"

"That's what people in Brewster County call the southern portion of the county. Not too many people live down there, even today."

"How well did you know Ray?"

Solange laughed. "Maybe a little too well. We got to dating when I was a sophomore and he was a senior and we spent a lot of naughty time in that apartment on the days his mother wasn't there. I guess that means we have something in common. You are sleeping with him aren't you?"

"Once," she said, turning leaves of lettuce over to find the right size piece of grilled chicken. "I hope more."

"We got married right after he graduated."

Chigger nearly choked. She put down the fork she had in her hand and pushed her chair back a little. Her eyes were even wider than before. "Married?"

"Yes, dear," Solange said with a smile. "I was his starter wife."

"Really?" Chigger said. "W.T.F.? Or maybe L.O.L. And you're still friends? I thought Trey was his friend and you were just Trey's wife."

"Just Trey's wife?"

"You know what I mean. Like you didn't have a relationship with Ray except through Trey."

"Ray introduced us."

Chigger was shaking her head as she spoke. "Seriously? Like, how did that happen?"

Solange scooped up a french fry dripping with cheese. "Long and boring story. They worked together at the *Post* in Houston and I happened to be at a bar they happened to be at and Trey was leering at me and Ray asked him if he'd like to meet that hot girl and Trey said sure and the rest is history."

"Epic," Chigger said, still shaking her head. "I take it you parted friends?"

"Pretty much. Ray was in the Navy after he got out of college and he was gone nearly all of the time and that doesn't bode well for a marriage."

"Let me ask you this, how many times has Ray been married?"

"Enough to know better. There've been times I thought he was married but he wasn't, just living with some woman and other times I'd think he and some woman weren't married but they were but not for long. One of them lasted four months, I think. Difficult to keep up with Ray. He says he's your basic serial monogamist."

"Serial monogamist?"

"Yeah. He won't cheat on you but if he finds someone else he's interested in, he'll dump you for her. Over and over and over."

"You ever have any kids?"

It was Solange's turn to be quiet. Tears brimmed in her eyes.

"A daughter."

"Something happened?"

"Typical child of the Seventies. Got into sex, drugs, and rock 'n' roll before she was out of puberty. Ran away from home a few times. Last time was when she was 17 when she went off to Hollywood to become a star and you're an adult in Texas at 17 so there wasn't anything we could do about that. I don't know... well, she ended up making adult films. Ray... Ray saw her."

Chigger paled and whispered, "G.T.F.O.O.H."

Solange looked up at her and it was her turn to pale. She went white. Her hand went to her throat. Her eyes blinked wildly.

"What's wrong?" Chigger asked. "I'm sorry I brought up something painful—"

"Young lady, you can't ever sleep with him ever again. No. Don't. Oh, if he realizes it. He will realize it if he hasn't already. Oh, God."

"What?"

"You look just like Bonnie," Solange said, her stomach churning. "Just like our daughter. Why didn't I see it before? God. You're the wrong age. She'd be, what, in her fifties today. Fifty-two. Thirty years older than you, but neither of us has seen her since she was your age. You are what we remember."

They sat silently, the noises of passing cars and chattering shoppers crowding in on them. Chigger pushed what remained of her salad away from her.

"Let's go," Solange said, picking up her shopping bags. Chigger followed without saying anything.

They walked to Solange's white Honda Ridgeline. Solange cussed when she saw an old blue Chevy Astro van with dark tinting on its windows parked close to the driver's side of her pickup with barely enough room for them to open the front and back doors a little to put their shopping loot in the back and for Solange to slide into the driver's seat.

"Ah, did I park too close? I'm sorry," a tall woman said walking up to them. "Let me move."

"Thanks," Solange said, thinking she recognized the woman but couldn't recall from where.

But the tall, thin woman didn't move. Instead she raised a large pistol she had in her hand and pointed it at them while with her left hand she opened the sliding door on her van. "Get in."

"What?" Solange and Chigger said at the same time.

"Shut up and, ah, just get in and you won't get hurt."

"Just take our stuff and leave us alone," Solange said.

"I don't want your, ah, stuff," the woman said, poking Chigger in the ribs. "In the van." The women climbed into the van. The other woman got in behind them and closed the door. It was close quarters in the back seat but the tall woman reached down and got one end of a pair of handcuffs and clicked it on Solange's right wrist. She clicked the other end to Chigger's left wrist. A large chain draped over the small chain that connected the handcuffs and ran under the base of the seat. The tall woman placed her pistol on the front seat and got a roll of duct tape, placing a strip over each woman's mouth. She climbed into the front seat and drove away.

CHAPTER 30:
A CHAIN OF DISASTEROUS EVENTS

The familiar surroundings petrified Solange. They had been taken north to Pleasant Valley and to the back of Frontier Gulch. They parked in front of the garage door to the old warehouse and their kidnapper pushed a remote control and the heavy door slowly and noisily rose. The van moved into the cavernous garage area and parked near the old stagecoach that hadn't been used in years. If this woman wasn't worried about being identified, if she wasn't worried about them knowing where there were being held, Solange was certain this woman had no intention of ever letting them leave alive.

But what sense did this make? Why kidnap them? Who was this woman? Solange was certain she had seen her before, but where? She didn't think they had ever met. Had she seen this woman in a store, on the web, on television? Could this be some sort of oddball TV reality show?

The woman opened the van's side door and disconnected the large chain from their handcuffs. She pulled them out. Solange made as much noise as she could behind the duct tape, snorting heavily through her nose.

"What's your problem?" the tall woman asked.

Solange motioned with her head, trying to get the woman to pay attention to the duct tape across Solange's mouth.

"You want me, ah, to take the tape off?" the woman asked.

Solange nodded vigorously. "I will, but if you scream I'll put a bullet right in that open mouth." Solange nodded slowly.

The woman ripped the tape off quickly and Solange said, "Ow!" which echoed around the open garage.

"Shutup," the woman snapped.

Solange nodded and whispered, "I'm sorry. That hurt. But I couldn't breathe. I have sinus problems and I have a lot of trouble breathing through my nose. I thought I was going to suffocate with that tape."

The woman scowled. She pressed the remote to close the garage door. "Might as well do the same for you," she said as she ripped the tape from Chigger's mouth.

Chigger worked her chin back and forth a couple of times to regain feeling. "Why? What's this—"

"Shut up," the woman snapped. "You, ah, understand, 'shut up'?"

"Yes," Chigger said.

The woman slapped Chigger so hard that Chigger fell to the cement floor, dragging Solange with her. "I told you to shut up and that means no, ah, speaking. Get up."

The tall woman pulled them to their feet. She led them to a door where she punched in a series of numbers. The door opened towards them, the woman pushed them inside, the door shushed closed behind them. They were in a brilliantly white room. The woman guided them through what looked like a medical lab to another door. As she reached to open the door, it opened on its own. Out came a short, thin man in a white coat and ammonia fumes.

The woman waved her hand in front of her face. "Doc, doctor, did you spill something in there?"

"What? Oh, no, of course not," the man said. "I was just using the water closet to urinate. I heard unfamiliar noises and came out to see what was transpiring so I neglected to flush. Who are these people? You know no unauthorized people are allowed in here."

"Doctor, if that smell is just from your, ah, piss, then you need to drink more water. A lot more water. These ladies will be our guests until the, ah, project is completed. They'll be in there, chained, so they won't be, um, in your way."

"If you and Jason or whatever his name is feel that is necessary, then fine. That's not my job. But where will I go when I have to, well, go?"

"In the pisser like always. If you're modest, then just put a paper bag over they heads so they won't, ah, see anything."

"Even if they can't observe, I'm unsure whether I will be able to perform the necessary functions with people standing nearby."

"You've gone in a public toilet, right? Same thing."

"I have never used a public restroom in my life. The thought alone is disgusting."

The woman shook her head, the man strode away, and she pushed Solange and Chigger into the small room. Solange looked around. A commode was in the far left corner, but all the walls were lined with shelves on which were cleaning supplies and many boxes and bottles of various sizes. The boxes and bottles had labels, but Solange couldn't read them. A bucket and mop were near the commode, along with a broom and large trash can. The woman led them to within a few feet of the commode and attached their handcuffs to a chain that had been prepared for this—it was anchored on a ring bolted to the floor. The chain was just long enough to allow Solange and Chigger to use the commode, but they would be several feet from the door. The room had no windows. The woman flushed away the ammonia smell.

Chigger sobbed.

"I gotta go make ah, a phone call," the woman said. She turned off the light just before closing the door.

•

It was late Saturday. After his day playing cowboy, Ray came home, showered, shaved, put on clean clothes, then drove to his office. Normally he worked half a day on Saturdays. On those Saturdays when he wasn't shooting, he worked from about nine in the morning to noon. When he did shoot, he came in after getting cleaned up, checked for messages and e-mails, spent some time doing routine work like rewriting press releases or making calendar entries then went home to clean up his weapons.

Four seconds after he walked into the office the phone rang. He dropped his keys on his desk and answered.

"This is Mrs. Cunningham on Huth Lane," the voice said. Ray rolled his eyes and sat down. Gladys Cunningham was 92 years old, lived alone, and called him at least twice a week complaining about something or demanding an investigation into something else.

"What's up, Mrs. C?" Ray said.

"I've asked the city for action and they've ignored me so that means it's time for our village newspaper to take up the cause and insist something be done."

"About what?"

"There's a deer crossing sign right on the corner where my little house is and that sign needs to be removed and it needs to be removed immediately."

"Why would that be?"

"Because," Mrs. Cunningham said. Her pause indicated that the reason should be obvious. "*Because* way too many are being hit out here. The precious little deer are everywhere it seems these days and when cars come by they aren't even frightened anymore. I watch them, Mr. Strider, I know. They're tame now. Just yesterday some hooligan came speeding down the road and ran right into one of the deer and the boy didn't even stop. I don't know how long that poor deer suffered before she finally died. And later some county crew comes by and just unceremoniously picks her up on a shovel and tosses her into a trailer and takes her off. Just yesterday, mind you. There have been at least a dozen, maybe two dozen, deer have died right here in the past month or so it seems. That deer crossing sign needs to be removed. It needs to be moved somewhere else safer, Mr. Strider, because these deer need to cross somewhere else. Not here. It's just too dangerous here."

"I'll see what I can do, Mrs. C., but I'm not promising anything."

"Humpf," she said and hung up.

Ray was thinking there was a thin line between mental illness and being a Texan when the phone rang again.

"Mrs. C—"

"Just listen," the voice said. It was an electronically synthesized voice with no inflection, the kind of voice recognition software that enables you to hear the words you type into a computer or that read e-mail to you. "We have taken Solange Burleson and Tiffany Montgomery hostage. They will be held unharmed if you do precisely what we say. First, you will destroy any files you have on City Manager George Wallace. Second, you will stop all investigations and inquiries into City Manager George Wallace. Third, you will stop all investigations and inquiries into any deaths that have occurred in Pleasant Valley in the past month. Fourth, you will not contact law enforcement about this. If you fail to comply, each woman will be sent back to you in several separate packages over several separate days. Do you understand?"

At first, Ray thought what he was hearing was a joke, but he could think of no one who would do such a thing. Perhaps back in Houston, but not here. Then he wondered, if this was serious, how anyone could be so stupid. But if this were serious, he realized, it would certainly work.

"Do you understand?" the voice repeated.

"Yes. But, lookit, I want proof of life. I want to speak to them. Now."

"That will not happen now. We will call back in one hour and you will hear them but you may not speak to them. Do you understand?"

"I'll be here. But if you harm—"

The connection was broken.

"Crap."

•

Diana told George what she had done. What she expected was to be congratulated for her initiative. What she got was a slap across the face. It wasn't just a slap. It was a slap with power and force behind it, a slap that sent her reeling backwards into the wall, a slap that burned her gums and would leave a souvenir bruise, a slap that instantly changed their relationship. She had never been touched in anger before. No one had ever slapped her. No one had ever punched her. No one had ever kicked or tripped her. No one had ever grabbed her.

"You stupid-stupid-bitch," he said. His eyes had narrowed. His jaws had tightened. "Stupid, Christ, stupid." His muscles tensed and he brought up his right arm to backhand her. She caught it at the wrist and twisted, forcing him to his knees. "God damn it, you stupid..." She applied more pressure and he stopped talking. What she wanted to do was break the wrist, knowing that just a little more pressure would do it. What she did was release him and let him up. This man had meant everything to her until just a moment ago. Now he meant nothing.

"The paper guy won't, ah, do anything now," she said.

"Maybe. Maybe not," he said, his jaw muscles still flexing. "The call wasn't yours to make. We talked about this. He's not some typical small town newspaper editor. He's got friends all over the place. If anything happens to him, years will be spent by his friends tracking us down. Christ!"

"That's why, um, this will work. We're not doing anything to him. This will work."

He sighed as he rubbed his arm and wrist. "All this will do is confirm any suspicions he had and they had been just that up to now, suspicions. Nothing could be proven. Now… Damn it all, how could you be so stupid? It's going to have to be cleaned it up."

She looked down at the floor. "I had it planned out—"

Without thinking, he backhanded her. Hard. "This must be ended now and all the loose ends must be cleaned up. Damn it all to Hell. Some heat may come our way but that means the paper guy, too, now. You're great at making accidents happen. You're going to have to create a masterpiece to clean this fucking mess up."

She looked up at the ceiling, then down at the floor, anywhere but straight at him. She clenched her fists. She ground her teeth. She set her jaw. "I'll, I'll clean up everything."

•

"It's been two hours," Trey said. He stood facing a window in the *Pleasant Valley Picayune* office, but he saw nothing outside.

Ray sat behind his desk, leaning way back in his chair, his legs crossed and his feet on his desk. "I know."

"We should call LeRoi."

"Not yet. We don't know what's going on."

"What the hell you *reckon's* going on?"

"We don't really know yet. Patience is a virtue right now."

"Yeah? Who says?"

"Patient, virtuous people."

Trey whirled on his heel to face Ray. "Oh my gravy. This ain't the time."

"Do I look like I'm laughing?" Ray sat up straight in his chair. "Sit down."

"I'm as restless as a hen on a hot griddle."

"That's why you need the patience. We go off half-cocked,

letting our emotions carry us, no telling what'll happen."

"We got bupkis. Call LeRoi," Trey said throwing his body into a chair.

"Think. We call LeRoi and he has to be all official and call the high sheriff and then the sheriff calls in SWAT from San Marcos, maybe the Rangers, and that alerts all the media and all of a sudden we've got an incident on our hands and, trust me, incidents never end well."

"We have to do *something*. You said they said they'd call in an hour. It's way on past that." Trey's phone rang and he rushed to get it to his ear. "Yeah, Greg.... Yeah. Soon as I can." He shoved the phone back into his shirt pocket and said to Ray, "Greg's worried that his mother isn't home yet. His mother, Ray. He's worried that I'm not there. We'd have had supper by now. He's knows something's wrong, he senses those kinds of things."

"OK, let's go to your place," Ray said, standing.

"What about the call?"

"Lookit, if it hasn't come by now, I don't think it will. But I've got Call Forwarding. I'll punch in your phone and we can wait up there. Besides, what if she gets loose or this is all some big mistake somehow, that's where she'd go. Come on." Ray transferred his office phone to Trey's cell and they left.

LOOK TO THE SKY

Here he was at last, where he was supposed to be, in the sky and in action, no longer the back-up pilot, no longer second string. He was the better pilot, certainly, and now he would have the chance to prove it. The number one pilot, the one who should have been number two, was suffering with the flu. They said he was in ICU Isolation. What a weenie! Couldn't even handle a little flu bug. Now command would know who should have been number one all along.

It was a skittish ship and needed a strong hand in charge of it. He'd played with it a little on the way from the Bio Safety Lab Four in San Antonio and knew he needed to show it who was boss.

This X-57 Caracara was a single-seat vertical-take-off-and-landing craft with a top speed of 300 miles per hour, three gyroscopic sensors, and two 75-horsepower electric motors driving its five-arm tilt-rotor propellers on the end of each wing. It could perform in the air the way Sandra Izbasa could on a gymnastics mat. Up, down and all around. The ship had the speed of a plane, the agility of a helicopter, and the silence of the wind. It was painted in the latest black stealth paint, absorbing radar and becoming nearly invisible to the naked eye in the night sky.

Its mission now was to fly supplies in to a clandestine landing zone and be gone before anyone knew it was there.

He switched on his microphone.

"Rat's Nest, this is Thunder Chicken. Over."

"This is Rat's Nest. Go ahead."

He'd been told Rat's Nest was a woman, a woman with a sexy voice, but this was a man who sounded uncertain and didn't know proper protocol, as if he didn't communicate on the radio very often. He guessed it must be the boss at Rat's Nest.

"Rat's Nest, this is Thunder Chicken. ETA zero two minutes. Repeat. ETA is zero two minutes. Conditions are green. Over."

"This is Rat's Nest, Thunder Chicken. OK."

"Rat's Nest, this is Thunder Chicken. I am going hot on my mark. Mark. Over."

"This is Rat's Nest. OK. You're acquired. Come ahead."

He was low now and hovering. His training taught him how to land, but he was more used to regular aircraft and this one had a split personality, sometimes acting like a fixed wing and sometimes acting like a helicopter. He had never flown a helicopter. He pushed the controls forward, just a little he thought, but the ship reacted too quickly and he pulled back. The tail went down and the ship lurched to his left. He pulled quickly to his right and the ship reacted too quickly again.

Damn this ship, he thought as it touched the ground at 269 miles per hour—that was the readout on his holograph display that was the last thing he ever saw.

CHAPTER 31:
CLEANING UP

Diana did not know, did not comprehend, compassion or empathy. She understood the quick and the dead. She would always be quick. She didn't care if the lab was in place to discover a cure for all cancers or to create a plague that would devastate the human race. She simply didn't care. What she felt now was new. At first she thought it was what people called a guilty conscience, but she knew she didn't have a conscience so that couldn't be it. She considered the feeling for a while and decided it was regret. She didn't know how to react to regret. What she craved was stimulation. Action. She needed her adrenaline to flow in prodigious amounts as often as possible.

She drove the stolen van over the country roads at twice the posted speed limit, kicking up gravel when she hit the shoulders and running over a buzzard that couldn't get away from his roadkill breakfast fast enough. She laughed feeling the little bump of the buzzard's body under her right front tire. "You are what you, ah, eat," she laughed.

She opened the garage door with the remote, slowing down the van just a little. The door was barely above the van's roof when she drove in. She got out of the van and walked to the lab door, punched her code into the door's keypad and went inside. It was dark so she flipped on the lights, glad the doc wasn't in yet. She wouldn't have to explain. She wouldn't have to talk to the little weasel. She walked quickly to the bathroom. The women woke when she opened the door. They looked like they had both cried themselves to sleep. She held her .50 caliber Mark XIX Desert Eagle pistol at port arms in her left hand, watching as the women staggered to their feet. Diana walked to the commode and turned off the water supply valve to the right of the bowl, near the floor, and then flushed the toilet. She took a bottle of bleach down from one of the shelves and poured it into the empty bowl. She looked around, found another bottle of bleach and poured that in. She added small portions from a couple of bottles of other flu-ids, enough to nearly fill the bowl. She closed the lid. She unscrewed the caps of all the bottles on the shelves in the room. She took a folding knife out of a pocket, opened it, and cut Xs into bulging paper containers on the shelves and stacked on the floor.

"What? What are you going to do?" Solange said.

"Shut up. Remember?" Diana folded up her knife, put it away, and then unfastened the chain from the women's handcuffs. "Don't say a word. Walk on out ahead of me," she told them. They did.

In the garage, Diana waved them into the back of the van and Solange said. "We've got a right—"

Diana popped Solange in the forehead with the barrel of the pistol.

"Ow!" Solange squealed, echoing around the now open garage.

Diana placed the barrel of the Desert Eagle directly on Solange's right eye. "Shut. Up."

Solange looked down and nodded. The women got in the van, Diana fastened them to the floor chain, slid into the driver's seat. She drove off without bothering to close the garage door.

•

"Well?" Trey said. Ray was quiet.

Ray and Trey had spent the night on the deck of Trey's hilltop home, staring off into the murkiness, listening to a occasional dog bark or cat squeal or frog croak. A cordless phone stood on the small table between them. Their cell phones were in their shirt pockets. On the deck around their chairs were empty beer bottles, a partially empty bourbon bottle, two apple cores, and doughnut crumbs. Trey caressed a hot cup of coffee in his hands. Ray held a glass half full of orange juice.

"We can't just sit here," Trey said. Thin fingers of sunlight crept over the hills into the valley.

Ray shook his head, put his glass on the table. He got his cell phone and punched in a number.

When LeRoi answered, Ray could barely hear him over the sounds of sirens and what sounded like heavy machinery in the background.

"I am busy, Ray," LeRoi said.

"We need to talk to you. Confidentially. We need some advice. But it's urgent, LeRoi, and I mean as urgent as possible. We're at Trey's. You've got to come over right now."

"I cannot. I am up to my ass in alligators at this moment. We have a plane wreck out here. We have pieces of the plane and pieces of the body scattered all to Hell and gone just west of Wallaceville. We have every deputy, every firefighter in our county, all of EMS, and it seems like half the firefighters from Comal County. It is a true mess, Ray, and I am going to be out here for a long time."

"Crap," Ray said.

"Biggest thing to happen around here in a long time, you better get your ass out here while there is still something to take pictures of."

"I can't. I can't. Call me when you're free." Ray punched off the phone without waiting for a response. "Crap."

"What?" Trey said.

"Big plane crash near Wallaceville. He'll be out there all day."

"So we're a day late and dollar short."

Ray shook his head and slumped in his chair. The sun was now fully up.

Daddy," Greg said from the doorway.

"What is it?" Trey sighed.

Greg walked out onto the deck, one hand touching the railing. "I heard it again."

"I'm worried about her, too," Trey said.

"Daddy, I know you think I'm just hearing things or it's all in my head. Well, I guess either way it'd be in my head, but I'm not hearing things. I heard it."

"What'd you hear?" Ray asked.

"Mommy," Greg said. "Yesterday I heard the same thing."

"What's she telling you?" Ray said.

"She's not talking to *me*, Uncle Ray. I just heard her. Both times, yesterday and today, it was the same. Louder today, though. She says, 'Ow,' and another lady says, 'Shut up.'"

Ray and Trey stood up at the same time.

"You're sure of this Greg?" Trey asked.

"I heard it, Daddy. Both times. Coming from the Gulch."

"Crap," Ray said. "Trey… we figured something was going on in the old warehouse, could that be where our damsels in distress are? How reliable do you think what Greg thinks he heard is? We didn't hear anything."

Trey walked over to his youngest son and put his arm around his shoulder. "Very. You know what they say about blind people, their other senses get heightened. He's always had great hearing. Don't believe me?"

"Sounds odd."

"You've got to make a leap of faith. Make the leap and a net'll be there."

"Who's Annette?"

Trey rolled his eyes. "Well?"

Ray told Greg LeRoi's cell number then, "If we're not back here pretty soon, you call him. Tell him we went to the Gulch warehouse and it's life or death and to get his butt down there and rescue us. Do that?"

"Sure, Uncle Ray. Is that where my mom is?"

"Don't know, Greg, but we're going to go find out."

•

They drove to the garage in Ray's old pickup and were surprised to see the door open. Ray turned the truck around and backed up to just outside the doorway. He grabbed his satchel as they got out of the truck and as they walked into the garage he took his pistol out of the bag and racked a round into the chamber.

"I guess you know what you're doing," Trey said as they walked to the white door in the back wall of the garage.

"I don't know what gave you that idea," Ray said, trying the locked door then staring at the keypad. Ray punched in a few random numbers but only succeeded in activating a red light on the pad.

"What're the odds you can just smooth guess the right numbers? Billion to one?" Trey said. "Look around. If you can't see what's staring you square in the face, you're cross-threaded between the ears. You've got problems."

"When I was growing up I rode in a car with the windows

rolled up and my mother smoking like a chimney and I lived in a bedroom slathered with lead-based paint and went to a school that had asbestos ceilings. I pedaled a bike without a helmet or knee pads. In the summertime, my mother would kick me out of the house at seven in the morning and tell me she didn't want to see me again until dinner time and she didn't care that my friends and I were playing with snakes in the cactus across the river in a foreign country or were climbing down old mine shafts and rolling around in mercury dust. When I was eleven, I had my own rifle and shotgun and hunted coyotes. Problems? Yeah, who wouldn't? I'm surprised I survived. Now, you got a better idea about getting in?"

Trey took a Swiss army knife from his pocket and pulled up the screwdriver blade.

"You think you can disassemble the key pad and get us in? Doubt that'll work either," Ray said.

Trey rolled his eyes and said, gesturing with the knife, "See, the trouble with you academic schmucks is you've got no practical understanding of how things work. So step aside."

Trey reached up to the top hinge on the door and worked the blade between the hinge and the pin. Slowly at first, then quicker, the pin rose up. Trey pulled it out. He did the same for the bottom hinge then lifted the door off the hinges and set it aside. "Door opens out. Pretty dumb thing if you're looking for security. No lock in the world makes much difference if the door opens out."

Ray shook his head. "Lookit, fifty years ago I knew everything. Today I know nothing. That's what education'll do to you."

They stepped in. Ray pointed his pistol a little ahead of him as they walked around the lab. "Geezum crow, will you look at all of this?"

"Never seen the like," Trey said.

They walked slowly around the lab. They couldn't open the door to the Clean Room because that door was locked and opened inward but the top half of the room's walls were glass and they could see all around it. No one was inside. They saw only one other door. They opened that and switched on the light.

"Oh, my God," Trey said, jumping back quickly. "What is that smell?"

"Bleach," Ray said, stepping into the room. "Looks like a combination bathroom and cleaning room. Somebody must have spilled some bleach. They're not here." He left the room and shut the door behind him.

"Don't they use bleach to cover up crime scenes? Wash up blood, wipe out DNA, or whatever it is they do?" Trey asked.

"I didn't see any blood inside. I think somebody just spilled a bottle of bleach. Keep looking."

They looked everywhere in the small lab but found nothing except machines they didn't understand and sealed test tubes they didn't dare touch. In a small adjacent room with an open door, they found two cages. One with about a dozen chickens who looked drugged or asleep. The other cage had snakes in it. Ray stuffed his pistol in his waistband then got his camera out of his bag. He took a picture of the snakes, turned around and took more photographs of the lab.

"Why're we wasting time?" Trey said.

"This is important," Ray said. "Billy's cause of death was snakebite and here we've got a box of vipers. I need to document as much of this as I can. These photos will shine a light very brightly on these cockroaches."

CHAPTER 32:
FIREWORKS

Ray and Trey drove back up to Trey's house. In the driveway was Solange's white Ridgeline. The two men looked at each other as they rushed inside. Solange stood in the doorway between the living room and kitchen, holding Greg as closely to her as she could, his chin resting on the top of her head as he hugged her back. Chigger stood off to one side.

"Baby," Trey said, rushing to her side. They kissed and became a three-way hug. Chigger, shaking, looked down at her feet.

"You OK?" Ray asked.

I'm still terrified, but I'm OK," Chigger said.

Ray almost went to her, but stopped after taking a step. He turned to Solange. "What happened?"

"This woman grabbed us at the mall, cuffed us, drove us to the old Gulch warehouse and chained us up in a bathroom. We were there all night. This morning she shows back up, puts us back in the van and drives us back to the mall parking lot and uncuffs us and says, 'Have a nice day,' and drove away. I mean, that's actually what she said, Ray, 'Have a nice day.'"

"No explanation?"

She shook her head. Trey noticed the bruise on her forehead and brushed back her hair to get a better look. "It's OK," she said. "Still hurts, but the skin isn't broken. I guess I talked out of turn after she warned us not to and she hit me with her pistol. Biggest pistol I ever saw, Ray."

"Who was she?" Ray asked.

Trey, Solange and Greg moved to the sofa and sat down. Chigger sat in one of the chairs. Ray remained standing. "I don't know. She seemed familiar, but I don't think I ever actually saw her before," Solange said.

"Describe her," Ray said.

"Tall. Thin. Blonde. Mean," Chigger, shaking, said. Solange

nodded agreement.

"You've seen her picture," Ray said. "In the *Picayune* when we ran the photo of the new city manager and his wife. Right?"

Chigger, shaking, nodded. "That's *her*."

"Why would she want to kidnap us, and then let us go? Crazy," Solange said.

"Sure is crazy," Ray said. "She kidnapped you to keep me from investigating this guy Wallace whose real name is Frass and whatever is going on in the warehouse. I got a threatening phone call last night. Why she'd let you go is beyond me. It's my guess she already killed Fred and Billy and Sarah and Jubal T."

"The place was weird, like a hospital," Chigger said, shaking a little less now.

"Research lab," Ray said. "Biological research if I'm not mistaken. From what a friend of mine says, they're experimenting with the flu."

Solange pulled Greg a little closer to her. "Why here?"

"Small town. We're all ignorant rednecks in a sleepy little town. Nothing happens here. They can keep things hidden much easier here. All of that," Ray said.

"Why let us go? We can identify her and now we know where their hidden lab is. Nothing's a secret anymore," Solange said.

"They're acting like they're one taco short of a combination platter," Trey said.

Ray took out his phone and called LeRoi. "Don't argue. This is life and death. Get over to Trey's right now. It's an emergency. Bring a friend or two if they can spare anybody else, but *di di mau*, Nguyen."

"I don't speak Viet—" Ray didn't let LeRoi finish, punching his cell phone off.

Chigger stood up, no longer shaking. "I quit."

"Probably best," Ray said.

•

Professor Doctor Farvel Jerome Perittomatopolis, MD, PhD, AMORC, DDSM observed the garage door wide open and the door to the lab removed and pronounced it a bad day.

This would not do. He shook his head and clucked his tongue as he surveyed the lab to see if anything was damaged or missing. He saw nothing out of place. A raccoon scurried under one of the tables and out the doorway. He opened the door to the water closet. The women Dinah? Delores? had chained up the night before were now gone. He was thankful for that. He didn't like to get involved in those sorts of things even though he knew they had to be done. He was also thankful they were gone because he had a severe urge to urinate. He walked to the commode, flipped open the lid, and let loose a strong stream into the bowl. Just as the urine hit the fluid in the bowl, the professor doctor wondered what Dianne? was complaining about yesterday. He didn't believe he smelled any ammonia in his urine. Since coming to the Texas Hill Country his sinuses had been stopped up because of the preponderance and variety of allergens in the air, but he refused to believe he couldn't smell as well as he always had. He didn't have time for a second thought.

The ammonia in his urine struck the chlorine in the bleach and mixed the other chemicals confined in the toilet bowl together and the combination flared up. It wasn't really an explosion, just a flash of fire that singed the hair on his testicles and gave him the surprise of what was left of his life. He staggered backwards in pain and shock. The newly-formed, deadly chlorine gas surrounded him and sent him into a state of wild confusion. He backpedaled, his arms waving around him like wings. He howled. He staggered into one of the shelves and knocked chemicals off and onto the floor. He fell into another shelf and did the same to more chemicals, cleaning materials and gardening supplies. He jumped up. He tried to run but his vertigo was overwhelming so he smashed into several other shelves, sending more liquids and powders flying. He fell to the floor just as the floor burst into flames. His mind was in a whirling miasma. His body was in terrible pain. Covered in chemicals, rolling on the floor that was covered in more chemicals, adorned in man-made fiber clothing, he burst into flames. The flames licked around the room seeking something else to ignite. They found the dried out and rotten plywood and ancient drywalls and the walls burst into flames.

The fire spread quickly, engulfing the lab in less than half a minute. The flames reached the ceiling, the ceiling that was also the floor of the eastern boardwalk of shops in Frontier Gulch. In little time, the flames consumed the plywood ceiling, licked the wooden rafters, consumed the plywood floor and polyester carpeting above.

The flames wanted more and found their way between the old warehouse and the better maintained office area where Margie Gruntle and her two pirate boy toys were enjoying themselves on the day bed in her office. A can of black powder used by the Pleasant Valley Gunslingers that was stored in the security office exploded in the flames, spreading the fire faster, further. A beam fell on Margie's bed igniting the polypropylene material the trio sprawled upon. The flash of the bedspread bursting into flames burned the hair from their bodies before Bass and Red were able to pick Margie up and pull her out of the office, out of the building, up to ground level. Bass rolled her in the dirt of the main street of Frontier Gulch.

They all sat for a moment, catching their breaths, wondering what had just happened. They watched as the east side of the street caught fire and burned. Only when they heard people screaming behind them did they realize today was a tourist day and Frontier Gulch was full of people. Tourists came running out of the shops on the burning east side of the street, joining other tourists on the west side of the street to watch the conflagration. None of the tourists noticed the bald, naked bodies of Margie and Bass and Red scrambling to the west boardwalk. Bass and Red ran off to the parking lot. Margie sat, her back against the outside wall of the Indian-themed souvenir shop, facing the fire. One of the shops along the east boardwalk was the photo/print shop where tourists could have their pictures taken and printed on wanted posters and the chemicals in the shop exploded while the flames gorged themselves on the paper stacked in the shop.

•

Ray saw LeRoi drive up to Trey's house just as they heard the explosion from down in the Gulch. They all rushed to the deck and looked on as they watched most of Frontier Gulch burn to the ground. LeRoi called 9-1-1, but Ray knew all the volunteer firefighters and all the emergency medical technicians were up at the plane crash site and it would be many minutes before any of them arrived here. It would be too late to save the Gulch.

Ray ran to his pickup to get his camera. As everyone else watched the fire in terror, Ray snapped as many photos as he could from the deck.

This sort of thing was old hat to him. Heck, he'd snapped pictures squatting on the wooden deck of the *Battleship Texas* when it was engulfed in fire many years back, smoke and flames all around him. How many explosions and fires at refineries along the Houston Ship Channel had he covered? More than he could count. His reactions were on automatic in situations when others were paralyzed by what to them was the unknown.

Satisfied he had everything he could get from the deck, Ray ducked under the railing and ran down the hill and across the field to the burning fake Old West town, taking more pictures. LeRoi followed him. Ray saw a naked, bald woman cowering on the boardwalk and snapped a couple of photos before he recognized who she was. Ray stood in the doorway, keeping an eye on the fire, the crowd, and on LeRoi. LeRoi pulled Margie into the shop. He looked her over as well as he could but she didn't say a thing.

"Ray, get your ass in here," LeRoi bellowed. Ray wanted more photos outside, but he went in. "Get some blankets."

Ray and LeRoi went to the wall of the shop to pull down Mexican copies of Navajo rugs, then wrapped Margie in them. Ray didn't know if covering someone who had been burned was the right thing to do, but followed LeRoi's lead.

"She has got some burns, but not too badly. All her hair is gone, though. Must have been a flash of fire. If she did not inhale any flames, she should be OK. She was lucky. I would be more worried about shock right now than burns."

LeRoi went into the back of the store, found a refrigerator, grabbed three bottles of water, gave one to Margie and one to Ray. Ray stuffed the water into his shoulder bag and went back outside, taking more pictures.

CHAPTER 33:
A PIRATE ROAD TRIP

It began raining late in the afternoon, just a drizzle at first then steady, heavy drops. They weren't going anywhere anyway.

"I never watched a movie standing up before," Red said. "I think my legs are going to sleep."

"Lean on the back of the couch like I'm doing," Bass suggested. "Takes the weight off. Just switch around every now and then."

"I sure hope this sunburn lotion works."

"It's got aloe in it and that works wonders. Just be glad we got out alive."

"At least we've still got most of the hair on top of our heads."

"Singed some, though."

"Yeah, but Margie doesn't have any. Anywhere. Matey, when that beam fell down I thought we were all goners. I saw that fire flare up like that, I thought it was like a preview of Hell and that was where we were headed right then."

"Aye, but we didn't, so relax. Watch the movie."

Bass's semi-ensemble at the time was a black crew neck Oakland Raiders pullover with a giant logo in a shield on the front. Red was wearing a red and pewter and white Tampa Bay Buccaneer long-sleeved T-shirt with a large Buccanner flag logo on the front. Neither of them was wearing any trousers or underwear but from the waist down they glistened from the Solarcaine they had covered themselves with. It was too painful right now to wear clothing down there. It was too painful to sit.

They were watching *Abbott and Costello Meet Captain Kidd*. "I never thought these old flicks could be this funny, especially about pirates," Red said. "That Puddin' Head guy, he's hilarious. Expressions he makes crack me up."

"That's Costello," Bass said. "The sourpuss guy is Abbott."

"He's not funny at all. But this Costello, shiver me timbers if he couldn't be a TV star today. Big time. Imagine him on SNL, he'd blow everybody else away."

They watched as Puddin' Head accidentally switches a love note with a treasure map from Captain Kidd. His buddy Rocky ends up with the map and blackmails Kidd into taking them aboard his ship so they can find the treasure and get a share of it.

"What makes them think ol' Cap'n Kidd is going to share any booty with them? He'll run them through, first chance he gets, me bucco. And this babe pirate Cap'n Bonney… why in Davey Jones's Locker would she ever fall for a loser like Puddin' Head?"

"That's why it's a comedy, matey. Nothing makes sense. If you try to logic it out, you'll miss the laughs."

The doorbell rang.

"That'd be the pizza wench," Bass said, rushing to the door. Red joined him.

They opened the door and put on their friendliest smiles, forgetting what they weren't wearing. The delivery girl handed them the large, warm box with a bill taped to it. As she told them the cost she looked up for the first time and saw them. She rolled her eyes. "My grandmother's Chihuahua's got a bigger pecker than either y'all. Hope y'all're having fun."

"We got sunburned," Red said.

"Riiiight," she said, frowning. "Y'all got sunburnt in April. Sure."

"Stick around and we'll show you some real fun," Bass said.

She stepped back a bit and surveyed the boys' exposed body parts. "Y'all *do* look pretty well burnt, junior. But I kinda doubt either y'all could do much even if I came in, stripped down, and gave y'all a lap dance. Y'all so burnt if I looked at it seriously most likely would hurt so much y'all'd scream for mercy. Ain't no fun happening here for a while."

Bass gave her money for the pizza, including a generous tip. "More tip money in it for you if you do come in and strip down. Maybe we can't do anything right now, but we could always use a show."

"I gots other pies in the car getting cold and I hate driving around the rain so I gots to go. I'll take a raincheck on y'all," she said, amused at her own joke, spun on her heel, and hurried away.

Bass open the box. Red took a slice. Bass put the box on the sofa, took a slice for himself, and then closed the lid.

Captain Kidd's ship is sailing to Skull Island and while Kidd tries to get the treasure map away from Rocky, Captain Bonney tries to get Puddin' Head to make love to her—in the 1952 sense of the phrase, of course, not the modern sense. Neither captain succeeds.

"We need our own treasure expedition," Bass said munching on his second slice.

"Where to, matey?"

"Galveston. I read where Jean Lafitte buried a huge treasure somewhere in the island. We could go look for it, eat shrimp, drink beer, frolic in the surf during the day and frolic with wenches at night."

"That sounds like a plan," Red said, wiping pizza sauce from the corner of his mouth with the sleeve of his shirt. "But... but we don't have much money. Most of what we had was in our pants and they got burned all up. The big treasure Margie was going to give us for the favor she thinks we did her, we never got because of the fire."

"We can camp out on the beach. We can buy cheap beer. We can probably cop some shrimp from a grocery store and cook up our own on a campfire."

"Great, matey, but I don't think we've even got enough gas in the car to get there. Sure not there and back, too."

Bass nodded. "Arrr. We've still got that siphon stuff in the trunk."

"We can't steal gas around here, it's too crowded. We tried it that one time. Remember?"

"Aye, but we've got enough gas to get back up to Pleasant Valley. Not many people there, especially not during a weekday. We can siphon off a tank full easy, get on the road to Galveston."

"And search for Lafitte's treasure."

They smiled and said in unison, "Pirates!"

CHAPTER 34:
LISTEN TO THE RHYTHM
OF THE FALLING RAIN

The rain carried the smells of the smoldering tourist trap all around the village. Ray was alone at the Fork, eating a Big Roll and drinking orange juice. He sat at an inside table next to one of the windows looking out over the deck that looked out over the Dark Fork of the Bigfoot River. The rain bounced hard off the deck. Ray listened to the music of the rain and watched the drops dance on the surface of the river. He felt warm and comfortable. He could sit here all day—and just might. Leaving here meant work. It meant a lot of work. It meant working again like he had at the *Post*, putting together the pieces of puzzle well enough to form some sort of lucid narrative then punching it up with pithy quotes and a snappy turn of phrase to turn it into something a reader would spend the time to actually read and not just scan the way most newspaper readers did. What paper readers were left in the world anyway.

His trouble was two-fold. First, he just didn't want to do it. He couldn't muster the energy. His anger at the kidnapping had subsided into an aggravation, but his rage over the deaths remained and that rage consumed all of his energy. Second, too many of the pieces remained missing from the puzzle. That was the trouble with being a reporter, you were rarely in on the action and you had to figure things out based on reports and what others said and what few facts you could discover. At least now he was sure what the flying saucer was and was convinced what the spaceman Chicken Charley saw was—but he couldn't prove either one.

When his trousers played *The Good, The Bad, and the Ugly*, the ringtone echoed around the empty restaurant.

"*Kelly's Heroes*," the caller said.

"Too easy, Monica. World War II comedy with Clint Eastwood, Don Rickles, Donald Sutherland and Telly Savalas."

"I didn't ask for the actors," she said. "What were the characters' names?"

"Kelly, of course, Big Joe, Crapgame, Oddball, Cowboy, Turk—"

"OK, OK. What'd you do, watch it last Friday when it was on the movie channel?"

"Of course. Ask me a week ago and I might have gotten Kelly and Oddball but none of the others. It's not a movie that usually just pops into people's heads. I'll bet you saw it then, too, and that's where the idea to ask the question came from."

"You're right again," Monica said.

"So what's up?"

"I got your e-mail with the files. I e-mailed you back but haven't gotten an answer so I figured you were out of the office. Great pics of the fire. So I called. E-mailed you back a few new things from Bonavita, government flaks doing their non-denial denials, distancing themselves from a failed operation. His CI says that Frass's boss actually did not know what was going on, but I find that difficult to believe."

"Nobody knew what Ollie North was up to, so I guess it's possible."

"Yeah, sure. Reagan didn't, he never knew anything, but somebody had to be the mastermind. And that was so long ago nobody today cares or even remembers."

"Mon, when it comes to governments, nobody is a mastermind. Regardless of when it happens. It's all just one confusing mess after another until some historian comes along thirty years, fifty years later and makes sense out of things nobody had a clue about while they were happening."

"Human beings do tend to see order in things."

"Yeah, we even see elephants in clouds."

"I see you've got a ton of clouds today. Finally ended that drouth, huh?"

"About time. The cows around here were starting to give powdered milk. It's rained steadily since yesterday afternoon and they say we can expect this system to squat over us for another day or two."

"How long's it been?"

"Last measurable rain we got here was August last year. So we've been dry for more than seven months. West of us has had storms off and on the entire year but it seems like all the rain gets dumped out there before the system ever reaches us. Lookit, last month New Braunfels got three inches, but we didn't get a drop of it and you know how close that is to us."

"So what are you going to do about Frass?"

"I don't know. I can't decide right now whether to kill him or ask him for an interview."

Monica was quiet for so long that Ray thought he'd lost the connection. Finally she said, "I know you, Ray, and I know you won't do anything rash. So don't. I want to work with you on this story, not write about you."

"No worries, Mon."

"Well, you e-mail or call me once something new comes up. We should be nearly ready to put this all down on paper."

"I will. And thanks to you and Tony."

"That's our job, Ray. Yours, too. Remember that. Bye."

He placed the phone on the table, went back to watching and listening to rain. He listened to rain music playing in his head. Gordon Lightfoot's *Early Morning Rain* for a bit. The music fit his mood but the lyrics didn't. He wasn't at an airport. *I Love a Rainy Night.* Couldn't think of the singer–George Strait? Eddie Rabbitt? The metronomic music worked, but the lyrics didn't. They promised a sunny day and right now he didn't believe in one. Lou Christie's *Rhapsody in the Rain.* Naw, that was so obviously about sex that the Catholic Church got it banned on a lot of radio stations. *It's Rainin' in Paradise.* Neil Young? He wasn't sure. The voice he heard sounded like Neil Young: "It's Rainin' in Paradise/Here come the clouds/There's a big wind blowin' through town/The rooster crows/But we're sleepin' in past dawn/It's rainin' in paradise." Almost. He made an effort to clear the music out of his mind and just listen to the real rain. It was better.

Ray had rarely been so personally involved in a story before. One time, an attorney friend of his got elected to a new Congressional district, but that was it. He'd covered murders, too many murders, but he never knew the victims or the murderers. He'd covered graft and corruption, but it was never in a city he lived in. He'd done Iran/ Contra and some of the Iran Hostage Crisis, but at top levels of government things always seemed more abstract than real. This was all too personal. He knew each of the people who had died—except for the unidentified burned skeletal remains from the Gulch. He lived in the town being misused by unfeeling government bureaucrats–the sort who always believed their desired end justified their means. And all he was going to do was write a story about it.

He watched the downpour. The hypnotic tattoo of the rain was interrupted by the sounds of Tom coming in to work with two waitresses who cleared the breakfast buffet and made certain the restaurant was ready for the lunch crowd. Of course, the lunch crowd on a Monday was likely to be small.

On weekends, Tom worked only as the manager. On weekdays, he worked as manager, cook, dishwasher, and occasional busboy.

Ray looked at his watch. It was nearly eleven. He had been sitting here for three hours and could remember only about three minutes of it. Tom said hello. One of the waitresses, Debbie, said hi. He didn't know the other waitress; she was new and would train with Angie. He picked up his phone and called Trey.

"You want to do lunch?" Ray asked.

"Sorry I missed breakfast, but Solange needed some extra attention this morning. She's still shook up. Came to work, though, and I know she'll be all right. It's kind of schmaltzy, but I just wanted t'be around her 'til I was sure."

"I understand. Can you do lunch?"

"Shit, I reckon, but I want t'beat the crowd."

Ray laughed. "Then just name your time. You've got until noon on Friday."

"Eleven-thirty. I'm hungry. All I had for breakfast this morning was coffee."

"I'm here. See you." He put the phone back on the table. He wanted to call LeRoi but figured the deputy was either still working or sleeping in after working all day Sunday.

His attention went back to the rain. It was coming down even harder now, large drops with enough force that they sounded like hail. But they weren't. He heard rumblings of thunder to the north and west. The towns of Blanco and Dripping Springs were probably getting pounded with storms, he guessed, and when all that water started flowing downstream the Bigfoot River was going to flood. More work lurking. He was glad his house was on a hill—a small one, but a hill nonetheless—and far enough away from either branch of the Bigfoot that flood waters had never threatened the house. He watched the dark waters roiling under the rain in the Dark Fork and thought back several years ago when he was covering the search for a missing boy out near the town of Comfort when a school bus was swept away off a bridge. All the S and R people found was the carcass of a cow. Thirty feet up in a tree. Now *that* was a flood.

"What d'you know good?" Trey said when he sat down.

Ray shifted his chair around to face Trey instead of the river. "I'm pert near out of good."

Angie and the new waitress, who Angie introduced as Shari, came up to the table and Angie offered Trey one of the Big Rolls, but he declined. "Just bring me a BLT and tea," he said.

"Ray?" Angie asked.

"Coke and, what, a cheeseburger I guess with–"

"Mustard instead of mayonnaise and no onions," Angie said.

"I guess I'm too predictable," Ray said.

"That's a good thing," Angie said. "I get confused less that way." She and Shari walked back to the kitchen.

"How's Margie?" Trey asked.

"Ambulance came in six minutes, I timed it because I thought it would be much longer given the attention to that plane crash. They gave her oxygen and hauled her off. She's at CTMC listed in stable condition with second-degree burns. Had some damage to her lungs, but not much. She was pretty lucky. How's the wife?"

"About as good's you can figure. Neither of us slept much last night. But she's a strong woman."

"That's your fault. You and raising all those boys. When I first knew her, she was shy and timid."

Trey leaned in, lowered his voice, and spoke each word carefully. "We want them hoppin' over coals in Hell, Ray."

"Me, too. That's Plan A. Maybe it'll get done officially. LeRoi called me late last night and said they'd brought in Frass and were detaining him on suspicion of arson and murder. If it doesn't happen the right way… well…" Ray patted the side of his satchel that was propped up in a chair next to him. "We'll just see."

"What about the woman?"

"Disappeared."

Their lunches arrived and they ate, hearing nothing but the rain.

"One good thing," Trey said. "We did need this rain. It was so dry so long that water was becoming a gas, creek beds were becoming a solid, and asphalt was becoming a liquid." Ray nodded.

Angie and Shari arrived to clear their empty plates.

"You save me a roll?" LeRoi asked Angie as he walked over. They hadn't noticed him enter the restaurant.

"Sugar, I'll always have a Big Roll for you. Coffee?"

"I have had so much coffee already I will be awake the rest of the week. Apple juice, if it is not too much trouble," LeRoi said.

"Cider? Closest we have. Tom brought some from Medina last time he was there," Angie said. LeRoi nodded OK. She and Shari left and LeRoi pulled out a metal chair that rattled over the floor like a skeleton breakdancing. He moved Ray's shoulder bag from the seat to the floor and sat down. Ray rolled his eyes, grabbing the satchel and stuffed it beside him.

"What's up?" Ray asked.

"First thing you should know is that crispy critter they found down there has no ID yet, and that may be next to impossible. Nothing left of him to identify. I saw the pictures and he–well, I guess it could have been a she–was nothing but burnt bones and a little bit of skin. The Austin ME will be able to tell us a rough age and whether it is a man or woman, but I think that is going to be about all we are going to find out about it."

"You think it's Mrs. City Manager?" Trey asked.

"I have no opinion on it. I wait until the evidence tells me what to think and I am afraid the evidence will not tell us much at all. For the body anyway. This rain is not going to help the arson people nor the Ranger we called out to help. What we have is an intense fire with much of the debris washed away by this rain. The river is rising and Frontier Gulch is right on the Dark Fork bank like this place is. This place is on a hill, but the Gulch is, by definition, much lower. And the fact that the main portion of the burned area we are interested in was below ground and, if it does flood, everything just goes down the river. This is not a good thing."

Ray was thankful he had taken the photos of the lab when he and Trey were in it yesterday. If he hadn't, and it did flood, no one would ever have known what was there.

"Last murder we had in Pleasant Valley was nine years ago when a meth head killed his girlfriend. In a couple weeks we've had five deaths. Six if you count the pilot in the plane crash." Ray said. "In Houston, five murders in a month is routine, in Pleasant Valley that's a massacre. Plus we've had flying saucers and crop circles and that plane crash and a top tourist attraction burned to the ground. These weren't all coincidences and you know it."

LeRoi's roll and apple cider came and he smiled, sipped a little from the glass. He cut off a small piece of the cinnamon roll with his fork and ate it slowly. "That is what we think, but we do not *know* any of it. Fred and Jubal T. were preliminarily ruled accidental. Even Billy's was because of an accident. Snake bit him when he was unconscious from a fall. Sarah died of the flu. Bird flu, by the way, which was odd. No other reported cases of that around here. We do not *know* any of them were other than what they have been ruled. Preliminarily."

"You said you were holding Frass pending arson and murder charges?" Ray said.

LeRoi nodded. "The body in the lab. If the fire was arson, anyone who died in it was murdered. And speaking of Mr. Wallace, you are not going to like the rest of the story."

"What now?" Ray asked.

"We released him an hour ago."

"Why?" Ray spat.

"What the fuck?" Trey echoed.

"Cider, hard cider, was the top alcoholic beverage during the American Revolution," LeRoi said, sipping his non-hard cider. He shook his head and settled back in his chair. He paused. "I brought Mr. Wallace up to the office and we had him in the interrogation room. Me and the sheriff and Captain Rea and Sergeant Shannon the sheriff's little girl, and the second that the sheriff asked him for ID he whipped out this business card."

"A business card," Ray said, look down and shaking his head slowly. He knew what was coming.

"A Get-Out-Of-Jail Free Card," LeRoi nodded. He took a bigger drink, set the cup down, pulled a folded piece of paper out of his shirt pocket and handed it to Ray. "I made a copy for you."

The card was simple. Centered on the top line were the words "Law Enforcement Personnel;" centered on the second line were the words "Please Call;" on the third line was a telephone number beginning with the area code 703; centered on the bottom line were the words "Provide Code GJF814abf."

"Virginia area code," Ray said, slumping a little.

"If you say so. We went to the sheriff's office and he put the call on the speaker phone and it is recorded if you want to hear it. I wrote down some notes."

LeRoi consulted a small notepad he took from the same shirt pocket. "The receptionist who answered the phone said it was the Office of the Director of National Security. Sheriff told her we had a man in custody who gave us this card and she asked for the code. He read it in and was connected to a Ken Keppen who said he was the Special Assistant for Public Affairs for the Preventative Actions Office of the Deputy Mission Manager for Biological and Chemical Weapons Operations and Investigations for the Mission Manager for the Deputy Director of the Office of Acquisitions and Technology in the Office of the Principal Deputy Director of National Security. This Mr. Keppen said we should release the man in question immediately as it was top priority in a matter of national security and that this man was acting on behalf of national security. From what he said, and the sheriff could not pin him down on this, he was not clear whether this man was working for that particular office of National Security or was working for national security in some general sense. You know this DNI, Ray?"

"Not much. Got started after 9/11. I thought it was just some new agency that was supposed to coordinate efforts but essentially just added another level of bureaucracy between the actual intelligence agencies and the White House. Ninety-nine percent of bureaucrats give the other one percent a bad name, so I didn't think this one actually did anything."

"Sounds like a lot of buck passing going on," LeRoi said. "I mean, a Special Assistant for Public Affairs to a deputy manager under a manager under a deputy under another deputy of the director?"

"Keppen's just a flak," Ray said. "He'll just regurgitate whatever he's been told to when someone calls in a situation like this and provide a different version from the facts. Frass could be working–"

"Speak of the devil," Trey said, pointing to the door that just opened. George Jefferson Frass walked in. He sat down at the first table inside the front door and looked over the menu. He gave no indication he had seen them across the room. Ray looked around for Diana, but no one followed George in.

Ray strained to see into the parking lot, to see if Diana was in George's car. He saw three cars. LeRoi's patrol SUV, Frass's Tesla, and an old Chevrolet of some sort with two kids in it. The black cherry Chevy had a skull and crossed swords painted on it. *What's the matter with kids today?* he thought.

"Nothing you can do t'that piece of shit?" Trey asked LeRoi. The words "piece of shit" were loud enough to be heard in the kitchen. The waitresses all looked over to their table. George gave no indication he heard the remark. The deputy sheriff responded to Trey's question with a shrug of his eyebrows and shoveled a large piece of his roll into his mouth.

Ray stood, pulling his shoulder bag onto his lap. He reached in. LeRoi grabbed his arm. "Don't do it, Ray."

Ray smiled. His hand came out holding a notebook and a camera. "Don't sweat it, man. Time for Plan B."

LeRoi still held Ray's arm. "Whatever you do, you come right back here and tell me what I saw."

LeRoi let go of the arm. Ray smiled and walked over to George's table. Plan B in Ray's mind was to provoke George into a fight so that it would look like Ray acted in self-defense and the result was unintentional. He ran over the procedure in his mind. He learned how to do it in the Navy. He would strike upwards with the heel of his hand, putting as much force as he could muster into the blow. His hand would strike George's nose in just the right place and drive the septum directly into George's brain, killing him instantly. He rehearsed this four times in his mind before he made it across the room.

"How does it feel being the piñata at the party?" Ray asked, sitting down.

George looked up from his menu, scrunching his eyebrows together. "I have no desire to speak with you. You spare me the we-must-do-what's-right speech and I'll spare you the ends-justify-the-means speech. I'm leaving your charming little village after I eat. You won't see me again and I won't see you again."

Ray didn't bother with the pretense of opening his reporter's notebook. His pen remained clipped into his shirt pocket. He knew George wouldn't say anything anyway. The man just sat there and smiled the pleasant smile that Ray wanted to rip from his face. Ray brought up his camera and snapped a quick picture. George lashed out, knocking the camera from Ray's hand. Ray smiled and cocked his arm back for the blow. But several things saved George's life. First was that George remained seated across the table from Ray so the angle of the blow wasn't direct. Second was the fact that as Ray threw his hand to George's face, he chickened out at the last minute and the force of the blow wasn't as strong as Ray originally meant it to be. Third was the fact that what Ray learned in the Navy turned out to be untrue—a blow cannot drive the septum up the sinus cavity into the brain because two bones in the skull happen to block the passage.

However, Ray's blow did pack enough force behind it to crush George's nasal cartilage and break his nose causing his eyes to tear up. Bone fragments made breathing difficult. Blood gushed from George's nose and he soared to his feet.

"You bastard!" George bellowed.

Ray smiled. "Yes, sir. In my case an accident of birth. But you, sir, are a self-made man."

George grabbed his napkin off the table and held it to his nose. Ray walked back to Trey and LeRoi.

"*The Professionals*?" LeRoi said.

"I've been waiting to use that line for decades," Ray said, sitting down.

George tilted his head back, the napkin covering his nose. He kicked the front door open. He walked out to his car through the pouring rain.

Chapter 35:
The Perfect Storm

George Jefferson Frass drove his Tesla Model X slowly, his head tilted back. One hand held the steering wheel; the other held the cloth napkin to his bloodied nose. The nose continued to bleed and the blood flowed down his throat, choking him a little.

He hoped Diana would be at the house. He hadn't seen her since he'd slapped her, an action he immediately regretted not just because he had genuine feelings for her but because he knew if she got angry enough she could easily kill him. He didn't think the odds were very high for that probability, though, because they'd been together for five nearly perfect years. He needed her skills.

He coughed. One of his favorite shirts was now ruined. Damn that reporter. And no action taken by the cop. He swallowed more blood. The car coughed a little, too. Must be the rain, he thought.

He saw no other vehicles on the road. He splashed over the low-water crossing at Bryce Hollow Creek, not that he knew the name of the usually dry creek. It was so narrow that, with his head tilted back, he never saw it before he was in it. The water was only a couple of inches over the roadway but it was enough to slow the car down with a jolt when he hit it. The jolt knocked the Bluetooth device off his ear into the back seat. The Tesla plowed through the water.

These stupid people need bridges, he thought as he coughed again and the car grabbed the pavement on the other side of the crossing. The car sputtered again, jerking him forward a little. *Damn this rain*, he thought.

His wipers were set on fast and their slapping back and forth annoyed him. The windshield started to cloud up and he stopped the car in order to see the dashboard so he could turn on the defoggers. He did so and turned the fan up and waited for it to work its magic, which it did in just a few seconds. It was such a well-made vehicle.

He looked over his seat for the Bluetooth, but didn't see it. It was probably on the floor somewhere. Blood dripped from the napkin over his nose. He cursed, turned to the front, and tilted his head back again. He drove on.

At the crossing of the Dark Fork of the Bigfoot River several things conspired against him.

First was the fact that George Jefferson Frass did not know how to treat a nose bleed. The best way was to sit in a chair and lean forward, putting a clamping pressure on the nose above the nostrils. Most people, like George did, tilt their heads backwards or lie down. This just allows the blood to trickle down the throat, causing people to choke. Plus, by tilting his head backwards he couldn't see the road ahead of him very well which meant he did not see that the warning sign at the Bigfoot crossing was a foot under water.

Second was the fact that George Jefferson Frass was unaware that two mischievous Texas State University sophomores dressed in matching Pittsburgh Pirates black T-shirts – the ones with the one-eyed pirate smiling in front of crossed bats on the front – had slashed the back tires of the Tesla and those tires had now completely deflated. If he hadn't walked out of the restaurant with his head tilted back, he might have seen the tires looking a little low and he might have checked them before he drove off.

Third was the fact that George Jefferson Frass did not know that as little as six inches of water can float a car away when the stream is flowing strong. And that's what happened as the car hit the water. Despite the Tesla being advertised as a vehicle that can handle adverse conditions with aplomb, it could not handle properly with two flat tires nor deal with water under all of its wheels and it floated off sideways. In a normal situation, with four working tires, the second he felt the jolt of the water he might have been able to stop, put the car in reverse and drive backwards away from the danger but at this precise moment the Tesla froze.

Fourth was the fact that George Jefferson Frass did not understand that water flowed downhill. This was important to him at the time because all of the rain that had fallen in the general area in the past day had been seeking the bed of the Bigfoot River so it could flow into the Blanco River which would flow into the San Marcos River which would flow into the Guadalupe River which would flow into the Gulf of Mexico and become one with the oceans of the world. All of the rain draining into the Bigfoot from upriver created a four-foot wall of flood water that flowed downriver and struck the low-water crossing he was now floating across at precisely that moment.

Fifth was the fact that George Jefferson Frass loved his Bluetooth cell phone earpiece. When the ear piece dislodged at the first crossing and landed somewhere in the backseat of the Tesla, it became impossible for him to call for help. As if that would have done any good.

Sixth was the fact that George Jefferson Frass was not aware of a simple law of physics that prevented him from breaking a window or opening the door because the pressure outside of the car was greater than the pressure inside of the car since it was under water. He tried to open the door and failed. He hit the door window as hard as he could but nothing happened. He hit it repeatedly as the water started to gush inside. But the glass refused to break. The Tesla was such a well-made vehicle.

Seventh was the fact that George Jefferson Frass had taken one of Diana's "go pills" as he left his rental house that morning. Without her by his side he felt he needed something to keep him at his best through the day even if the day was going to be nothing but discretion being the better part of valor. The 3-quinuclidinyl benzilate with a small amount of diamorphine to take the hallucinogenic edge off had some adverse reactions that he was not aware of including anxiety and panic, confusion and constipation, and heart arrhythmia. The constipation and arrhythmia were meaningless at this point in George Jefferson Frass's life, but the other reactions were critical. He panicked as his car was carried away, quickly filling with water. And because he was confused, the thought never occurred to him to just punch the window-down button, which he probably couldn't have done anyway because the electric power was now completely dead. However, when the car did fill with water, which it was doing with alarming speed, he would be able to open the door and get out then. All a normal person would have to do is hold his breath for a few seconds and not panic.

But George Jefferson Frass was anxious, confused, and panicked, flailing wildly inside the Tesla full of water as it floated down the Dark Fork of the Bigfoot River just under the surface of the water.

CHAPTER 36:
A TURD FLOATER

It was a turd floater.

Ray, Trey and LeRoi watched the wall of water flood down the Dark Fork. Ray said, "Crap," and LeRoi said, "Shit." The three of them rushed out of the Fork restaurant to their respective jobs.

Trey's part of the print shop had no pending work and he knew they would have no other business during a storm like today's, but that's where his wife and one of his sons were so he went there.

LeRoi called in to the sheriff's office asking about which roads needed to be closed and was dispatched to various low-water crossings in the area to help road crews set up barricades to prevent some cactus-licking idiot from driving into water that was too deep to ford in a typical car.

Ray drove to Trey's house so he could snap photos of the floodwaters from the deck on the hill that overlooked the river and what was Frontier Gulch. The back half of Trey's deck was covered and that provided his camera good protection from the rain. He was thankful the wind wasn't blowing. The flooded river moved like a stain, quickly overflowing its shallow banks. He switched his normal lens out for a telephoto and pulled the cheap collapsible tripod out of his shoulder bag, screwing it into the base of the camera and pointed the lens at what remained of Frontier Gulch. He took pictures of the water flowing into the Gulch, then over the dark remains of the burned out section, washing away nearly everything. The water looked like it had stopped, but Ray realized what he was seeing was the water dropping into the underground warehouse. Soon it would float all the debris from down there up and that, too, would float down the river. He waited for that to happen. It took a half-hour, much quicker than he would have imagined, telling him the volume of water now pouring down the river was perhaps a hundred-year flood. He hoped it wouldn't turn into a five-hundred-year flood—that would likely lift the river to the base of the Fork's deck and too close to the very deck he was standing on.

The rain eased up into a drizzle. Ray waited another hour, until the waters stopped rising and started to recede a little. He wondered about the people living further downstream. If the flood was this bad in Pleasant Valley, it would be much worse in Wimberley and at least twice as bad in San Marcos. He stored his camera gear and drove to his office.

It was still raining when Ray walked into the office. He stomped water from his shoes, shed his jacket onto the coat rack by the front door, placed his bag on his guest chair, tossed his drenched cap onto the window sill, slumped into his chair running his hands through his hair. He took his glasses off and placed them by the computer, turned on the machine. Only then did he notice Chigger. She was putting the last of her things in a cardboard box.

"You're really leaving?" he said.

"Really? You're kidding, right? You actually think I might a stayed?"

"I wasn't sure. But I do think it's the right decision."

"Hell, yes. I get kidnapped, nearly killed. I find out I remind you a your daughter and you only figured out the resemblance once you saw me naked. You're a piece a work, Ray."

He looked down. "I only saw her that way in a movie."

"Seriously? What sort a guy goes to see his daughter in a porno, for Christ's sake?" She folded in the top of the box and put on her raincoat.

"Lookit, it's not like we knew she was going to be in it," he said. "When I was at the *Post* one of the theaters in town, Cinema West, decided it was going to show adult films and cater to a couples crowd. Trying to make it all respectable. Didn't work. But anyway, they sent out passes to all the media in town and I was assigned to do a feature on the place. Me and… Crap, which one? Doesn't matter. Anyway, me and my wife went and the first scene she's in she gets out of a hot tub naked. I froze at first because I didn't believe it was her. I watched some more and realized it was and I left."

"Whatever," she said. She lifted up the box. "Have a friggin' nice day."

Ray sprinted to the print shop. It was too near his office to bother taking his truck, but in just three steps he wished he had. The rain got strong again, coming down in sheets, as if God were pouring out the chamber pots from Heaven. His Lost Maples State Natural Area ball cap and light raincoat provided no protection whatsoever. He burst into the print shop door, stomping his feet and shaking his arms.

"You look like a drowned rat, Uncle Ray," Ben said.

Ray walked to the counter. "I feel like one."

"You're nuts running around in weather like this, darlin'," Solange said, looking up from her computer. Ben was perched on a stool, reading a magazine flattened out on the counter while Trey was cleaning one of the small presses. For some reason the clackety-clack of the press didn't seem as loud as it often did and Ray guessed it had something to do with the rain dampening the noise. A dehumidifier was also running full blast in the midst of the three presses in the back.

"Chigger quit," Ray said to Solange.

"Figures. She'd be nuts to stay," Solange said.

"I know. I know. But that leaves me in the lurch," Ray said. He turned back to Ben. "I was hoping that you might be willing to jump in and help with ad sales until I find a new salesperson."

"Sure," Ben said. "Be OK if I ask Robby to help out? He could use a few extra bucks and the shop's been busy so I can't always spare the time like I could before."

"You got it. Just have your dad print up some of my ad rate cards for y'all."

"Same percentage?"

"Naw. How about an extra five percent?"

"Sure. And take your time looking."

"Absolutely," Solange said. "Take your time and make sure you hire someone who's going to be around longer than a few months this time. I think maybe you need to stop hiring single women. Hire some guy. You go through women sales reps like Trey goes through print rags."

"I love you, too," Ray said. He waved to Trey who waved back. He walked to the door, shuddered a moment then walked into the driving rain.

•

Back in his office, Ray checked his e-mail. As he was looking them over, a new e-mail popped up in his inbox. It was from Monica with an attached file with more information from the Washington Bureau. Only a couple of paragraphs in, the office phone rang.

"Best biker flick?" the voice said.

"Easy. *Breaking Away*. Dennis Christopher, Dennis Quaid, and that actor I just love who doesn't work enough... Jack Haley? Jackie Earle Haley."

"No, Ray. Biker movie not biking movie," Monica said.

"*Wild Hogs*. John Travolta, Tim Allen, Martin Lawrence."

"I would have guessed you'd say Brando's *The Wild One*."

"Too pretentious," he said. "What's up, Mon? I just got your e-mail."

"I wanted to make sure you got this info as soon as possible. It's in the file with correct spellings. The guy heading up the medical research is a Doctor Farvel Jerome Perittomatopolis."

"Farfel? I'll bet he got made fun of every day while he was growing up. Wasn't Farfel the name of that dummy dog Paul Winchell had? The ventriloquist?"

"Way before my time, Ray."

"Come on, Paul Winchell? Invented the first artificial heart?"

"Give me a break. A ventriloquist invented the first artificial heart?"

"You could look it up," Ray said.

"Besides, it's Farvel, with a V. Don't know where he's from but records say he was a plastic surgeon in Boston until his medical license was suspended after a number of botched operations. He left the U.S. and taught for a while at some med school in Guatemala. Important part of that is he had to give Guatemala fingerprints, a urine sample, and a blood sample before he could work there."

"So we can match up the DNA if the Evidence Chick here got enough from the crispy critter in the lab."

"Should be able to do it."

"Probably. We're lucky they got the remains out immediately because everything else washed away in the flooding. Those bones are the only evidence they'll ever have. I'll bet it's the doctor, though. I checked with the S.O. earlier and they said the remains are male."

"So it's not Frass's girl friend," Monica said.

"Nope. And it's not Frass because I… I had a run in with him after the Gulch burned down. Almost has to be the doctor."

"Just find an official to speculate. We'll need to have his name in the story."

"I doubt the Evidence Chick will. She's all about the evidence. The high sheriff might if I ask him the right way. If he won't… well, I always have 'sources close to the investigation,'" Ray said.

"Meaning you," Monica laughed.

"I'm as close as you can get to this one," he said. "Keep me posted, Postie."

"You, too," she said and hung up.

Ray dialed LeRoi's cell phone.

"I was just going to call you," LeRoi said. "I had my phone in my hand."

"What's up?"

"George Jefferson Wallace—"

"Frass, LeRoi. Frass," Ray interrupted.

"We may think that is his real name, but the only ID on his body was a driver's license that said 'Wallace' so that is what we go by until we know differently through official channels."

"Body?"

"The man drowned."

"*Chu ay qua song.*"

"Ray, I keep telling you that I do not know any Vietnamese."

"How'd you know it was Vietnamese?"

"I recognize the word *song*—river."

"Means 'He crossed the river.' What they say in the old country when a person dies. We used it, too. Too often. So where'd they find him?"

"Inside his Tesla this morning, floating gently down the Blanco. Right under I-35."

"Getting over some of those low-water crossings downstream

from here, the river must have *really* been high," Ray said.

"Happened right after he left the Fork is my guess."

"Texas ain't no place for amateurs."

"Amen, brother. What is your news?"

"The crispy critter in the Gulch underground is probably a Doctor Farvel Jerome Perittomatopolis. He was the lead researcher."

"Name like that, he got teased more than I did as a kid," LeRoi said.

"Good news is that his DNA is on file in Guatemala. He taught in a med school down there. I imagine the Evidence Chick can coordinate with whoever keeps that stuff in Guatemala."

"She will appreciate that. Thanks, guy."

"See you in the morning."

•

Ray didn't realize he was exhausted until he sat down and turned the TV on. He had a Shiner Bock and a bowl of cheddar Goldfish on the table next to the remote.

He was watching the Boston Red Sox play the Texas Rangers in Arlington. The game started off with a whimper then a bang. Three bangs. The Ranger pitcher retired the first three Sox batters on nine pitches. Three straight strikeouts. The first three Rangers then hit home runs. The last thing he remembered was smiling after taking a long drink of his beer. Next thing he knew he woke up to a tie ballgame in the bottom of the third inning. He had dozed off so suddenly that it now frightened him a little. He hadn't felt sleepy when he sat down. It was as if a switch had been thrown—one second he was awake and alert, enjoying the game, and the next second he was gone. He got up and walked to the bathroom, rubbing the back of his neck. He returned, drank more beer, munched on Goldfish, watched the game.

It was a good game, tied for the next three innings, with excellent defensive plays made by both teams. In baseball, he preferred dazzling defense to homers. One play was the sort he loved. The BoSox shortstop lunged for a hard-hit ball, catching it in the webbing of his glove, rolled on the field and fired the ball to the second baseman for one out on the runner from first, and then the second baseman jumped and whirled in the air, rifling the ball to first for the second out just as the runners' foot hovered over the bag. The double play was a thing of beauty. No ballet could possibly surpass it. "Yeah!" he said.

He relaxed as the game went to a commercial. He thought he heard something outside the house. Probably a cat, he thought. Too many feral cats in the neighborhood. Or deer. He groaned to his feet to get another beer and walked to the living room window and looked outside. It was too dark to see anything and he didn't hear the noise again. He returned with the beer and made it last to the final out in the top of the eleventh inning.

Watching the game, he felt like he was being watched. Every now and then he looked at the window.

CHAPTER 37:
STRANGERS IN THE NIGHT

Ray woke up at four in the morning to Henry Mancini's theme from *Peter Gunn*. He thought he smelled honeysuckle. His first thought was that he must have set the alarm wrong, but then the honeysuckle got stronger and he looked at the foot of his bed where a black form stood outlined against the dark gray of the night. His mind raced with possibilities. None of them good. Without a conscious decision, he decided to go down fighting. He tossed his body toward the bed stand.

"It's not there," a soft voice said.

His hand froze at the drawer knob. "Hunh?"

"Your Colt Auto. It's not there."

"Where? Who?"

"It's in my hand right now with a round in the chamber and the hammer cocked back so if you, ah, breathe wrong it could go off and that would be a shame."

The CD continued to play. Cozy Cole's *Topsy Part 2* filled the bedroom. Ray now understood a phrase he'd never believed in before—petrified with fear. He couldn't move. The shape edged a little closer, almost touching him. All he heard was the music. Low volume. This was his CD, a mix of instrumentals. This wasn't the CD that had been in the player. It had been in a stack by his computer. Not even on top. Whoever this was had been here before. Whoever this was knew what was on his CDs. Whoever this was had replaced the Gypsy Moon CD that was in the player with this one.

He couldn't move, but he felt his muscles relaxing. The honeysuckle smell was strong now, mixing with the gun oil from his Colt Commander. The barrel of the pistol stroked his cheek. He jerked away, finally moving. He was now on his back.

The figure stood. The nightlight seeping through the open bathroom door was just enough to cast whoever this was in silhouette—long, faint fingers of light playing over the dark figure. It was a woman. He forced his eyes to see her face. No details, but he knew who it was. The missing Diana. She was naked. His pistol was in her left hand. With her right hand she pulled back the bed covers. He was naked. She knelt on the bed, placing his Colt on the stand. She slid down next to him, running her left hand along his side, across his belly, down. Her hand lingered a moment then caressed his stomach again, up across his chest, to his chin. She turned his head towards her and kissed him.

The kiss was all it took. *Autumn Leaves* played—his favorite of all the songs on the CD. More music, more foreplay. He did nothing but react. *Theme From A Summer Place, Ebb Tide, So Rare.* His mind was on the music. His body reacted to the touch, the tongue, the kiss. She rolled on top of him and settled in. He felt it all, but he didn't feel a part of it. He was watching others do this. He wasn't participating, but it was happening to him. Ahh... Mr. Aker Bilk's *Stranger on the Shore.* She moved up and down, back and forth, around. She gasped. *Moon River. Love is Blue.*

He gasped. She collapsed on him, caressing his face, kissing him, running her fingers through his hair, a frenzy of kisses. She rolled to the side, between him and his pistol, running her hand down his chest and belly and into his crotch. Her fingers played there for a moment, then she rolled off the bed and stood there. *Wonderland by Night.*

"I knew I'd like you," she whispered. She picked up the Colt. She ejected the magazine and jacked back the slide to eject the round in the chamber. Even in the dark, she caught the round. She returned the pistol it its drawer and stepped to the computer desk where she fingered the extra round into the magazine, and then placed the magazine next to his mouse.

She returned to the bed, kneeling on it, reaching a hand out to his body.

"How?" he managed to say.

"I am *kunoichi*," she said. "I am invisible. I disappear into the shadows. I appear from the shadows. No doors hinder me."

"Female ninja," he said.

"Oh, more than that. Because *kunoichi* are women, we are more than, ah, ninja. We are subtle. We are seductive. Hmmm? We move anywhere. We move into your house. Into your bed. Into your head. I have been inside of you, Ray. You have been inside of me, now. We are one. Always, we are, ah, one. I'm going away, but I will be back." And she melted into a shadow.

Suddenly the player rang out with a song he knew was not on his instrumental mix CD. She must have switched the CDs with one she had made. He hadn't heard this song in at least fifty years. Maybe sixty. He didn't have any CDs, tapes, or LPs that had this song on it. She must have brought it with her. It was the Spike Jones song *I Search For Golden Adventure In My Seven Leaky Boots*, but she had edited out the long travelogue satire that preceded the music. It was just Jones' cacophonous version of *Quiet Village*. Instead of Martin Denny's soft, seductive Polynesian music, here was a jumble of noise with the same melody—jazz trumpets, native drums, Sirena the Fire Goddess, whistles, sneezes, car horns, clown horns, bird whistles, honky tonk trumpets, triangles, police whistles, explosions, car crashes, talking parrots, waves crashing on the shore. Some quiet village.

She would be back. Did that frighten him or thrill him?

CHAPTER 38:
IMPALE YOURSELF ON REALITY

Ray and Trey sat around a table on the soaked deck at the Fork. The rain had stopped moments before they arrived and Angie had just dried off the metal tables and chairs on the deck. They ate their Big Rolls. Trey finished half of his while Ray managed to eat only two small bites. The Dark Fork rushed below them in a frothing, brown confusion, it's banks under four feet of water.

The sky was mostly clear—a soft blue that reminded Ray of the old Houston Oilers' uniform jerseys. His attention was riveted on the sky, watching wispy clouds appear, change, disappear. It was something his Uncle Tony had shown him when he was a child, a way to make time pass without having to think. He sipped from his second cup of hot chocolate. It wasn't cold out. It wasn't even chilly, just cool, but he held the warm of the chocolate close.

"Hey," LeRoi said, sitting down. Angie came over immediately with a roll for him and a cup. She poured his first cup of coffee from the carafe on the table, hefted it a little, noticed it was nearly empty, and took it away to fill it.

"Hey," Trey said. Ray continued to stare off. "Maybe you can get our boy here involved in a conversation. I've failed miserably. Hasn't said three words all morning."

"I will bet I can get him to say more than three words," LeRoi said.

"You lose," Ray said.

LeRoi cut off a large piece of his roll and managed to shovel it into his mouth. His words were well-mumbled but understandable. "Well, I have good news and bad news. Which do you want first?"

"Good news," Ray said.

"See?" Trey said.

"Doria spent the night with me," LeRoi said.

"Bull," Ray said.

"She surely did," LeRoi said, washing down the roll with a

long swallow of coffee. "She and Pastorette Sylvia had a bad argument last evening and Doria stormed out. She packed all of her things and left. She had no place to go and knew I have always been interested in her so she showed up at my place. Soon as I answered the door she cried up a storm. We talked for hours."

"She do more'n spend the night?" Trey asked.

LeRoi smiled. "Indeed she did. We put down a bottle of bourbon and she ended up crying on my shoulder and, well, one thing let to another and that led to the bed. She was purring softly when I left this morning."

"She's just trying to make Sylvia jealous," Ray said, turning around to face his friends.

"Told you I could get more than three words out," LeRoi said. He drank more coffee. Angie brought a full carafe over and left it on their table. "I think that is partly what she was doing, yes. Quite frankly, I will take what I can get. But I will bet now that she has slept with me, she will not be rushing off so quickly to get back to Sylvia."

"The World's Greatest Lover LeRoi?" Ray said with no humor in his voice.

"In a manner of speaking, yes. I lose my ego completely when I am with a woman. I am a patient lover. I do not have sex with women; I make love to them. I make them feel special. They appreciate that."

"Good on you," Trey said.

Ray nodded agreement. "I hope she's still there when you get home."

LeRoi nodded. "Me, too." He pushed his half-eaten roll away a little. "Want the bad news?"

"Why not?" Ray said.

"I had to get started a little early this morning, just after sun-up, and when I drove by your place I noticed that Wallace woman lurking around outside. Diana. The one we think kidnapped Solange and Chigger then disappeared after she let them go? She was walking to a car almost hidden in the trees on the north side of your house. I flip on my overheads and she is gone. I mean, she put the pedal to the metal like I have never seen, tires smoking and rear end wiggling—"

"Smokin' rear end." Ray said in a dead chuckle.

"She flew up the road. I am chasing her. Before I know it, she is on 12 heading north and pulling away from me. She must have been taking some of those curves at seventy-eighty miles an hour and it was still raining. Damn good thing no one else was out there. I hit the siren to warn any other cars that we might come up on. I call Hays County S.O. for assistance and they send a unit from Dripping. Trouble is, I never got a good look at the car. The rain and the light are bad and she is too far off so all I can tell is that the car is dark. Could have been blue or green or black. Maybe even a dark red. I cannot tell.

"I pass the medical clinic and she is one curve ahead of me and the Hays deputy just turns south on 12 from the light in Dripping Springs so I figure we have her trapped, but then all we see is each other. Our best guess is that she turned into the Home Depot there, so we go into that parking lot but she is not there. She must have gone out the other entrance on 290. We do not see a thing. So I call Travis County S.O. for assistance because we do not know which way she turned. The Hays deputy goes north on 12. I let the Travis deputies handle the east and I go off west on 290. I call Blanco S.O. for assistance and I meet up with that deputy around Henly. You know how many back roads go off from 290—west and east. She could have gone anyplace.

"We put a BOLO out, but that is a waste of time because my description of the car sucks big time. I do not even know if the car was foreign or domestic. Dark compact is all I know. I could not even tell if it had Texas plates."

"She got away?" Ray said.

"If she had not, I would be at the jail right now processing her and writing up reports, but I am sitting with my friends eating Big Rolls and drinking coffee on this deck overlooking a flooded river and looking forward to going back home."

Ray shook his head. He stared deeply into the remains of his now cool chocolate.

"At least I came by before she got into your house," LeRoi said. "No telling what she was planning."

"How do you know she didn't already do it?" Ray said.

"She was outside. I saw a light come on in your bathroom so I figured you had to be OK enough to do that. Then we never got a 9-1-1 call so I figured you were not injured. So I chased her. Did she do something?"

Ray looked up.

"Did she?" Trey asked.

Ray looked down at his roll and without looking at them said, "I think I was raped."

"What?" LeRoi said.

Trey's eyes got wide and his mouth went slack. "Real life ain't like this."

"I don't know," Ray said. "Maybe that's what happened, maybe not. I honestly don't know. Right now, I feel like I've been pulled backwards through a knot hole."

"Do you want to tell us about it?"

"Not much to tell," Ray said, looking at them. "I woke up around four. She was in the bedroom holding my Colt on me. She turned music on. She was naked, got in bed, and we had sex."

"Christ, Ray. Did she force you?" LeRoi said.

"How could she force him? It's different with a guy. If he's scared he ain't getting up."

"I was so scared my ass pulled five pounds of cotton out of my mattress," Ray said. "But, no, I don't think she did force me. She put her gun down and mine came up. It was like some dream. I'm still not certain it happened."

"Why would she do that?" LeRoi said.

"You tell me," Ray said. "Who knows who she might have killed? Billy? Jubal T.? Whatever was going on in the lab sure caused Sarah's death. The man in the lab? Fred?"

"Except for our crispy critter, none of those deaths was ruled suspicious in any way," LeRoi said.

Ray pointed a fork at LeRoi. "Preliminarily."

"They will need much more evidence than we have to rule them any other way," LeRoi said.

"You know better," Ray said. "Plus, she kidnaps the girls then lets them go. She disappears. The Gulch burns down. Frass drowns. She shows up at my place, has her way with me, then disappears… Yeah, she disappeared into the shadows."

"We'll find her," LeRoi said.

Ray shook his head no. "You'll never find her."

"What about you? Do we add rape charges?" LeRoi said.

Ray shook his head no.

"I've never seen him look like this before," Trey said, shaking his own head slowly. "He's in love."

"You in love with her or are you in love with the risk?" LeRoi asked.

"What's the difference?" Ray said, pushing away from the table and standing up.

"So what're you going t'do?" Trey asked.

"I better get to the office," he said. "I've got work to do."

The following story appeared in the April 22 edition of the PLEASANT VALLEY PICAYUNE, COLORADO SPRINGS TODAY, on the Elmore Newspapers Corporation wire and on-line, and on various wire news services. The byline was reversed in the TODAY edition. Several photographs by Ray W. Strider accompanied the story.

The Pleasant Valley Flying Saucer Massacre

By Ray W. Strider, *Pleasant Valley Picayune*
and Anthony Bonavita, *Elmore Newspapers Washington Bureau*

PLEASANT VALLEY, TX—What happened in this small Texas town was like a massacre.

In just over two weeks seven people died under suspicious circumstances. In all of last year, four people died in this village of 1,707 in the Central Texas Hill Country—none of them under suspicious circumstances. The last murder recorded in Pleasant Valley happened nine years ago when a meth-amphetamine addict killed his girl friend in a dispute over drugs.

The deaths alone weren't all that thrust Pleasant Valley into turmoil.

The village's main tourist attraction, Frontier Gulch, burned to the ground. Two of the village's prominent citizens were held prisoner in a secret laboratory at Frontier Gulch after being kidnapped by a woman reportedly connected to a federal agency.

During the same time period, citizens reported numerous UFO sightings and crop circles. A secret, experimental government aircraft crashed, killing the pilot. An Air Force spokeswoman identified the wreckage as that of an X-59 Caracara, but said this particular aircraft was not assigned to any of the armed forces.

All of this, including the deaths, can be connected to that clandestine biological laboratory allegedly experimenting with deadly new strains of flu and anthrax. The lab, which was destroyed in the same fire that destroyed Frontier Gulch, was run by federal agents, but government spokesmen deny any official sanctioning of the lab's activities by any Washington agency.

Those denials haven't deterred area members of the U.S. House of Representatives from asking for a Congressional investigation into what happened at Pleasant Valley and what the level of involvement by federal agencies may have been.

U.S. Rep. Scott Winters, R-Dist. 25 of Texas, called recent activities in Pleasant valley an "outrage."

"This is the sort of thing that we must get to the bottom of and get to it quickly," he said. "What happened in Pleasant Valley was devastating enough, but if any government agency had anything to do with any portion of it, we need to make them fully and publicly accountable to the American people. I am calling for an immediate investigation and I am certain my colleagues, on both sides of the aisle, will join me in denouncing this outrage."

Winters spoke at a press conference on Wednesday in the Rayburn House Office Building in Washington, joined by Texas Representatives Jesse Hancock, R-Dist. 11, and Giselle Bourque, D-Dist. 21.

"The United States government does not prey on its own people. If any federal involvement did, in fact, occur then the individuals involved, at all levels, need to be brought to swift justice," Bourque said.

Texas authorities continue searching for remnants of the biological lab after it was burned on April 18 and all the debris was washed away in a flood that happened the next day. Based on photographs taken by *Pleasant Valley Picayune* editor Ray W. Strider, experts believe the laboratory had state of the art equipment for such a small facility and was fully capable of creating deadly pathogens. One of those photographs shows a serpentarium where several venomous snakes were kept. Another photograph shows the remains of a large coop and burned bodies of chickens.

"We have absolutely no knowledge of any such lab operating in Texas or anywhere else in the United States," said Ken Keppen, Special Assistant for Public Affairs for the Preventative Actions Office of the Deputy Mission Manager for Biological and Chemical Weapons

Operations and Investigations for the Mission Manager for the Deputy Director of the Office of Acquisitions and Technology in the Office of the Principal Deputy Director of National Security in Washington, D.C.

Although government laboratories do create various deadly viruses, they are done in highly controlled environments in attempts to create vaccines or antidotes in case of epidemics or biological terrorist attacks, Keppen said.

George Jefferson Frass, who drowned in the recent flood in Pleasant Valley, was an agent in the Office of Biological and Chemical Weapons Operations and Investigations, a sub-agency of the Majority Agency for Joint Intelligence in Washington, according to a high-ranking source in the Central Intelligence Agency.

Keppen acknowledged that Frass did indeed work for that office but that anything he did in Pleasant Valley was unauthorized and "any inappropriate action that was taken was an error of judgment on Agent Frass's part and not the responsibility of this office."

He said personnel files indicated Frass was on vacation for the past month.

"The fact is that an inquiry into the matter will be embarked on by this office as soon as practicable," Keppen said, "but more research needs to be undertaken to determine precisely which actions he was, in fact, involved in."

Frass had identified himself to Pleasant Valley city officials as George Jefferson Wallace, producing recommendations from a previous job in Ocean City, Colorado, a city that does not exist. Papers on his body also identified him as Wallace.According to Keppen, Frass lived in Upper Marlboro, Maryland.

Mayor Jubal T, Gruntle brought Frass to Pleasant Valley to be the village's first city manager, but both Gruntle and Frass died before that appointment became official.

Gruntle fell to his death down a stairway in his home.

Frass drowned when his Tesla Model X was swept away from a low-water crossing near his rented home during the flood.

Frass's partner, Diana Slingerland, was posing as his wife. She has disappeared and Bigfoot County Sheriff Lank Fischer speculated that she may have died in the fire that burned down the lab and that her body may have been washed away by the flood before it could be found. She was reportedly sighted after the lab's destruction, however. Keppen denied any knowledge of Slingerland.

Solange Burleson, 69, co-owner of a local copy, graphics and print shop, and Tiffany Montgomery, 24, until recently the advertising director of the *Picayune,* identified Slingerland as the woman who kidnapped them on April 17 from an outdoor mall in nearby San Marcos.

The two Pleasant Valley women were brought back to Pleasant Valley and held in chains in a room in the lab until they were released the next day, hours before the fire destroyed the lab and Frontier Gulch.

The *Picayune* received a computerized telephone call April 17 warning the newspaper from conducting any further investigations into Frass or the lab.

The women could give no reason for their release.

"She just let us go," said Burleson. "She seemed angry, but not at us. I've never been more frightened in my life."

Burleson and Montgomery identified Slingerland and a researcher they saw at the lab through photographs.

The CIA source said Frass, Slingerland, and a Dr. Farvel Jerome Perittomatopolis were attempting to weaponize a highly deadly version of the H5N1 bird flu by creating a chimera, blending the flu virus with a type of anthrax to make it even more contagious. It is unknown whether they accomplished this goal since all evidence was obliterated by the fire that destroyed the lab and the subsequent flood.

Burleson identified the researcher she saw as Dr. Perittomatopolis. A body found in the aftermath of the fire in the Frontier Gulch warehouse was identified through DNA evidence as Dr. Perittomatopolis. Records show that Dr. Perittomatopolis, 37, originally from Maine, had his medical license revoked in Massachusetts for several problems relating to a plastic surgery practice he owned in Boston.

Those records indicate that two of his patients died while undergoing routine liposuction procedures, that a breast implant exploded in a woman's chest while she was in an airliner, and several other patients filed complaints about post-surgery complications including loss of voice, incontinence, and several for nasal septal perforation. NSP is a hole in the nasal septum and is often impossible to correct.

Until last year, Dr. Perittomatopolis was employed as a professor of anatomy at the Juan José Arévalo Autonomous University Medical School in Huehuetenango, Guatemala.

DNA records acquired from Guatemala enabled Bigfoot County officials to identify the body of Dr. Perittomatopolis.

The fatal airplane crash just west of Pleasant Valley on April 18 was likely related to the clandestine lab and the numerous flying saucer reports, according to sources close to the investigation. The pilot of that aircraft was identified as Air Force Captain Reynaldo Cruz Martinez, 29.

The plane in question was a X-59 Caracara. The Caracara is an experimental single-seat vertical-takeoff-and-landing craft with a top speed of 300 miles per hour, according to an article by Russell Myles in the January issue of *Aviation* magazine this year. Until it's crash, the Caracara was a classified Air Force project.

Lt. Col. Wesley DeSoto, an Air Force spokesman at the Pentagon, acknowledged that the Caracara could perform as either a fixed-wing aircraft or a helicopter, and used all the latest Air Force stealth technology.

DeSoto said only two of the craft were operational, one at Lackland Air Force Base in San Antonio and the other at Groom Lake Experimental Aircraft and Weapons Air Force Facility in Nevada.

DeSoto said he had no information on what the San Antonio Caracara's mission was. Officials at Lackland AFB have not responded to requests for such information.

Sheriff Fischer said the aircraft's mission might have been to fly supplies to the clandestine Pleasant Valley lab since a government Bio Safety Level Four Lab operates in San Antonio. The BSL-4 Lab has refused comment. A woman at the BSL-4 Lab who refused to identify herself said her lab engaged in research highly sensitive to the security of the United States and could make no comment one way or another on the situation.

Making the deliveries was what likely led to the various UFO reports in the area, a source close to the investigation said. A large circle of flattened grass observed near the underground warehouse where the lab was located was an indication of some craft landing vertically near the lab.

The flattened grass area was also surrounded by crop circles, including one of a pirate skull and crossed sabers, but officials cannot find any connection of those artifacts to either the lab or the Caracara.

Sarah May Colvin, 38, and her 14-year-old daughter Charlene May Colvin were apparent victims of whatever virus was being studied or manufactured in the secret lab.

Both were infected by a mutated strain of the H5N1 bird flu, according to Dr. David Oliveira of the Center for Disease Control in Atlanta. Sarah died of congestive heart failure from complications of the disease and pneumonia while Charlene was partially paralyzed.

Charlene is known locally as "Chicken Charley" because she raised free-range chickens in the back yard of her family home and sold the eggs to health food stores in the area. Charlene and Sarah had reported several of the hens missing over a couple of weeks and all were returned. A source close to the investigation speculated that since the clandestine biological lab was experimenting with the bird flu the missing chickens could have been used by the lab in the experiments and that is how Sarah and Charlene were infected.

The secret Pleasant Valley lab was located in an unused underground basement of Frontier Gulch, a reproduction of an Old West town that featured Westerns shops and fake gunfights on weekends.

The Gulch and most of the surrounding property are owned by Pleasant Valley Mayor Jubal T. Gruntle and his wife, Margie.

Gruntle, 52, died on April 15, as the result of a fall on a steep stairway in his home. The death was originally ruled accidental, but new evidence found at the scene and recent revelations about the lab prompted officials to reopen the investigation into his death. Texas Rangers are currently helping the Bigfoot County Sheriff's Office with that investigation, along with investigations into the lab and subsequent fire and another death.

The other death under renewed scrutiny is that of William Henry Faust, 80.

Billy, as he was known to everyone in the town, was the village character. His devilish grin and impish behavior were so renowned he was listed on the city limits sign that reads "Welcome to Pleasant Valley, Pop. 1707 and one Li'l Devil."

The official cause of Faust's death was listed as cardiac arrest, the result of a rattlesnake bite suffered when he apparently slipped, fell, and knocked himself unconscious in an old fifth-wheel trailer he lived in. The trailer had numerous holes in the floor and walls, allowing small animals such as snakes to enter the trailer. The secret lab at Frontier Gulch housed rattlesnakes for some unknown purpose.

Faust's small trailer is adjacent to the Gruntle property and near the entrance to the underground warehouse at Frontier Gulch.

Faust also owned Bigfoot Toobs, a facility that rented inner tubes for tourists running the famed Dark Fork Rapids along the Bigfoot River during the warmer months of the year.

According to records filed with the Bigfoot County Clerk's office by Gruntle and his business partner Raymond "Bubba" Thibodeaux, the rental facility was scheduled to be demolished along with Billy's trailer to make room for a housing development built by the Gruntle-Thibodeaux partnership.

Retired from the Marine Corps on a disability pension suffered from stepping on a mine in Vietnam, Faust performed in nearly every small theater production in the Hill Country and had several small parts in films. He also performed in the gunfights at Frontier Gulch.

Lance Chafin, the award-winning actor who worked with Faust on the productions of *A Perfect Life* and *The Alamo*, both filmed in areas near Pleasant Valley, called Faust "an American treasure. He was one-of-a-kind and his kind is unlikely to be seen again in many lifetimes."

Gruntle was the only mayor the city of Pleasant Valley had ever known, stepping into the post when the village was incorporated 13 years ago. City Council member Doris Pirtle, who was mayor pro-tem, took over the office of mayor on Gruntle's death.

"Jubal T. will be sorely missed in our little village," Pirtle said. "He was the sort of man who got things done and the sort of man you could rely on."

The first death that may be connected to the clandestine lab happened when Frederick Wayne Salgado, 44, was killed when he lost control of his 1200-cc Nightster Harley-Davidson motorcycle on Huth Lane sometime after midnight on April 5. Sheriff Fischer said the accident was the result of Salgado swerving in the road while traveling at high speed.

"We do not know what or who Fred swerved to avoid hitting," Fischer said. "Wild animals such as deer are frequent hazards on Pleasant Valley roadways."

A photograph taken at the scene appears to show the footprint of someone wearing a hazardous materials suit, the sort that would be worn in a biological laboratory, but Fischer said it is impossible to say whether that was what caused Salgado to lose control of his motorcycle, but was a possibility he and the Rangers were looking into.

Lamar Pendergrass, the Pleasant Valley Volunteer Fire Department Fire Marshal, said the fire that destroyed Frontier Gulch began in the old warehouse and spread quickly throughout the warehouse, adjacent offices, and the shop buildings above. The cause of the fire remains undetermined, he said.

Margie Gruntle said Frontier Gulch would be rebuilt and that the Pleasant Valley Historical and Cultural Preservation and Beautification Society would designate the area surrounding the Old West town as a nature preserve in honor of her dead husband.

Thanks

Although this is a work of fiction, I must thank a few people who made it possible.

- Chicken king Jesse Huth.
- Justice of the Peace Andy Cable.
- Constable Darrell Ayres.
- George Colvin for his unwavering enthusiasm over the years.
- Larry Morris for his help and friendship.
- My wife Madonna for her steadfast love and true friendship.
- My grandmother Charlotte Aines Kimball who gave me her best stationery and fountain pen one rainy day when I was nine years old, sat me down by an open window overlooking a lilac bush, and told me to write whatever I wanted to.

Books by the Author

- *Big Bend Guide*
- *Rainbows Wait For Rain* trilogy
    Calamity Creek
    Woman Hollering Creek
    Second Coffee Creek
- *Texas Museums of Discovery*
- *Texas 107 Best Walks*
- *Texas Redneck Road Trips*
- *Texas, the Capital of Capitals*
- *The Legend of Fort Leaton*
- *Who Is Mother Neff and Why Is She a State Park?*

About the Author

Allan C. Kimball is the author of five Texas travel books, four historical novels set in the Big Bend of Texas, and a book on the history of Texas state parks.

He is a member of the Western Writers of America.

Allan is also an award-winning journalist and photographer with a long career as a reporter and editor at daily newspapers in Texas. Over the years he has interviewed several presidents, discovered clandestine airstrips, and covered stories as diverse as chili cook-offs, prison boot camps, disastrous tornadoes, sea turtle rehabilitation, gubernatorial races, and beer-drinking goats,

As a member of the Baseball Writers Association of America he covered the Houston Astros and Major League Baseball for several years. And he has chased killer bees throughout South and Central America. His articles have appeared in many national and state magazines.

Allan and his wife Madonna live in Wimberley, Texas.

Made in the USA
Lexington, KY
11 December 2019